THE INSIDER'S GUIDE TO

HONGKONG

THE INSIDER'S GUIDES

AUSTRALIA • BALI • CALIFORNIA • CHINA • EASTERN CANADA • FLORIDA • HAWAII •
HONG KONG • INDIA • INDONESIA • JAPAN • KENYA • KOREA • MALAYSIA AND SINGAPORE •
MEDITERREAN FRANCE • MEXICO •NEPAL • NEW ENGLAND • NEW ZEALAND • PORTUGAL •
RUSSIA • SPAIN • THAILAND • TURKEY • VIETNAM, LAOS AND CAMBODIA • WESTERN CANADA

The Insider's Guide to Hong Kong
(Second Edition)

© 1995 Novo Editions, S.A.

Moorland Publishing Co Ltd
Moor Farm Road, Airfield Estate, Ashbourne, DE61HD, England
First Published 1987
published by arrangement with Novo Editions SA
53 rue Beaudouin, 27700 Les Andelys, France
Telefax: (33) 32 54 54 50

ISBN: 0 86190 564 4

Created, edited and produced by Novo Editions, S.A.
Editor in Chief: Allan Amsel
Designt: Hon Bing-wah/Kinggraphic
Picture editor and designer: Delian Bower Publishing
Text and artwork composed and information updated
using Ventura Publisher software

All rights reserved. No part of this publication may be reproduced, stored in
a retrieval system, or transmitted in any form, or by any means,
electronic, mechanical, photocopying, recording, or
otherwise, without the written permission of the publisher.

Printed by Samhwa Printing Co Ltd, Seoul, Korea

THE INSIDER'S GUIDE TO

HONGKONG

by Derek Maitland

Photographed by Nik Wheeler
and Alain Evrard

MPC

Contents

HONGKONG

(PEOPLE'S REPUBLIC OF CHIN

Guangdong Provinc

Shenzhen

Lo Wu

Deep Bay

Ponds

Lau Fau Shan

Yuen Long

Shek Kong

NEW TERRITORIES

Tai
Sh

Tuen Mun

Castle Peak
Bay

Tsuen Wan

Kw

Ma Wan

Tsing Yi

Sto
Isla

Chek Lap Kok

Discovery Bay

PENG CHAU

Tung Chung

Mui Wo

Tai O

LANTAU ISLAND

Silver Mine Bay

Hei Ling Chau

Lantau Peak

Sunset Peak

Chi Ma Wan Peninsula

Yeung Shui Wan

CHEUNG CHAU

Shek Kwu Chau

Soko Islands

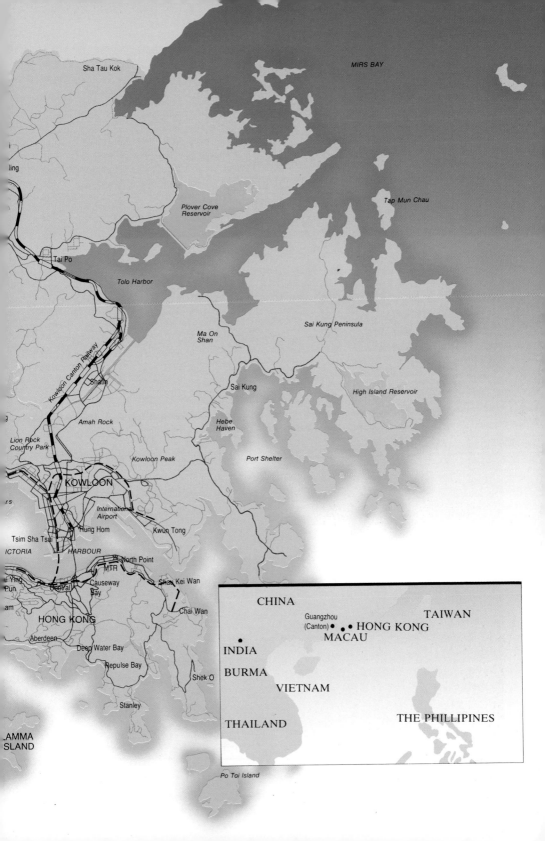

Images
of Hong
Kong

THE RESOUNDING BOOM

Every day on the stroke of noon, a cannon is fired on the waterfront of Causeway Bay on Hong Kong Island, marking the passing of another 24 hours of high-paced business and pleasure in this, the world's most incredible and exotic center of capitalism.

The Noon-Day Gun doesn't just mark the time, it announces achievement and change — for at the frenetic pace at which business goes on in the tropical heat and business as it does about the business itself. It's believed the cannon was first fired a century ago in a ceremonial welcome to one of Jardine & Matheson's cargo clippers, loaded with opium, as it sailed into the harbor. It was this nefarious trade in "foreign mud" with China that gave birth to Hong Kong, that nurtured its founding business and trading houses in its infancy, that set the swashbuckling and quite disreputable tradition and tone of its business world and the sort of people who inhabited it. And, while that world is infinitely more

humidity and urban clamor of Hong Kong, that past 24-hour period may have seen a new multi-storey hotel or a new restaurant open its doors in a celebration of gongs and tom-toms and prancing dragons and lions, a new consortium formed to drive a new tunnel under the harbor, break the ground on a new multi-million dollar high-rise commercial and residential development, or build a new futuristic banking headquarters. And while the cannon signals the end of that day's business race, it's also the starter's gun that triggers the Hong Kong business world out of its blocks for the next mad 24-hour dash for profits. The origin of this noon-day ritual says as much about the philosophy of Hong Kong's approach to respectable, image-conscious and even virtuous today, it still has a faint ring and clash of cutlass blades, a whiff of musket powder and a slight swagger of the self-made buccaneer in its boardrooms. It is still a place where each noon-day boom on the Causeway Bay harborfront triggers the pursuit of one thing: the fast buck.

FIRECRACKER ISLAND

There've been so many booms in Hong Kong's 150-year flicker of history, that to study its development is like watching a fizzing firecracker, waiting for the next bang. Every five years or so this tiny island

and small wedge of mainland territory, this little ant-hill of probably fewer than seven million people, bursts its seams with ambitious and even impossible business dreams, and five years later it's not only achieved every one of them but is about to do it again.

In 1841 when the island itself was annexed by the British as part of their imperial booty from the first Opium War with China, it was dismissed as an insignificant "barren rock" with hardly a hope in the world of becoming much more than that. But almost from that first historic crack of the Noon-

the colony's second major attribute, its nineteenth century British and European adventure capitalists — dour ledger-worshipping successors to the "merchant princes" whose cannon-bristling East Indiamen had first forced China to open up to trade — Hong Kong couldn't help but make money.

Its magnificent sheltered harbor and its position as an offshore haven, distanced from the collapse, chaos and civil conflict into which China was sliding, gave it some advantage over the mainland treaty ports,

Day Gun it astounded everyone by burgeoning into a major trading center and "Emporium of the East," taking advantage of a number of crucial factors that the jaundiced mandarins of Whitehall had obviously failed to anticipate and which have underpinned its various development booms since.

First, from the moment the British flag was hoisted on January 26, 1841 the island was flooded with Chinese from Canton (Guangzhou) and the southern provinces fleeing famine and the harsh rule of the Manchu Qing dynasty, most of them with nothing to lose and thus, with thrift and hard toil, everything to gain. With this grabhappy cheap labor force harnessed by

where there was always the threat, and often the fact, of "native" unrest. As British maritime power grew, as steam replaced sail, and as the first transoceanic flying boats began linking the capitals of the Far Eastern and Pacific empire, Hong Kong's strategic position made it one of the busiest crossroads of the world.

From the turn of this century until World War II, only one treaty port outshone it, and that was Shanghai with its vastly bigger, even cheaper labor market, its huge textile industry and its direct access via the Yang-

Hong Kong then and now — OPPOSITE Pedder Street and Old Clock tower in late 1860s, and ABOVE modern-day eventide view of Manhattan style skyline of Wanchai.

tze River to the resources and trade goods of central China. But even then Hong Kong was virtually "twinned" through business links and joint investment with the "wickedest city on earth" — through the Hongkong and Shanghai Banking Corporation and the wealthy, powerful Kadoorie and Sassoon hotel families, for example; and when Shanghai collapsed, first in the horrific Japanese bombing and wartime occupation, then in the communist revolution of 1949, Hong Kong was there to pick up the pieces.

It became an offshore refuge and new business base for Shanghai textile barons and their money, fleeing the communist revolutionaries. With the many millions of dollars and even manufacturing equipment that they brought with them, the colony re-tooled, fattened and diversified — no longer just a huge island emporium and port of free trade, but an emerging manufacturing center too, churning out textiles and toys. By the 1960s it had not only gone through a new development boom but was in a near-permanent state of change. Again, Southeast Asia was in the grip of a violent convulsion, and again Hong Kong was in the right place and ready at the right time to take advantage of it.

That convulsion was the Vietnam war, a conflict to which the United States committed more than half a million military personnel and an immense amount of arms and supplies. By 1966, Hong Kong was not only the main Southeast Asian transshipment point for Vietnam war materials — its harbor packed with freighters — but it was also one of the most popular R&R (Rest and Recreation) venues for the American troops, and for the next decade was playing host to something like 3,000 free-spending GIs a month.

WINDOW ON THE WORLD

But by then the colony had also been taking advantage of a far greater and even more lucrative conflict, and one that underscored not only its innate, imperishable instinct for survival but also its fundamental survival policy — business above all else — and its unique ability to turn even the most unlikely situations to its own favor. While, in the 17 years since the Chinese revolution, it had become an off-shore life-preserver for almost two million mainland refugees, it had also quite incredibly become the communist government's main international trading base, communications center and source of something like US$5 billion a year in desperately needed foreign exchange.

The American embargo on "Red Chinese" exports had fallen like a ripe plum into Hong Kong's lap. It became a "laundry" for Chinese products, vast amounts of which went in one end of its port and emerged the other end as Hong Kong products with new certification to prove it. With China's own transport and trading infrastructure still struggling to repair itself after the many years of civil war, Hong Kong was also the key transshipment point for "legitimate" exports to other countries. On top of that, Hong Kong provided a base, or enclave, for Beijing's trade and diplomatic negotiations and capitalistic endeavors that lay conveniently outside the walls of the revolutionary socialist society.

If the prospect of a communist society practicing capitalism in Hong Kong was surprising enough, Hong Kong's own wheeling and dealing was simply amazing — it was playing international high stakes poker with almost every card in the pack marked. It was a sovereign British colony on the surface, but quite prepared to accept instruction from Beijing on key issues behind the scenes. It was anti-communist and a haven for many anti-revolutionary Chinese, yet it was acting as banker, business agent and sales rep for the communist government. It was supporting the American Vietnam war effort on the one hand as a funnel for war supplies, and on

Its late-fifties' image of the "World of Suzie Wong" had slipped into a micro-skirt, false eyelashes and Mary Quant eye-shadow, put a Beatles record on and headed for what was then called the *discotheque*. With its unique blend of Chinese character and red London buses, Hong Kong was "Carnaby Street East."

The island's Wanchai bar district fronted directly on to lapping harbor waters, sampans and American warships, and at night it was teeming and jumping with hordes of United States servicemen and their military

the other it was helping circumvent the United States embargo on mainland Chinese products. And it was making a fortune out of it all.

CARNABY STREET EAST

This was Hong Kong of 1966, the year that I first arrived there, fell in love with the place and began an intimate affair which continues with considerable passion to this day. In 1966 it was at the height of its first resounding boom, and the face of the society reflected it. It was a time of wealth, youth and a burst of hedonism after the post-war and post-revolutionary austerity.

police, tourists, local expatriates and young Chinese office workers. Its bars and discotheques were packed with bar-girls, hostesses and seething masses of dancers. The most popular, crowded, exciting "in" place, and the one with the loudest pop music, was the Cave. Its main rival was The Den (now a Japanese restaurant) at the Hong Kong Hilton, where you could leap about to the beat of the Stones or the Beach Boys or sway gently in the late hours to Paul McCartney's "Michelle" or Frank Sinatra's "Strangers in the Night."

OPPOSITE Chinese artist in Wellington Street studio specializing in "photographic" portraits. ABOVE Typical stall at fish market.

The Hilton was the most popular business and recreation hotel for tourists, American military officers and executives and Vietnam correspondents, and one of three hotels at that time that dominated the Hong Kong scene. On the island's Central District waterfront, massively impressive in that era of comparative low-rise development, the Mandarin (today it's called the Mandarin Oriental) was for British businessmen and visiting Foreign Office bureaucrats who liked a bit of brass and leather with their roast beef and gin.

And on the Tsimshatsui waterfront on the other side of the harbor, almost monumental in size, architecture and reputation, famed throughout the whole world for its guardian lions, its fountain, its unending streams of Rolls-Royces and its cavernous gathering place of the international jet-set — its lobby coffee lounge — stood the Peninsula Hotel.

Amid tall columns, crisp linen tablecloths, potted plants and bustling teams of waiters and uniformed bellboys, you could sit in the lobby of The Peninsula, on the very southern tip of "forbidden" China and the main overland routes of the entire Eurasian landmass, and watch the "in" people of Hong Kong and the rest of the world go by — wealthy ex-Shanghai industrialists, Shaw Bros movie starlets, the great stars of Hollywood, United States Congressmen, Commonwealth Prime Ministers, United Nations officials, British aristocracy, Indian princes, Asian and Western tycoons and the new giants of the British business world, the pop idols. Marlon Brando was there, so

was Danny Kaye, and so too were Steve McQueen, Doug McClure and Richard Crenna, filming *The Sand Pebbles.* And from the same soaring lobby windows you could gaze out across the twinkling lights of the harbor and its shipping and ferries to an absolute fairyland scene — the island and its rising Mid-Levels and Peak and the eastern reaches of Wanchai, Happy Valley and Causeway Bay, all of it ablaze with lights as though it were a huge diamond, encrusted with millions of precious gems — many of those gems, at the eastern end of the island, the lights of thousands of hillside squatter huts, shanty dwellings of tin, scrap timber and even cardboard, built on the hillsides by the thousands of refugees who had poured across the border from China.

In that year of 1966, Prince Charles paid a visit and the colony's British community went wild, filling the So Kon Po Government Stadium and the streets with thousands of Chinese schoolchildren waving Union Jacks. A "Buy British" trade drive was launched and the Union Jacks came out again, along with British food, industrial and consumer displays, British fashion shows, British beer, British pop stars and a lot of British pomp. The Australians left their mark on the colony that year too — a whole team of Aussie journalists working on one of the daily newspapers abruptly picked up and departed Hong Kong en masse, taking thousands of dollars' worth of tailored suits and other clothing with them, along with radios, cassette recorders, television sets, watches, jewelry — even a brand new car — and leaving a lot of Hong Kong merchants stuck with nothing more than some hire purchase deposits.

It was that kind of year and era, the swinging era when fortunes were being made and flamboyantly shown off in public, when you could sit and work at your office desk while a man traced the outline of your stockinged feet on a sheet of paper — and come back two days later with a pair of brand new hand-made high fashion, and cheap, shoes; when the same nineteenth century free-wheeling laissez-faire principles that had guided the colony's business and prosperity since the first shot of the Noon-Day Gun were still manifestly successful.

And it was also the year of reckoning, when the special laissez-faire license and "borrowed time" that had built the colony's fortunes suddenly ran out.

RED GUARDS AND REALITY

Two calamities hit Hong Kong in 1966 — one a natural disaster (or perhaps, in the context of that time, an act of God) and the other a momentous political act that sud-

house entrances over torrents of water that were raging down the gutters and foot-paths to the harbor. At the bottom of the street lay a huge junk yard of cars that had been washed down in the night and piled up on top of each other at a pedestrian barrier. On that same night two British journalists had tried to get across a flooding viaduct and one had been carried away and drowned in the Mid-Levels.

It wasn't that disaster of that scope was particularly new to Hong Kong — landslides were a regular occurrence in

denly brought home to people the implication of all those "fairyland" shanty lights in the squalid squatter areas that spilled down many of the colony's hillsides.

In June, one of the heaviest unbroken monsoonal storms in Hong Kong's history dumped so much rain that parts of the slope of The Peak and Mid-Levels, and the hillside above Causeway Bay, collapsed. The mud-slides caused incredible damage, and even loss of life, at one point smashing into the foundation pillars of a high-rise block of flats and tearing the building to the ground. I remember walking down Tin Hau Temple Road to the Causeway Bay harbor front in the pounding rain and watching people trying to leap from their apartment

monsoonal storms, and so too were violent and destructive typhoons, which boil up out of the Pacific to smash against the South China Coast from July to October every year. But what the 1966 tragedy showed was that Hong Kong could no longer go on simply making money and ignoring its own infrastructure, safety and welfare. The immediate lesson of 1966 was that a huge and costly public works program was needed to shore up and strengthen all hillside places where land slips were likely to occur.

OPPOSITE Neon signs festooned entrance of tram terminal in Happy Valley. ABOVE Old world grace and charm at afternoon tea in the renowned Lobby of The Peninsula.

The second calamity was the launching by Chairman Mao Zedong (Mao Tse-tung) of his Great Proletarian Cultural Revolution and the unleashing of the Red Guards, some of whom immediately began denouncing the imperialist regimes of Hong Kong and Macau. The Cultural Revolution ignited just as public outcry and unrest were coming to a head in Hong Kong over a proposal to hike up the fares on the Star Ferry. Both fire and tinder came together in violent riots in the teeming, tenement-packed streets in the urban hinterland of Kowloon.

For two weeks, in the interminable rain, the tourist mecca of Tsimshatsui and the deeper districts of Mongkok and Shamshui-po looked like an urban battleground. Police and army Land Rovers veered through the almost deserted streets with riot-clad crews and anti-missile metal grids over their windscreens and doors. The stately colonial stone and glass façade of the Peninsula Hotel was boarded up, and riot shutters guarded the hotels, stores, banks and money-change kiosks along Salisbury and Nathan Roads.

In the backstreets, fires blazed in the night, casting a hellish glare over huge mobs of screaming, chanting, rock-throwing rioters and, confronting them, deep, heavily-armored and shielded ranks of police and Gurkhas — the British Army's long-standing strike force of Nepalese mercenaries — advancing under big banners emblazoned with Chinese characters warning the crowds to disperse or be gassed, or possibly shot.

Again, Hong Kong was no stranger to civil unrest — there'd been labor strikes in the 1920s and riots in 1952. But, like the rains and mud slides, the 1966 outbreak exposed the bare bones of social neglect, exploitation and discontent that lay under Hong Kong's swinging image. When, in the following year, there was another natural calamity — this time a crippling drought — and even more violent and prolonged riots, including an incident in which a mob besieged Government House chanting slogans from Mao Zedong's "Little Red Book," it was obvious that radical and fundamental reforms had to be made to the way in which Hong Kong conducted its business and its community.

Thousands of its people were without homes, and many of those who were crammed into the packed tenements of back-street Kowloon were without adequate sanitation, health care, education, social welfare and many other facilities and amenities. The police force and civil service had a growing reputation for corruption. Chinese salaries were ridiculously low compared with those of the British and other foreign expatriates — less than one-tenth of the *gweilo* (foreign devil) incomes even at middle management levels (if, indeed, Chinese employees could break into middle management positions anyway).

Momentous and inevitable decisions were made at that time. Laissez-faire had to end, or at least be moderated and reformed to produce a caring, rather than exploitative, society. Hong Kong had to shed its buccaneering attitude and begin to regard itself as a serious and possibly permanent society, not a temporary dwelling and business house living on borrowed time. And in typical Hong Kong style, it threw itself headlong into major reform — and another huge development boom began.

GOING FOR BROKE

By 1974, when I returned to Hong Kong for what was to become another five-year "live-in" romance with the place, it was already well into a massive building boom that was completely changing its physical character and social attitude. Suzie Wong had thrown away her stiletto heels and slinky cheong-sam, settled down, got an office job and joined the PTA. If the transformation aroused a twinge of indignation and regret among the hedonists, it offered a new sense of hope and inspiration to thousands of immigrant Chinese families who, only a few years before, had crept across dark, guarded borders, run the

OPPOSITE Modern futuristic entrance to a shopping plaza in Tsimshatsui East.

coastal waters in packed sampans and junks, or swum across Deep Bay or the inlet south of Shataukok, and now demanded and deserved a society with some permanence and sense of concern in which they could build decent lives. Also, it had not escaped the calculations of the government and business world that Hong Kong could not succeed in its next stage of development — from trade, textiles and toys to trade, international banking and finance and electronics — without a vastly improved housing and public transport infrastructure

Mass Transit Railway (MTR), a high-speed subway that would switch the bulk of Hong Kong's public transport underground and solve the enormous "people pressure" in its urban streets.

Two other gigantic projects, the Plover Cove and High Island reservoirs, were under way in the New Territories to solve Hong Kong's chronic high-summer shortage of fresh water. Kai Tak Airport was being expanded, its harbor runway — streaking out into the harbor waters on reclaimed land — already one of the

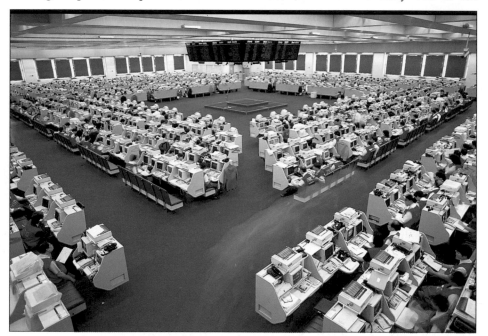

that would keep its working population reasonably happy.

So, by 1974, the first Cross-Harbour Tunnel had been built, providing speedy, direct access between the island and the mainland districts. The Lion Rock Tunnel had been blasted through the tall hills just north of the Kowloon urban sprawl to free the traffic bottleneck that had existed on this key route to Shatin and the New Territories. On Hong Kong Island, initial work had already begun on the Aberdeen Tunnel, carving through the island's central mountain to Aberdeen, Repulse Bay and Stanley on the southern side. And an even bigger, far more ambitious tunnel system was also under way, the US$2.2-billion

world's most thrilling examples of space-saving engineering, providing a spectacular touchdown right in the heart of a high-rise beehive. Work had started on the huge Kwai Chung container terminal, destined to become the main export conduit for China trade.

THE NEW CITIES

But all this paled against the central showpiece of the development boom — a multi-billion dollar resettlement scheme to develop three rustic, sleepy rural centers in the New Territories, Shatin, Tsuen Wan and Tuen Mun, into huge New Towns, or satellite cities, providing public housing and full social amenities for one million people. When the first blueprints were made public it looked like another urban nightmare — the plans calling for a population of 90,000 in one gigantic skyscraping housing estate alone.

There was an echo of Hong Kong's old laissez-faire attitude in the arguments that were put up to defend this, one of the most massive, tightly crammed high-rise public housing projects on earth. The Chinese were accustomed to living this way, one argument went — they even preferred it. Its promoters were on much more realistic ground when they pointed to the space-saving factor — Hong Kong's largely hilly terrain, making it difficult to create sprawling low-rise tract housing. But even then it was apparent that one million working people were going to be poured into huge industrial dorm-itories, thrown up relatively cheaply on reclaimed land, while the hillsides were to be kept free for high-profit luxury private condominiums. Of all the development schemes under way in 1974-75, the New Towns had the biggest question mark over them.

There were costly development projects under way on the social and recreational fronts too. New sports stadiums to be built in Wanchai and on the roof of the new Kowloon-Canton Railway terminus at Hung Hom; a new ultra-modern Space Museum and Planetarium on the water-front at Tsimshatsui; a huge US$25-million marine playground, Ocean Park, featuring aquariums, marine zoology, wave tanks, whale and porpoise shows, a cable car sys-tem, fairground rides and cultural gardens, on the Brick Hill headland between Aber-deen and Deep Water Bay on the southern shore of Hong Kong Island.

On the island and in the tourist and com-mercial centers of Kowloon, the face of Hong Kong in the latter half of the 1970s was one of noise, overcrowding, stress and chaos. Whole streets were being excavated and districts ripped apart in the work on the MTR and other projects; pneumatic pile drivers shrieked and thumped on dozens of building sites right through the day and sometimes into the night; cherished

landmarks of the colonial era, notably the old Kowloon-Canton Railway Station Tsimshatsui, disappeared in the frenzy of redevelopment, adding to the trauma of some of the more traditional sections of the British community. And amidst it all, some two million tourists a year poured off the Jumbo 747s at Kai Tak Airport and 70,000 Vietnamese boat people struggled ashore from leaking ramshackle sampans and junks — and cargo freighters that had rescued them at sea — to be herded into makeshift refugee camps, and, as their numbers swelled, locked up in concentra-tion centers. Not surprisingly, the general health of the community suffered — a report in 1979 claimed that between 20 and 50 percent of the population was suffering from some degree of stress-related mental sickness.

But already, the signs of a new, far more just and realistic community were begin-ning to appear. With the combined pressure of Beijing and local outrage, and a couple of notorious court cases, the Royal Hong Kong Police has been brought to heel with the setting up of the watchdog Independent Commission Against Corruption (ICAC). The Hong Kong Festival, launched in earlier years to counteract the adverse pub-licity of the Red Guard confrontations and riots, had now been turned into the annual Hong Kong Arts Festival, combining public relations with a bid to lift the community out of what had been a profit-oriented cultural wasteland.

What had been a colony was now a "trading territory" — it distinctly said so in all Hong Kong Government Information Service releases. The government's Infor-mation Officers were also under distinct notice that anything questionable they wrote about Hong Kong would be dis-cussed over tea in Guangzhou or Beijing that same day. There was a coincidental and gradual breaking of the political and commercial umbilical with the "Home Government" in Whitehall. First, a decision by Hong Kong to break away from sterling and link its currency to the United States

OPPOSITE Hong Kong's population watches movements on the Stock Exchange of Hong Kong.

dollar, then a certain distancing of this burgeoning enclave — now one of the top 20 trading and industrial centers of the world, and potentially its third richest financial capital — from the staggering, crisis ridden, and comparatively impoverished economy of Britain.

The "territory's" own economic structure began to change significantly, with high-tech production rising to dominate the manufacturing sector. Its financial structure saw an even more significant change — mainland Chinese investment moving in,

and "communist" corporations suddenly challenging the long-established Old Boy network of British and Western corporate powers that had enjoyed almost divine authority in the rich property and development fields.

Another momentous change was about to take place in Hong Kong, and one that explained everything — the sudden massive social development, the slow but steady erosion of its ties with the British Crown. It was a change that would, once and for all, test Hong Kong's unique ability to turn every challenge to its own advantage. It was more than just a change, it was a crisis. Hong Kong was to be returned to the sovereignty of China.

CHINA'S FRONT DOOR

When Hong Kong had been grabbed as a colony in 1841, the Union Jack had flown only over the island itself. In 1860, after the second Opium War, China's Qing dynasty government had been forced to cede the waterfront district of Kowloon up to what is now Boundary Street, and 38 years later the British took a 99-year lease on the hinterland, what is now the New Territories, and 233 more islands.

After the 1949 revolution the communist government in Beijing disowned all colonial agreements, quite rightly pointing out that they had been obtained under military duress. But, for reasons that have already been explained, Hong Kong was allowed to continue existing and serving Beijing's interests under British administration. The internal rule and day-to-day running of the "colony" were left to the British, but most key decisions on defense and diplomatic affairs required Beijing's approval — and, just in case the British were tempted to exert full colonial autonomy, Beijing occasionally demonstrated the sort of overwhelming *fait accompli* Hong Kong faced by flooding the people with thousands of "illegal immigrants."

It became apparent from the moment that Mao Zedong died, when the ultra-revolutionary Gang of Four were crushed and imprisoned and when the head of the Chinese "revisionist" moderates, Deng Xiaoping, rose to power, that the status of Hong Kong was in question. China's sudden swerve to the semi-capitalist path was accompanied by a new open, but more aggressive, foreign policy in which Deng himself made it clear where the future lay by donning a Texan ten-gallon hat at a rodeo while on a visit to the United States, during which time the Chinese military turned its jets, tanks and guns on neighboring Soviet-backed Vietnam to put it in its place, and when it was made clear

ABOVE Wide-beamed junk-style harbor lighter hauls cargo from mid-harbor freighter. OPPOSITE Yaumatei typhoon shelter displays a colorful array of lighters. OVERLEAF Cross-harbor ferry passes high-tech facade of the Victoria Hotel.

that the futures of Hong Kong, Macau and even nationalist Taiwan were now to be settled.

In Hong Kong, word rippled down through the expatriate business community that it was time to begin a strategic retreat. Outside the highest levels of government, the feeling was that Hong Kong's value to China, and thus its reason for existence, had run its course — a capitalist China flinging its door wide open to the rest of the world would hardly need a special offshore trading base and diplomatic window any more.

the Hong Kong Chinese there was a sudden rush for immigration to the United States, Britain, Australia and just about any other non-communist country that would take them, and up to 40,000 a year have since been leaving in what has become a serious drain of middle-management expertise. In Britain, the "Hong Kong lobby" of parliamentarians and business chiefs, bolstered by the Falklands victory, fiercely rattled their sabers against this cowardly sell-out in the face of one billion mainland Chinese.

That feeling rose to panic when, in 1982, British Prime Minister Margaret Thatcher visited Hong Kong on her way to the first talks on its transfer back to Chinese control in the year in which the lease runs out on the New Territories, 1997.

The Hong Kong stock market slumped, the hugely inflated property market took a nose-dive with it. Some of the biggest Hong Kong corporations, headed by Jardine & Matheson, let it be known that they were transferring their financial bases elsewhere. Two major property companies collapsed and had to be bailed out, and there was a temporary run on a leading bank. Capital flew out of the territory with the speed of migrating swallows. Amongst

But in fine traditional style, Hong Kong recovered quickly from its initial panic, took a good hard businesslike look at the situation and did what it had done in the midst of all crises of the past — looked for the opportunity for profit. A new restaurant opened in Central District, for example. Its name? "Nineteen 97."

THE CITY STATE

As any visitor to Hong Kong will immediately confirm today, the much-feared Anglo-Chinese agreement didn't sink the territory at all, nor did it even make a dent in its phenomenal economic growth. Hong

Kong has continued to boom in the face of the Beijing takeover. Indeed it has taken vigorous advantage of the economic expansion that its absorption with the mainland economy promised.

The territory's economy has more than doubled as Hong Kong manufacturers, sidestepping escalating labor and property costs, have shifted their operations across the border to the Shenzhen Special Economic Zone and other key low-cost sites of Guangdong province. The Pearl River delta, embracing Hong Kong, Macau and southern Guangdong, is now regarded as the front-runner of another wave of Asian economic "tigers." An even more powerful industrial and trading axis comprising China, Hong Kong, Macau and Taiwan is seen as a possible generator of Asia-Pacific growth and investment in the 21st century.

Chinese corporations have continued to invest heavily in Hong Kong, particularly in the property market. The huge Bank of China building, a monolithic architectural hybrid of steel, glass and Chinese imperial arrogance, has planted Beijing's standard right in the heart of the territory's business community. Despite increasingly exorbitant office rents and real estate costs, foreign corporations have continued to pour into the territory, heeding the words of one business commentator in the South China Morning Post that "the only reason to be based in Hong Kong today is China."

But this new economic explosion has been underscored by dramatic confusion and confrontation on the political front, in the shaping of the territory's crucial relationship with its new landlord, Beijing. And much of it has been caused by the realization that despite Beijing's pledges on its control of Hong Kong after 1997, despite its assurances on "one country, two systems" and its promise that Hong Kong's fundamental business, political and social structure will be left intact for the next 50 years, the territory may well be shedding colonial power only to face a form of rule far more authoritarian and iniquitous in the years to come.

The moment of realization was a brutal one. On the night of June 2 1989 the Beijing authorities sent tanks and troops into Tiananmen Square to crush the student pro-

democracy movement. Up until that night when mass killings that took place, Hong Kong's business community and a growing number of its people took the view that despite the prospect of coming under Chinese Communist Party rule, the "Open Door" policy and rapid economic changes in China would lead to political and social liberalization as well. The Tiananmen Square massacre proved that despite all the other fundamental changes taking place in China, the Communist Party had no intention of relaxing its grip on the country.

Hong Kong's reaction was equally dramatic. Mass demonstrations of more than a million people at a time, Chinese and expatriates together, poured through the streets in protest against the Tiananmen crackdown. An underground escape system went into operation to help Chinese democracy activists on the run from the authorities to get out to the West. There was another emigration panic, with Hong Kong Chinese — mostly skilled middle-management people — seeking citizenship in Canada, Australia, Britain and any other country that would

OPPOSITE High-rise public housing at Shatin.
ABOVE Sampans hustle between moored fishing trawlers and junks in picturesque Aberdeen.

admit them. Beijing's view of Hong Kong perceptively shifted: while it was still a much-coveted political and economic asset, come 1997, it was now also a potential hotbed of resistance and possible insurrection against authoritarian rule.

Since Tiananmen Square, Hong Kong's relationship with its new masters has followed two distinct tracks. On the economic track, even the horror of Tiananmen and a subsequent hardening of communist party rule have been largely ignored in the clamor to take advantage of business opportunities

Foreign Service mandarins who tended to bow to China's demands as though it was still the fashion to bear tribute to imperial Beijing. In a sense, they were right: first Mao Zedong, then Deng Xiaoping, both elevated to cult status at the tip of the Communist Party pyramid, simply copied the imperial structure of authority and administration that had existed for many centuries before the 1949 revolution.

But under Patten's governor ship, the scholarly myths of 5,000 years of Chinese history and culture were swept away. Far

in China. On the political track, the collapse of world communism, leaving China and North Korea as the last bastions of Marxist authoritarianism, produced a British-led administration in Hong Kong, with wide domestic and international support, which, far from being the caretaker government that one might have envisioned diligently putting the books in order for Beijing's triumph in 1997 — actually began redefining and reforming Hong Kong's political institutions to strengthen its hand in the inevitable power-play with Beijing after the takeover.

The appointment of Chris Patten, a tough British Tory Party strategist and former MP, as Governor of Hong Kong in 1992 brought to an end a tradition of British

from being the Middle Kingdom, endowed with innovation, wisdom and exoticism that have fascinated China scholars for years, China was seen as a politically and socially backward, over-populated, under-educated Third World monolith with a brutally self-protective ruling structure that lacked the worldliness, experience and insight required to safeguard Hong Kong's basic freedoms after 1997.

It was Governor Patten's most fundamental step to safeguard those rights — a move to reform and shore up democratic rule in Hong Kong through expansion of elected representatives in the Legislative Council that finally tore Beijing's veil away. The Chinese unleashed such a ferocious, vilifying campaign to personally undermine Patten and to rein in all major political and economic development in Hong Kong particularly the new International Airport project at Chek Lap Kok — that the territory saw for the first time how radically life could change after Beijing's administrators and public security people strode in.

There were other more immediate changes that altered the public view of life after 1997. Major crime spiraled in Hong Kong during the early 1990s as armed gangs from Guangdong, alleged to have the

magazine of life after 1997, the analysts who contributed to the article generally agreed that increasing lawlessness and corruption were two prime epidemics to be expected after the takeover — spurred by mainland officials and business interests whose interpretation of capitalism was simply the means to get rich quick.

But for all this, Hong Kong has continued to prosper, and in development terms has outshone even the great social and commercial booms of the 1970s and 80s. The prospect of enormous wealth in the

tacit support of corrupt provincial officials, launched a spate of raids on banks and jewelry stores, fighting deadly gun and grenade battles with the Hong Kong police. A wave of car thefts, in which mainly luxury vehicles in the Mercedes Benz class were stolen and smuggled across into Guandong, was followed by a surge of cross-border thievery involving luxury yachts and cabin cruisers — some of which were later found operating as public ferries on the Guangdong river network. Hong Kong's Independent Commission Against Corruption (ICAC) reported an alarming 40 percent rise in commercial corruption, most of it committed by mainland Chinese interests. Indeed, in a scenario published by one Hong Kong

economic partnership with China has far outweighed the real and nagging fears of post-1997 rule. The thousands who fled the territory in search of foreign citizenship after the Tiananmen Massacre have been drifting back, weighing up any fears that they still may have against the lack of qualified jobs and aggressive Hong Kong-style business opportunities in the recession-hit West. Hong Kong's endemic pragmatism and flexibility has triumphed again. And while that is both its drawback and its strength, depending on one's own moral

OPPOSITE Hong Kong's colonial style legislature framed by Central District's modern high rise offices. ABOVE Aberdeen waterfront LEFT and Wanchai tram.

view, it cannot be denied that much of this tiny, ultramodern, ever-burgeoning territory's special allure is its belief that nothing short of catastrophe should stand in the way of a fast buck.

The Hong Kong that now welcomes more than seven million visitors a year, including over one million business travelers and package tourists from mainland China, is a thriving, highly efficient city-state. Where the great social programs of the past two decades have given it an ultramodern infrastructure — public transport, telecommunications, parks and playgrounds, social services and business facilities — the most visual development trend of the 90s seems to be to transform, once again, the territory's commercial skyline.

They're calling it ego architecture — a multibillion dollar scramble by the territory's new tycoons to outdo each other in the scale, design and sheer audacity of new skyscrapers and commercial malls. No sooner had the 70-storey Bank of China thrust skyward over Central District than an even bigger, architecturally grander monolith, Central Plaza, streaked upward out of the new harbor front business district of Wanchai this one setting a new trend for Hong Kong in early Manhattan neo-classicism combined with an after-dark look of something reminiscent of the movie *Ghost Busters*. It's a design trend that you'll see right along the Central-Wanchai-Causeway Bay commercial corridor in new high-rise creations like Number Nine Queen's Road (The Galleria) and the Entertainment Building in Central District, the giant Times Square in Causeway Bay and a host of other smaller commercial and office complexes that have sprouted up on both sides of the harbor.

While Hong Kong has been roundly accused of ripping up its history, it is creating a new architectural heritage that is evident in the landmarks of the past three decades — buildings like Jardine House near the Star Ferry and the cylindrical 66-storey Hopewell Centre in southern Wanchai representing the first great burst of growth in the 70s, supplanted in the 80s by the enormous steel and glass citadel of Exchange Square and the novel futuristic architecture

of the Lippo (formerly Bond) Centre and the main headquarters of the Hongkong Bank, and now all of them giving way to the granite towers and turrets of the neo-classic 90s. Where shopping malls like The Landmark, with its vast atrium, in Pedder Street Central was the last word in a luxury, multifunctional shopping environment in the 80s, now the huge Pacific Place complex, with two lofty atriums, three sprawling levels of shops and department stores, restaurants, office towers and three hotels the Marriott, Conrad and Island Shangri-La

— and the equally dramatic Times Square have become the new showplaces.

In infrastructure, too, the second Cross-Harbor Tunnel linking Kowloon Bay with Quarry Bay is to be joined by a third from western Kowloon to Kennedy Town on the western harbor front of Hong Kong Island. This project, in turn, will link with a complex and costly highway, harbor bridge and new MTR system supporting the most ambitious new development in Hong Kong's, the new airport. Meanwhile, what's

OPPOSITE Aberdeen and its famous floating restaurants. ABOVE Faces of Hong Kong development — Corinthian Arch decorates shopping mall. OVERLEAF Hong Kong's skyline from Victoria Park.

reputed to be the world's longest public escalator system has been built up to the Mid-Levels from Central District to make getting up and down the steep streets easier for walking commuters. It also tries to reduce Mid-Levels traffic congestion. If anything, it is a testament to Hong Kong's role as a wealthy, ego-driven super-city, and it reflects the corresponding change that has taken place in the role that Hong Kong sees for itself as a tourist attraction as we approach the 21st century. Where the contrasting lion and dragon of colonial and

a day on three routes — one running along the east-west corridor of the Hong Kong Island harbor front from Sheung Wan to Chai Wan, the second linking the island with mainland Tsimshatsui and western Kowloon and the other running through the second Cross-Harbour Tunnel between Quarry Bay and eastern Kowloon. A warning, though: try to avoid it at peak travel times, when demand is so fierce that Japanese-style "people-pushers" have been considered to pack passengers on to the trains.

Chinese culture was the main tourist draw card for many years, now it is simply the fascination of a rich, spectacular, hard-driving major Asian metropolis.

The Mass Transit Railway

Nothing has revolutionized Hong Kong's public transport system more than the underground Mass Transit Railway (MTR). It's taken the people-pressure off the streets of the main tourist districts on both sides of the harbor and also considerably reduced what was once a costly and aggravating travel problem caused by the territory's island-mainland geography. This fast, clean and constantly growing MTR system carries upwards of two million passengers

The New Towns

Gigantic clusters of high-rise housing estates, shopping malls and manufacturing zones have transformed former mainland and New Territories market and fishing centers like Shatin, Tsuen Wan and Tuen Mun into self-contained satellite cities. Built to resettle squatter populations and boat people who poured into Hong Kong in the 1950s and 60s, they've also taken some of the pressure off the urban beehives of Kowloon and Hong Kong Island. And at night they are awesome to behold — glittering mountain ranges and soaring peaks of light, an astonishing mixture of Disney castles and the extraterrestrial visions of Star Wars. They've decentralized shopping, too, with vast commercial malls like Shatin's New Town Plaza and a series of malls at one of the later residential developments, the huge Whampoa Gardens complex near Hung Hom, rivaling anything found in Tsimshatsui or Hong Kong Island.

Tsimishatsui

This bustling commercial center right on the tip of the Kowloon Peninsula has long been Hong Kong's main tourist district, the site of most of its tourist hotels and the key

shopping area for visitors. During the 1970s and 80s, the area expanded on to reclaimed land in the harbor This formed a completely new tourist area, Tsimshatsui East — the area where hotels like the Royal Garden, Regal Meridien, Holiday Inn Crowne Plaza Harbour View and Nikko are now situated.

But for all its reputation and growth, along with its famous Golden Mile of shops and department stores, Nathan Road, Tsimshatsui has never really matched the high-rise architectural drama of Hong Kong Island's Central District and other harbor front locations. The reason: a long-standing restriction on building heights because of the mainland approach by aircraft landing at Kai Tak International Airport.

Images of Hong Kong

All this is changing. With the new airport at Chek Lap Kok under construction, and with the vast area of ready-formed flat, open land at Kai Tak already slated for massive redevelopment when the new airport opens, building restrictions have already been relaxed and Tsimshatsui is starting to mushroom with new skyscrapers.

The new tower wing at the famed Peninsula Hotel, opened in 1994, reflects something of the skyward explosion that's going to take place right through Kowloon in the coming years. Until the tower was

built, this grand dame of hotels was almost lost in the welter of new (if low-rise) business and recreational development that transformed the Tsimshatsui waterfront — including the spherical dome of the Space Museum and Planetarium, the sweeping roof of the Hong Kong Cultural Centre and the giant Regent/New World hotel and commercial complex.

Meanwhile, a wide swathe of reclamation off Yaumatei, west of the peninsula, has extended the waterfront of what used to be a typhoon shelter so deep into the harbor that old Hong Kong hands joke about the days

OPPOSITE and ABOVE Tsimshatsui East is Kowloon's newest tourist area.

to come when you'll be virtually able to step back and forth from Kowloon to Central.

The Hong Kong Island

If you think the image of the Incredible Shrinking Harbor is a bit beyond the pale, take a look at the new reclamation and development that's going on in the harbor front in Central District. It's only 20 years since the Mandarin Oriental Hotel on Connaught Road was virtually at the water's edge. Then it somehow shrank amid a burst of new development that saw the water-

front extended and buildings like the Victoria Hotel/Shun Tak Centre, Exchange Square, the GPO and City Hall, the Ritz-Carlton Hotel, the giant Admiralty, Lippo and Far East Finance centers, the avante-garde HongkongBank and adjacent Standard Chartered Bank, the Bank of China and nearby Citibank buildings, not to mention the huge Pacific Place complex to the east, turn the area into Hong Kong's Wall Street.

Now, all this new high-rise expansion is receding into the urban hinterland of Central as the new waterfront reclamation is prepared for new office blocks, government buildings, parks and recreational centers — and the cross-harbor Star Ferry trip, surely one of the last touches of tranquillity in this booming city, gets shorter again. As for Wanchai, once famous for its bars and brothels, I can remember the time in the late 60s when Queensway ran right alongside the harbor waters. Now, the great towers of the Lippo Centre and the office blocks and hotels of Pacific Place provide a kind of triumphal introduction to a district that's not

only streaked right out into the harbor on reclaimed land but has also become a financial and business hub rivaling Central.

On this harbor frontage, Central Plaza building stands like an architectural champion, challenging Central District, amid development that includes the Hong Kong Academy of Performing Arts and Arts Centre, the vast Hong Kong Convention and Exhibition Centre — flanked by the deluxe Grand Hyatt and New World hotels — three towering government offices, including the new Immigration Department headquarters — and the China Resources complex. If you knew Wanchai in the past, go to the 62nd floor revolving restaurant at the top of the Hopewell Centre, which once dominated this district, and take a look at all the breathtaking changes that have transformed Suzy Wong's old neon-lit beat.

Further east, Causeway Bay is now another small city in its own right. In the 1970s and 80s, the Excelsior Hotel and adjacent World Trade Centre (which itself may well have been demolished and replaced by now) rose up to dominate harbor front development overlooking the typhoon shelter and Royal Hong Kong Yacht Club. The big Japanese department stores — Matsuzakaya, Daimaru and Sogo — moved in to turn what was once a series of street markets and teeming tenements into a major shopping center. Now, Times Square, thrusting up out of the former tram depot, has added a nine-floor mega-mall full of shops, restaurants and cinemas, a cavernous piano-shaped atrium and commercial skyscrapers to the Causeway Bay/Happy Valley skyline.

From there, the Island Eastern Corridor, a long table-top expressway, streaks right along the waterfront to Chaiwan at the eastern end of the island. And, all along its route, some of Hong Kong's most famous old sea front landmarks — old residential tenement districts and fishing ports like North Point, Quarry Bay, Fortress Hill and Shaukeiwan — have burgeoned into high-

ABOVE: A promenade provides views of Hong Kong Island and harbor from Tsimshatsui East.
OPPOSITE: The Lippo Centre is Paul Rudolf's striking architectural contribution to the Hong Kong of the nineties.

rise housing estates and commercial centers every bit as dramatic as the mainland New Towns. One huge development along the way, Taikoo Shing, once an ugly industrial and warehouse district, is built around one of Hong Kong's biggest multi-storey shopping malls and includes an indoor ice-skating rink.

All this has made Hong Kong an exciting and efficient place to live and work in, even if it is overcrowded, hyperactive and surely one of the most exhausting environments on earth. For people like me, who've watched it go through a succession of building booms since 1966, it sometimes feels as though there's finally no more room, no more greed and vision, no more energy left, and that it cannot possibly expand any further. There must come a day, I keep telling myself, when, with a vast sigh, Hong Kong decides that whatever it decided to build itself into, the work is finally done.

But of course, that's not so. If anything, the territory has simply been preparing the ground for yet another momentous development boom, fueled by new vision and greed, when China's new capitalists have moved in.

The southern side of Hong Kong Island has undergone a similar development boom. With the Aberdeen Tunnel now virtually jetting traffic right through the island's mountainous central spine Aberdeen has been transformed from the crowded, rustic fishing port that it once was packed with fishing junks and floating homes — into a new satellite city. The small island of Ap Lei Chau, right across from the main Aberdeen waterfront, has also mushroomed into a high-rise residential estate.

All this has robbed Aberdeen of much of its former exoticism. But the harbor is still a fascinating sight — squadrons of new sleek-hulled, deep-sea fishing trawlers, some of which fish as far away as the Gulf of Tonkin off Vietnam, moored in neat rows where a pandemonium of junks and sampans once reigned. The Ap Lei Chau Bridge now separates the port into two sections, fishing craft at one end, and the city's most famous attraction, the huge

floating restaurants, along with a marina of luxury yachts and private cruisers at the Aberdeen Boat Club at the other.

To the east, a looming headland provides the stage for one of Hong Kong's biggest cultural and recreational attractions, Ocean Park. This sprawling playground, with one of the world's longest cable-car systems linking its lowland and headland sites, includes an Ocean Theatre, a Wave Cove with an artificial wave tank full of seals and other aquatic creatures, a vast shark aquarium, a funfair with one of Asia's biggest roller coasters, a 3.5 hectare (8.6 acres) walk-through aviary featuring some 2,500 exotic birds, a step back into old China at Middle Kingdom and a Disney-style Water World.

Beyond Aberdeen, Repulse Bay — once a rather sleepy bay where the famous Repulse Bay Hotel recalled Asia's more graceful days — is a high-rise citadel of luxury apartment blocks overlooking a beach which has been extended and widened with sand dredged from the sea. The hotel isn't there any more, but a public outcry managed to save its famous Verandah Restaurant, which is now incorporated into a residential and commercial development. In front of the beach itself is a sprawling complex of fast-food restaurants, including McDonald's, and a rather hideously designed "theme park" of traditional Chinese statues and shrines. This has turned Repulse Bay into something quite tacky. But the view of the bay is still quite exciting.

The village of Stanley, once a peaceful fishing haven, then a popular tourist market for cheap jeans and factory "seconds," is now an even bigger, far more crowded tourist shopping spot. It has also mushroomed with luxury apartment blocks and condominiums, with an entirely new up-market residential estate spilling down to its beach front from nearby Chung Hom Kok. Stanley has gone the way of Repulse Bay, and at weekends it's a struggle to get through the shopping crowds and invading hordes of barbecue picnickers. But like Repulse Bay, it still has fantastic views, even if you're likely to find reclamation barges and pile drivers blocking the way.

For an impression of what Stanley and Repulse Bay were like in calmer days, go even further south to Shek O, which features one of Hong Kong's best beaches. This seaside town, also once a little fishing port, hasn't yet come under the developers' jackhammers, and it's spending its last days of peace as a mecca for day-trippers and an off-the-track residential spot for young foreign expatriates. The Shek O Golf and Country Club, and another nearby beach community, Big Wave Bay, add to this area's resort potential.

The Outlying Islands

Even Hong Kong's biggest outlying islands are under development, with Cheung Chau now more of a New Town housing estate than what it traditionally was — a bustling fishing community with a bay packed with junks and its waterfront cafes providing rustic salons for its expatriate and Chinese community of artists, photographers and media people. But the biggest offshore development has taken place at Discovery Bay on the southern tip of Lantau Island — a largely undeveloped island that's actually one and a half times the size of Hong Kong. Discovery Bay has been turned in to a vast, constantly growing residential resort of high-rise apartment blocks and beach front condominiums, with its own shopping center, sports and social club, fire station and 24-hour hovercraft service linking its largely executive community with Central District.

A decade ago, the plan was to retain Lantau as Hong Kong's biggest parkland and nature reserve, but the pressure for new development particularly in middle- and upper-class residential property — and the advent of the new airport project at Chek Lap Kok off Lantau's northern coast, has put paid to that. While Lantau is still a comparative wonderland of soaring, untouched hillsides and mountain peaks, with tremendously inspiring views and hiking trails, it's days are numbered as a parkland. It is now seen as the site of the next big property boom.

The very prospect of all this development seemed daunting and even unnerving back in the late 70s. Even then, Hong Kong seemed to have crammed just about everything into one solid monolith of concrete and glass. It was feared that another development boom could only worsen what was already a deteriorating and stressful environment.

It has certainly caused a grave pollution crisis affecting the harbor, surrounding waters and most of the best beaches; and whether this will be tackled and eventually repaired depends on how the mainland Chinese view environmental matters when they get the key to Hong Kong. On past

performance, there's very little reason to feel optimistic about it.

But to objectively consider Hong Kong today, for all its concrete and clamor, you have to look at what all this development has done for its people. It has given them a sense of community and permanence that did not exist in its more anarchistic days as a colonial emporium. It has given them comfortable, if pressure-packed, housing. They now enjoy one of the finest integrated transport systems anywhere in the world and an exciting range of cultural, recreational and educational amenities. Their business world has been streamlined, computerized, coordinated and fitted neatly like a microchip into a social infrastructure that already anticipates the demands of the 21st century.

Thirty years ago a great many of these people were living in rude tin-roofed shanty towns where the huge apartment blocks, office towers and shopping malls now stand

ABOVE The electrified Kowloon-Canton Railway lins new towns with urban centers.

The British Flag Unfurls

THE "BARREN ROCK"

When Commodore Sir J. J. Gordon Bremer rowed ashore with a party of Royal Navy officers and ratings to plant the British flag on the Hong Kong Island foreshore on January 26, 1841, he can be forgiven if he thought he was adding a priceless new colonial jewel to the wealth and glory of the British Empire.

At that time of the year, Hong Kong would have looked its best. The sky would

cannon-packed sailing workhorses of the China and Far East trade, and the new faster slim-hulled American clippers which were beginning to slash days and even weeks off the long, highly competitive race from Baltimore and Liverpool to the South China Coast. With the mainland foreshore to its north and the mountainous island protecting it to the south, it was simply one of the finest harbors that Commodore Bremer and his men had seen anywhere.

Although it lay not much further than a cannon shot from the mainland, the

have been clear and the weather relatively dry and sunny. Being winter, a faint gossamer of early morning mist may well have lingered over the harbor waters, an echo of the mild seasonal chill of the night. The island itself would have loomed over the naval whaleboat in wooded slopes rising upward to the lofty 552 m (1,811 ft) high peak of a central mountain spine running along the island to the east — sunbathed and serene and lush, and no doubt achatter with bird life and possibly a troop or two of monkeys.

The anchorage itself would have excited Commodore Bremer's nautical appreciation — wide and deep enough to take three or four huge fleets of East Indiamen, the

island was virtually bare of human presence. It had been uninhabited until the fourteenth century, and even then had become only an occasional stopover for roving fleets of *Hoklos*, the "sea gypsies" of southern China. At some point in the century before Commodore Bremer's sea boots trod triumphantly along its sandy shore, small bands of mainlanders, driven by famine, had crossed over to it and established small fishing settlements on its eastern and southern foreshores in what are now Shaukeiwan and Aberdeen. Pirates had also used its sheltered bays as lairs, but even they had not regarded the island as a permanent base. Until the British arrived, the island and its "Fragrant Harbour" lay off the main trade route, ignored by all except an occasional junk on its way to or from Canton (Guangzhou).

As the Union Jack unfurled in the light breeze and prayers were said and the island claimed in the name of Her Britannic Majesty, little did Commodore Sir J. J. Gordon Bremer know that official wrath would ignite back in Whitehall, careers and reputations would be destroyed, contempt would be heaped upon the island and all involved in its seizure — and the Crown would even refuse to accept it — before it

If ever there was a more unlikely place for the birth of a huge, densely populated, highly prosperous trading and manufacturing city-state, it was this desolate, humpbacked island. When the news of its acquisition reached London, back came the imperious and indignant response which, to this present day, has been a catch-phrase of Hong Kong's incredible survival and development in the face of immense odds. Lord Palmerston, Queen Victoria's Foreign Secretary, dismissed it as nothing more than "a barren rock with hardly a dwelling upon it."

finally took its place on the official map of British colonial possessions.

It may also be that the Commodore had little idea of exactly what it was that he was committing brave red-blooded British men and fair womenfolk to. While the island lay in a pristine setting of clear dry skies and balmy winter sunshine on that historic January day, within a matter of months it would be like a steam bath, a furnace soaked in dense mist and incredibly high humidity, then hammered for days on end by strong torrential monsoon rains, and then, lashed and torn time and time again by the terrible *tai-fungs* or typhoons, that boil up each high-summer out of the northern Pacific.

"FOREIGN MUD"

It had been a far more dramatic and historic chain of events that had culminated in Commodore Bremer's flag-raising ceremony on the island's foreshore. Britain and China had gone to war in one of the most sordid conflicts of all time — one that was to end eventually in the total collapse

OPPOSITE Before the emporium — a view of modest skyline of Wanchai and almost barren Mid-Levels photographed around the year 1890. Lantau is still, for the most part, undeveloped and a getaway place for hikers. The Po Lin Monastery, part shown ABOVE provides vegetarian food for trippers.

of China's 5000-year-old tradition of imperial and dynastic reign.

The struggle had begun from the moment that the British, following on the heels of the Portuguese and Dutch, had first broken around the Cape of Good Hope and across the Indian Ocean to join in the rich trade pickings that were available along the China coast. The trouble was that, the trade was all virtually one way — there was a fierce British demand for two prized products, silks and tea, but there was nothing the British could tempt the Chinese with in return. As the Manchu Qing dynasty emperor Ch'ien-lung (Qianlong) bluntly informed King George III: "I set no value on strange or ingenious objects and have no use for your country's manufactures." Not only that, but the British "merchant princes" were banned from all Chinese soil except for a confined, segregated trading depot in Canton where they were at the mercy of a Chinese trading monopoly called the Co-Hong.

The Chinese would accept only one thing for their trade, and that was silver bullion. By the turn of the nineteenth century, the British taste for tea had reached the level of a national craving, and so much silver was being committed to tea imports that the treasury was close to bankruptcy. A commodity of some sort had to be found that the Chinese simply could not resist, and, as it turned out, there as one product that proved irresistible to thousands upon thousands of Chinese, from the most lowly, back-breaking, debt-ridden level of the peasantry to the effete, languishing refinement of the mandarins and aristocracy; and that product was opium from British Bengal.

By 1834, the Chinese were well and truly hooked. Opium was being shipped in through Canton at the rate of 16,000 chests a year. Five years later it had increased to nearly 40,000. Also, the silver flow had now completely reversed, and it was this threat of Chinese bankruptcy as much as the growing addiction to opium that finally galvanized the Qing Government into action. It imposed a ban on the opium imports and, when the British and other European traders tried to break the ban by smuggling

the stuff in, it ordered its commissioner in Canton to blockade the foreign depot and confiscate their opium stocks. To the bitter chagrin of the British traders, some 20,000 chests of "foreign mud" went up in smoke right before their eyes. And they promptly declared war.

The officer who led the attack was Britain's Superintendent of Trade in China, Captain Charles Elliot. He did a simply splendid job of it, leading a naval squadron up the Pearl River to Canton, blockading the city and forcing the Chinese to come very smartly to heel. He then sat down with the Qing emperor's negotiator, a Manchu viceroy named Kishen, and demanded trade concessions as compensation for the loss of the 20,000 chests of opium.

In hindsight, both men acquitted themselves quite admirably at the negotiating table. Faced with superior military power and an aggressiveness to go with it, Viceroy Kishen fobbed Elliot off with a "barren rock with hardly a dwelling upon it" and one that was conveniently separated from the Chinese mainland. As for Elliot, that's exactly what he was demanding, an offshore sovereign sanctuary from where British trade could be conducted free of direct Chinese interference.

But hardly had Commodore Sir J. J. Gordon Bremer raised the flag in the sands of what was to be called Possession Point than the roof fell right in on the deal, Elliot was lambasted by Whitehall for allowing himself to be conned into a virtually useless piece of real estate, and quickly transferred to an uncivilized backwater of the British foreign service as Consul-General in Texas. Kishen was similarly berated and punished for giving away sovereign Chinese territory, and was hauled to Peking (Beijing) in chains and then banished to Tibet.

EARTH, WIND AND FIRE

Even though the luckless Elliot's successor, Sir Henry Pottinger, was also in favor of

OPPOSITE Fun, amusement and excitement for all the family at Ocean Park.

The British Flag Unfurls

establishing Hong Kong as a major trading depot, for all of two and a half years the British Government dismissed it as a worthless embarrassment and unworthy of even being regarded as a British possession. And the island itself certainly offered nothing that would endear it to anyone, let alone the mandarins of Whitehall. In fact it gave the initial impression of being absolutely unsuitable for human settlement.

Within a few months of the flag-raising ceremony a severe fever epidemic gripped the tiny community, forcing it to embark upon its first public works project — a cemetery. Then a violent typhoon roared in and destroyed all its makeshift housing and tore huge merchant men from their moorings in the "sheltered" harbor. A few days later another typhoon struck, and this one caught Captain Elliot himself — not yet dispatched in disgrace to Texas — on a journey from Macau. He narrowly escaped with his life after taking control of the small ship and beaching it on an island. A month later, fire raged through the island's first squatter community built along its western foreshores by Chinese traders, craftsmen and laborers who had already begun pouring over to the island.

Despite these setbacks, Pottinger allowed surveying and land sales to begin as soon as he replaced Elliot, and then sallied north with a British expeditionary force to complete the task that Elliot had failed to do — force the Chinese to open up mainland ports, or a more suitable island, for free trade and compensate. Government for the confiscated opium.

By August 1842 his guns were trained on the key Yangtze River city of Nanking (Nanjing), and the Qing Government was cowed into signing the Treaty of Nanking which gave the British five Treaty Ports, including a rather nondescript coastal weaving and fishing township called Shanghai. Almost a year later, on June 26, 1843, Whitehall declared Hong Kong a British colony with Pottinger as its first governor. But it was still a rather reluctant gesture — the assigned role of this new British possession was simply to provide a port "whereat they may careen and refit their ships."

THE COLONIAL GEOGRAPHY

This early history of Hong Kong not only explains its birth, and the struggle, pain and humiliation that accompanied it, but also its geography — for the Hong Kong that exists today is really what those piously aggrieved nineteenth century merchant-soldiers made of it. They first took an island that covered only 68 sq km (26 sq miles) of landspace, with most of that space unsuitable for large-scale development, its 552-m (1,811-ft) -high backbone rising virtually from the water's edge. It had absolutely no natural resources beyond its 44 sq km (17 sq miles) harbor — but the harbor was immediately its most prized and potentially powerful asset.

Early *gweilo* development took place along the waterfront of Victoria, or what is now more commonly known as Central District, on the only immediately available skirt of reasonably flat land. Their Chinese camp followers erected their raucous, sprawling, densely packed shanty town further to the west, in what was for many years marked on the maps as Chinatown but is now known as Western District.

As development gathered pace it pushed in two directions, up the steep slopes, or Mid-Levels, of the tallest hill overlooking the harbor, The Peak, and east along the harborfront through Wanchai and another indent of reasonably flat land at Happy Valley — where another fever epidemic struck its first settlers, driving the British back toward Victoria and instilling all sorts of fears and superstitions in the Chinese. Above Happy Valley, a natural pass through the steep hills provided a vital road through what was named Wongneichong Gap to the island's southern beaches at Repulse Bay and Aberdeen.

As the first road cut through the ocher-colored soil of the hillside the Chinese protested that the British had severed the spine of a dragon that reposed in the hills,

OPPOSITE Trams and buses rumble along Queen's Road Central against a backdrop of the colonial-style Legco Building and towers of the Jardine House and Exchange Square.

destroying the island's *fungshui,* or natural harmony of spirits and elements, and laying the settlement open to great misfortune. They didn't have to look far for the evidence of the dragon's wrath — successive epidemics continued to cut like scythes through the merchant and military ranks, and lawlessness reigned throughout the infant colony, with constant violence, burglary, robbery and piracy. Hong Kong's second major geographical development came in 1860 when, as part of the final settlement of the first Opium War of 1841, the Qing Government ceded Kowloon Point, the mainland wedge of what is now Tsimshatsui, and the strategic Stonecutter's Island. This not only gave the colony a bit more elbow room and a mainland foothold but also more effective control of the harbor.

In 1898, having fought the second Opium War to force China to open her doors to trade, the British dictated another deal, this one a 99-year lease in which the present-day geography of Hong Kong was established — the island, the mainland Kowloon district, the hinterland New Territories stretching up to and slightly beyond the Shumchun River, now called the Shenzhen River, and 233 more islands. It gave the colonial government a total 850 sq km (328 sq miles) of territory.

THE HUMAN GEOGRAPHY

Nowadays, it is this aspect of Hong Kong which is the most little-known to outsiders and a constant surprise to them when they get here. Most think of it as simply one island — the bargain-shopping, joss-reeking offshore world of Suzy Wong. Often it's not until they arrive there that they realize how big Hong Kong really is. Aside from the main island and the large rump of territory across the harbor, two of the myriad other islands, Lamma and Cheung Chau, are big enough to support large mixed Chinese and foreign expatriate communities, while Lantau Island is a huge, relatively undeveloped opportunity for future expansion, twice the size of Hong Kong Island itself.

The tenacity with which the early British traders and settlers clung to this "barren"

place can be understood when you consider the territory's position within the geography of southern China. It lies at the eastern side of the mouth of the Pearl River, the major access to the sea for the key river of the south, the Xi Kiang, and part of a vast network of waterways that reaches right up into the heart of China. Canton (Guangzhou), the southern gateway to China and its most rapidly modernizing city, lies just over 100 km (66 miles) to the northwest — and this doorstep proximity is now of considerable value to both cities, giving Hong Kong a close, reasonably efficient trading and investment partner, and a source of food, and Guangzhou a ready supply of capital and much-needed consumer technology.

But it is the human settlement of Hong Kong that has really established its present-day geography. Just as the prospect of one billion people confined in 15 percent of the land-space can be regarded as the most fascinating topographical feature of China, Hong Kong's five to seven million population crammed into 10 percent of a relatively infinitesimal 1,070 sq km (328 sq miles) pimple of land has never ceased to amaze the outside world. A decade ago, the urban beehives of the island waterfront and Kowloon were so overcrowded that three square meters (32 sq ft) per person was considered to be an acceptable living space, and the district of Shamshuipo had a population density of 165,000 people per square kilometer (427,000 per square mile) — the highest the world has known.

It is this struggle to fit all its people in that has given Hong Kong its dramatic human topography, the massive high-rise development of its two main urban centers and the satellite towns of the New Territories. And, just as dramatically, the geography has been changed and re-sculpted over the past century in another continuing thrust for more living space — large-scale reclamation of harbor side and seafront land.

OPPOSITE Hakka women dressed in their traditional headdress are still a frequent sight in the New Territories countryside.

Engulf and Devour

When the first traders, merchants and soldiers began building the colonial settlement, Queen's Road was their first main thoroughfare on Hong Kong Island, and it ran right along the harbor foreshores. Before the island had even been officially declared a colony, trading depots, warehouses and wharves were being built on reclaimed land on the northern side of the road, and from that point on the water-

front was steadily devoured — and the harbor gradually narrowed — by successive waves of development.

As early as 1851, when a fire virtually destroyed the "Chinatown" settlement to the west of Victoria, new land was claimed from the harbor around what is now Bonham Strand to build a new community. Four years later the first reclamation work began along the eastern harbor front, extending the Happy Valley district into the sea. Over the next few years another reclamation project created a *praya* along the Victoria harborfront that pushed Queen's Road back from the water — but by 1890 this new land-space had become so overcrowded and unsanitary" that it was overtaken by another big reclamation scheme, and the old *praya* is now Des Voeux Road, deep in the heart of Central District. Successive reclamation schemes extended Kennedy Town and Wanchai into the harbor waters, and "pestilent swamps" on the foreshores of Causeway Bay and the mainland Yaumatei were filled in and quickly turned

over to commercial development. Right into the 1920s, the scramble for new land continued — the Wanchai waterfront was pushed further into the harbor, creating the teeming urban tenement area between Hennessy and Gloucester Roads; Kai Tak was extended into the harbor on the mainland side to create room for the colony's early land-based airstrip; and other reclamation work created new harborfront space at Shamshuipo and Laichikok. In the most dramatic reclamation project of all, the runway of Hong Kong International Airport, Kai Tak, was later built entirely on reclaimed land, creating what is virtually a fixed flight-deck in the harbor and, for travelers, one of the world's most awesome arrival and take-off experiences.

By the late 1950s, so much of the harbor front of Hong Kong Island was earmarked for reclamation that engineers began to worry about the effect it would all have on the harbor currents. It took a major research project to settle the fears — a 23 m (75 ft) scale model of the harbor, with electronically operated weirs creating "tides," was constructed at a hydraulic research plant in England. Tests showed where the land could be extended without damaging the colony's most valuable asset.

Since then, the harborfront around Central District has marched on beyond Connaught Road, creating land-space for the General Post Office, City Hall, British Forces headquarters, Mandarin and Furama Hotels and the soaring Jardine House and Exchange Square. In Wanchai, another massive reclamation scheme has doubled its area, creating the harborfront area on which the Academy for the Performing Arts, China Resources Building and Wanchai Stadium now stand. To the east, the Island Eastern Corridor streaks across reclaimed land that has doubled the land-space of North Point, Quarry Bay and Shaukeiwan.

On the Kowloon side, the Kowloon-Canton Railway Terminus, Kwai Chung container port and the huge Tsimshatsui East development all stand on land that was once harbor waters. Out in the New Territories, reclamation has provided much of the land-space for the huge New Towns of Shatin, Tsuen Wan and Tuen Mun. In all, more than 220 sq km (85 sq miles) of extra land has been squeezed from the sea bed over the past century and a half. And there's more to come. As Lantau Island is developed, easing pressure on the rest of the territory, more land will be reclaimed around its hilly coastline for more high-rise residential and commercial centers. And the geography of Hong Kong will change again. West of the Macau Ferry Terminal on Hong Kong Island, a broad strip of reclaimed land is about to radically alter the harbor front face of Western District.

monsoons that brought the British and European traders in the first place. In the days of sail, the huge canvas-laden merchant ships rode the summer monsoons north to the China Coast, stopping over in the "Fragrant Harbour" to take on fresh water and repair any damage before continuing up the Pearl River to Guangzhou. The winter monsoon, its winds originating in the frigid reaches of the Siberian steppes and blowing south right down through China and into the northern Pacific, carried the fleets on their first stage home to the West.

BETWEEN THE MONSOONS

If the struggle for living space has molded much of the topography and character of Hong Kong, the struggle with its distinctive climate has been just as dramatic. The island lies just south of the Tropic of Cancer, which makes it sub-tropical. But it also lies virtually at the point where the southern and northern, or summer and winter, monsoons collide over Southeast Asia — and that has made it a place where only mad dogs and Englishmen could probably have envisaged settling, survived, and developed the huge urban society that it is today. It was Hong Kong's position between the

Around March each year, as these mighty wind systems change, the warm southern monsoon meets the cooler, waning winter monsoon over the South China Coast, and the result is muggy moisture-laden air that blankets Hong Kong, settling in thick clouds over the Peak and the mid-levels of the mountains and drenching everything it touches. The summer months — May through September — see regular and sometimes torrential rains and, during the hottest months in July and August, temperatures soaring to between 27 °C and 34 °C

OPPOSITE Junk passes through Hong Kong harbor. ABOVE Harbor lighters have been the traditional method of unloading cargoes from moored ships.

(81 °F and 93 °F), along with humidity in the 90s.

Not surprisingly, Hong Kong is the answer to every air-conditioning salesman's dream, and its newest urban development, particularly in Central District and Tsimshatsui, seems to reflect the enervating climatic conditions — enclosed walkways and pedestrian flyovers connect many of the big shopping plazas and hotel arcades so that you can scurry from one frosty, blissful air-conditioned haven to another with only an occasional exposure to the sauna

winds of up to 200 km (125 miles) an hour and they usually cross the China coast to the east of Hong Kong, lashing the territory with their stormy outer bands. Mercifully, it's only on occasions that they hit Hong Kong head-on.

Two typhoons scored direct hits within months of Commodore Bremer's historic landing in 1841. On Tuesday September 22, 1874, a particular violent one almost devastated the colony, the *Hong Kong Times* recording this vivid description of the disaster: "The rain descended in torrents: the

outside. From October through December the northern monsoon takes over, its icy winds abating and softening by the time they reach this far south, moderating the climate to pleasant sunny days with 21 °C to 25 °C temperatures and a relatively parched 70 percent humidity. From there, January through March is cool, about 14 °C to 21 °C, and April in the mid-20 °C range.

But the most fearsome climatic feature that the territory has had to face, and still faces each year, is the typhoon season These powerful cyclones rear up out of the Pacific south of the Philippines each summer and surge northwards to hurl themselves one after the other at the Chinese mainland. They carry tremendous volumes of rain and

wind blew with the violence of a tempest, the rage of a whirlwind. Vessels staunch and strong were driven about the harbor or on to the shore like children's toy craft. Roofs were torn off as by the hand of a mighty giant; trees were uprooted by the hundreds; rows of buildings were blown down in a moment, many of the inhabitants beings buried in their ruins. The harbor water overflowed on to the Praya dashing aside and carrying away coping stones of tons weight. The work of destruction went on without intermission for hours; and it maybe said that there is not a single house in the Colony but what has suffered."

Altogether, 35 huge merchant men were either sunk, driven ashore or badly damaged, along with hundreds of junks and sampans. More than 2,000 lives were lost in Hong Kong and Macau. In the hinterland of Guangdong province, the death toll was an horrific 100,000. And in September 1906 an even more destructive typhoon hit — this one killing 10,000 people in just one and a half hours, sinking or crippling 141 British and European ships and destroying more than 2,000 Chinese craft.

The most recent destructive *tai-fung* (big wind) was Typhoon Rose in 1971, which hit the territory head-on with 150-knot winds that actually broke the anemometer and dumped 288 mm (11.23 in) of rain in just a single day. In 1979, when I was living in an apartment block on the seafront at Stanley, Typhoon Hope roared in and I was able to witness first-hand the full fury of these tropical hurricanes.

The winds were so fierce that they shook the nine-storey building. The view from the windows was, on the one hand, frighteningly bizarre — a howling, shrieking green blizzard of leaves stripped from the surrounding trees. On the sea front side of the apartment, the view was of raging seas, huge waves crashing over the sea-wall — and a beautiful "staunch and strong" pleasure junk belonging to one of my friends being torn from its mooring and hurled right up on to a beach and dashed to pieces against a brick and concrete public toilet.

But by 1979, Hong Kong had long been dealing with typhoons as an irritating but not necessarily dreaded annual weather disturbance. The territory now has a very advanced and effective early warning system that gives the community plenty of time to batten down for a "big blow." As a typhoon or "tropical storm" is spawned and begins its northward rampage, it is tracked by weather satellites and reconnaissance planes, and if it looks like coming close to Hong Kong a series of typhoon signals go up.

Signal number one means there's a typhoon building in the region. Signal number 10 means it's going to cross the coast close to or perhaps right over Hong Kong — and by then the entire population has gone home to sit it out. Windows are taped or fitted with storm shutters. Shop fronts and hotel façades are boarded up. Work sites are battened down to prevent what is now the main danger of these annual visitations — flying building material and debris in the streets. The radio and television network issues constant bulletins on the strength and direction of the storm. For tourists, snug and safe in their hotels, the only danger or inconvenience that a typhoon presents nowadays is the possibility of a delayed departure from Kai Tak Airport or the train and ferry terminals.

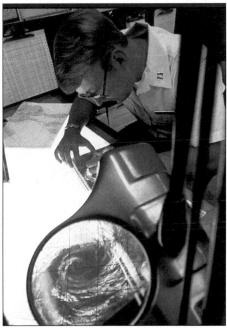

Somehow, against all these political and physical odds, Hong Kong has more than justified the faith and the colonial dream — however antiquated and piratical it may seem to be from these more honorable times — that fluttered with the Union Jack on the flag staff on Possession Point on January 26, 1841. Even more remarkably, that dream has been realized in the face of an even greater challenge — a partnership of what must certainly be the two most distinct and incompatible cultures on earth: the British and the Chinese.

OPPOSITE Hong Kong Harbor in twilight.
ABOVE At the Royal Observatory meteorologists interpret radar and satellite pictures of weather disturbance to give advance warning of typhoons.

The Lion and the Dragon

THE CULTURAL CONTRAST

Right up until the development boom and sudden political shift of the eighties, an integral feature of Hong Kong's vivid and most unlikely cultural character went on show each Saturday afternoon on a neatly trimmed and jealously exclusive oval of green turf right in the heart of Central District.

There, in the grounds of what is now a public park, Chater Garden, British creams and white cottons flapped in the damp breezes from the nearby harbor, and the sharp thwack of stitched leather on wooden bats — along with occasional cry of "Owzat!" — gave a faint, waning echo of British imperial tradition and power amid the general downtown clamor of traffic, trams and construction site pile drivers.

This Saturday cricket match, as religious to the British community as Sunday services in St John's Cathedral and the firing of the Noon-Day Gun, took place right under the towering, austere façade and red-lettered Chinese sign of what was then Maoist Beijing's main commercial and political base in Hong Kong, the Bank of China. This striking contrast of cricket and communism was for many years a much-photographed symbol of Hong Kong and the tenuous circumstances in which it existed — a borrowed place living on borrowed time.

But it also represented a much wider contrast, that of two largely alien cultures, British and Chinese, which had somehow managed to settle together and function side by side in Hong Kong, harness their various qualities and skills to a common goal — prosperity — and still retain their own cultural traditions and characteristics While the British enjoyed their sedate pursuit of maiden overs and silly mid-ons right below the bastion of Chinese communism, an antique Chinese sailing junk might have been tacking its way ponderously down the harbor, a traditional Chinese funeral might have been wending its way through the packed streets of Causeway Bay or Stanley in a cacophony of clashing cymbals and thundering tom-toms and wailing pipes; or thousands of Cantonese might have been flocking to pay their an-nual homage to Tin Hau, the Goddess of the Sea, pouring across the harbor in decorated sampans, fishing junks and lighters to Po Toi Island or Joss House Bay, on the southern shore of Clear Water Bay.

If there was any real measure of cultural exchange, it still placed each culture on the fringe of the other. The British and other foreign expatriate groups enjoyed the Tin Hau Festival and other Chinese cultural events just as the Cantonese enjoyed Christmas — but only as spectators, swiveling their camera lenses from the edge of the melee, never really to share the spiritual impulse of the occasion. If there was a point at which both cultures could actually find common ground and speak each other's language, it was in the business office or the boardroom, or in the one major "cultural" pursuit in which distinctions are blurred because it is another proving ground of the mutual lust for the fast buck — Hong Kong's paramount and incredibly wealthy gambling institution, horseracing.

Since the redevelopment of Central District and, significantly, since the gradual changing of the guard from Western to Chinese political and commercial power, the Cricket Club has moved to a more roomy but far less dominant site above Happy Valley on Wongneichong Gap Road. But the cultural contrast remains, and thankfully so, for it provides perhaps the most colorful and exciting of all Hong Kong's tourist attractions. And it also bears testimony to the extent to which the Lion and the Dragon have been able to lie down together, and each occasionally get a wink of sleep.

WIND AND WATER

In many respects, Hong Kong's colorful and often dramatic cultural character exists because of the tenacity with which the vastly predominant Cantonese population clings to its Chinese beliefs and traditions. In other respects, it prevails because of a constant and tenacious Cantonese struggle

OPPOSITE Traditionally costumed child "floats" on a pole over crowd secured by hidden braces, at Cheung Chau Bun Festival.

to drive a coach and horses through the slightest loophole or loose clause in the territory's British law.

In the midst of high-tech high-rise development, many Chinese cling, for example, to the traditional *fungshui* ("wind and water"), a mixture of belief, superstition, divination and geomancy which is aimed primarily at placing man in his most harmonious relationship with the physical and spiritual world about him. When a new apartment is being furnished and equipped, a *fungshui* geomancer may be called in to

because in their eyes it would weaken the southern capital by linking it directly with the inauspicious Nine Dragons said to be residing within the earthen bowels of Kowloon.

But even today, homes and offices in Hong Kong are sometimes evacuated and then exorcised by *fungshui* experts to get rid of "ghosts" and malevolent influences, as happened just a decade or more ago with an entire floor of the Inland Revenue Department. The movie tycoon Run Shaw is said to have consulted *fungshui* geomancers

position the furniture so that it conforms with the *Ch'i* or spiritual breath of the universe. Mirrors are often strategically placed in Cantonese homes to block or deflect the path of evil spirits and influences.

This 4,000-year-old science created havoc and apoplexy with Western attempts to modernize China in the early treaty port days. When the first railway line in China was built between Shanghai and Wusong it was bought up by Chinese investors and then destroyed for fear that the speed of the trains would disrupt the *fungshui* of thousands of people living along the route. When the first telegraph line was strung between Guangzhou and Hong Kong it aroused Chinese outrage and opposition

about the site of his huge production center at Clear Water Bay. When the Hong Kong Hilton rented its ballroom for a particularly important land auction, the development company conducting the sale brought in a *fungshui* man to check the ballroom's harmony before bidding began. He decided that the sale would be a big success if the ballroom doors remained open throughout the proceedings, several windows were blacked out to block evil spirits and the cocktail bar, of all things, was rearranged in an L-shape.

Fungshui enjoyed an upsurge of popularity during the initial New Towns resettlement and development in the New Territories. Any new home that didn't conform to the most propitious *fungshui* siting brought an immediate complaint — and a demand for compensation — from its occupants. It was a constant headache for the hard-pressed planners of the government's Public Works Department, and it may have been motivated less by spiritual concern than the opportunity for base coin, but it also tended to be an effective grassroots defense against a wholesale process of up-rooting and re-housing in which human comfort and needs may not on occasions have been given a high priority. It was taken

seriously, nonetheless, and especially when it became known that one of the PWD's Chinese departmental heads responsible for settling *fungshui* issues had himself brought in a geomancer to check the location and surrounding influences of an apartment that he was interested in buying.

It's difficult to say just how deep-rooted these beliefs remain in the present-day mini-Manhattan of Hong Kong, but it's estimated that there are still around 100 geomancers at large and still a fair proportion of the population that will not sign a business contract, take a trip, buy or build a home, select a grave site, bury their dead, or choose a wedding date without consulting the vital signs first.

THE BAMBOO RULE

But whatever its present-day strength, is an interesting cultural phenomenon for the role that it has symbolically played in the division of power in Hong Kong. Just as the British administration has often found it prudent and expedient to back down and pay lip service to its beliefs, so it has had to give ground on more major cultural and political issues over the years to accommodate its vastly overwhelming 98 percent Cantonese population and to keep the essential profit-making machinery of Hong Kong running smoothly.

In fact, for an undemocratic colonial government, ruling largely through the personal power of its governor and a non-elected Executive Council (with a partially elected Legislative Council responsible for passing policy into law), the British have been reasonably even-handed and non-interventionist in their dealings with the Cantonese, preferring to guide rather than govern and to bend like bamboo rather than stiffen like oak in the face of Chinese pressure. Their most obvious stamp on the society has been the civil law and order that has allowed the territory to develop to its present extent. They have also taken a hard and uncompromising line against spitting in the streets and other public places, much to the relief of visitors and young Chinese alike. They have discouraged littering, at least in the most popular urban tourist districts. Quite naturally, considering their obsession with "man's best friend," they've strictly banned the eating of dogs — or at least driven it underground. They've even managed to encourage the Cantonese to form British-style queues for buses, ferries and other public services and facilities — an accomplishment that can only really be appreciated when you experience the mob frenzy and struggle for any essential service throughout China itself.

But for the most part the British have allowed, and even encouraged, the Hong

Two faces of Hong Kong spiritualism: OPPOSITE Palmists read hands and fortune teller ABOVE awaits clients in Temple Street night market in Kowloon.

Kong Cantonese to be themselves, to freely observe their own traditions, rituals, beliefs and lifestyles. And it is this cultural freedom that has given Hong Kong its unique color and excitement on the one hand — and, on the other, preserved much of the most fascinating aspects of Chinese culture that were dealt a destructive body-blow in the Red Guard rampage of China's Cultural Revolution. The result has been a society that appears to be constructed almost entirely of steel, concrete and glass at first glance, but underneath is a constant and whirling pageant of Chinese social and spiritual life.

HONG KONG FIESTA

Hong Kong's spiritual calendar is full of observances, rituals and festivals that govern the Chinese reverence for life, death, good luck, good health, their forebears, their new-born and the various gods that preside over their interpretation of the universe and the firmament. On virtually any day, some ritual expression is being made somewhere in Hong Kong, whether it's the relatively simple slow-motion, highly controlled dance and calisthenics of traditional *Tai Chi* exercises, usually seen on Blake Pier on the Central District waterfront or along the harbor frontage of Victoria Park in Causeway Bay, or a full day's explosion of feasting, praying, joss-stick burning and gift-giving that marks a major spiritual event.

MAJOR FESTIVALS

Chinese New Year

The most important observance of the Chinese, their New Year, comes well after the Western event, marked by the first new moon after the sun enters the constellation Aquarius and falling somewhere between January 21 and February 19. It is a time of celebration and of reckoning, and it involves a full week of feasting, observances and rituals during which most business in Hong Kong grinds to a crawl or stops altogether. As the magic hour approaches, families, merchants and factory chiefs clean out

their homes and offices and settle all outstanding debts. Apartments and homes are decorated with peach blossom trees, kumquat trees, jonquils (Water Fairies) and chrysanthemums. It is at this time that the Kitchen God is believed to visit households to report on the families' conduct during the year, so pictures of the god are worshipped and smeared with sugar or honey so that the reports will be sweet and not sour.

For the visitor, the atmosphere of Chinese New Year can best be captured by

meandering around the enormous flower markets, erected specially for the occasion, in **Victoria Park** in Causeway Bay on Hong Kong Island and **Fa Hui** in Boundary Street, Kowloon. It is a carnival of jostling, jovial couples and families ambling around in search of flowering symbols fit to decorate their homes for the auspicious occasion. The most patient can be seen near dawn scurrying away almost hidden behind their bargains of enormous potted flowering trees which anxious sellers must clear at any price before the market closes.

On New Year's Day, the Cantonese dress in their finest new clothes — the children swaddled in brightly colored Chinese padded jackets — and go visiting close

The Lion and The Dragon

relatives, exchanging red envelopes, or *laisee* packets, containing "lucky money." On the second day it's time to visit and exchange *laisee* with close friends. It's also the time to reflect upon any late lunches, long sojourns around the water cooler or office mis-demeanors during the previous year. This has traditionally been the day when employers could inform any superfluous or unsatisfactory staff that their services are no longer required — either presenting them with a symbolic piece of chicken or greeting them with the words "Thank you for your

bals and, here and there, the crackle and splutter of fireworks — banned for all except official occasions in Hong Kong since the Red Guard troubles of the late sixties.

There are other festivals throughout the year that have less feasting and formality and far more fun and color.

The Dragon Boat Festival
Usually held in June, the Dragon Boat Festival is an ancient Chinese commemorative event that Hong Kong has turned into a combined sporting extravaganza and beer

assistance in the past year," which in the Cantonese tradition is equivalent to an American vice-president gently telling one of his executives, "You've done a great job. What you need now is a rest."

Although mainly a time of rest, reflection and family obligation, Chinese New Year has its pageantry and color too. In China itself, the period features huge Spring Festival parades in most major cities and towns. In Hong Kong, especially in the more "Chinese" villages and centers like Stanley, Aberdeen, Shaukeiwan and Cheung Chau Island, hundreds of people celebrate with almost continuous, day-long lion and dragon dances to the frenzied thunder and clash of tom-toms and cym-

fest — with the added underlying attraction of rivalry between Chinese and *gweilo* teams. The event has traditionally paid homage to the memory of an imperial adviser, Chu Yuan, of the Warring States Period (403–221 BC), who committed suicide by throwing himself into the Mi-Lo River in what is now Hunan Province in a desperate act of protest against official intrigue and corruption.

It is said that Chu was so popular and respected that the villagers, hearing of his death, rushed in their boats to the spot

ABOVE Rock singer performs in open-air concert. OPPOSITE Door gods and banners proclaim the approaching Chinese New Year.

where he'd disappeared and beat the water with paddles, banged drums and gongs and threw rice to keep the fish away from his body. It's been a custom since to make offerings of colored packets of rice on the day of the festival, and the symbolic beating of the waters survives in the very nature of the dragon boat races.

Today's dragon boats are anything up to 40 m (131 ft) long, have huge ornately carved and decorated dragon's heads on their prows and look very much like a hybrid of an ancient Chinese war canoe and a

modern racing shell. They're manned by as many as 80 oarsmen who lash at the water with their paddles to the heavy rhythmic beat of big drums carried in the middle of the vessels. There are many heats, culminating in a grand championship of the three fastest boats, and the races are held over courses that are packed with pleasure junks, launches, ferries and other small craft.

If there's an essential spirit to the competition it's making as much noise as possible. While hundreds of spectators on the surrounding vessels beat gongs to frighten evil spirits away, hundreds of others yell and scream encouragement from the shores as the boats leap and lurch through great

explosions and cascades of water thrown up by each massed strike of the paddles, the tom-toms pounding out a kind of primitive blood-curdling tattoo above all the hullabaloo and excitement. Some heats end with boats foundering and sinking with their crews, amid more waves of hysteria. The races are held at a variety of locations in the New Territories, Kowloon and on Hong Kong Island. The Hong Kong Tourist Association will give advice on the current year's program and venues, and these are also published in the daily and tourist newspapers. A week or so later, it's all done again, with crews from all parts of southeast Asia and even the West taking part in the strictly competitive International Dragon Boat Races, held on the Tsimshatsui East waterfront.

Moon Festival

In contrast, there are other traditional events and observances in Hong Kong that are noted more for their reverence and beauty than their decibel level. And none is more beautiful than the Moon Festival, held in mid-autumn on the 15th day of the eighth moon. Also known as the Mid-Autumn (Chung Chiu) Festival, it combines a Chinese version of the Western harvest celebration with a lantern festival and a fourteenth century tradition of preparing and eating moon cakes, a sweet confection filled with sesame seeds, duck eggs and ground lotus seeds. But it is also a moment of simple nature worship in which thousands of people make their way to beaches and the peaks of Hong Kong's many hills to picnic through the night and gaze upon the full moon.

For the Lantern Festival, there's no better venue than **Victoria Park** near Causeway Bay — the entire grounds festooned with thousands of lighted lanterns ranging from the traditional pot-bellied candle-lit paper designs to ornate laser-operated versions that revolve and play music. But, from my own experience, the location that offers the most romantic combination of lanterns and moon worship is **Stanley Beach.** There, in the full flat glow of the rising moon, the sands are packed with picnickers and moon-gazers; and there are not only lanterns of all shapes and designs to behold — everything from butterflies and fish to tanks and warships — but the children carve castles and ornate patterns in the sands and place hundreds of small candles in them, creating astonishingly sophisticated fairylands of flickering pools and caverns of light.

THE TEMPLE TRAIL

Other major cultural events in Hong Kong revolve around its temples, of which there

battle for supremacy, the two religions adapted to each other, virtually "borrowing" each other's gods, and have since stood alongside Confucianism as the paramount Three Teachings of the Chinese culture.

Hong Kong's oldest and most famous temple is the **Man Mo Temple** on Hollywood Road, below the island's Mid-Levels, built within a few years of the colonial land-grab of 1841. In typical Taoist style it's dedicated to the God of Literature and civil servants, known as Man, and the God of War, Mo.

are no less than 600, an amazing number for so small a place. Most of them are Taoist, and pay homage to animist beliefs and spiritual codes that sprang out of the early mists of Chinese history as a formula for that most crucial of all Chinese creeds — man's harmony with nature and the entire universe. Where ancient animism endowed all of the physical world with various guardian or malignant spirits, Taoism produced dozens of different gods and deities, all of them entrusted with the care and protection of some aspect of moral life. When Buddhism invaded China from India along the Silk Road in the fourth century, Taoism flexed and bent like bamboo in its path, and thus survived the challenge. Rather than

Tin Hau Festival
The most revered of all Hong Kong's deities is Tin Hau, the Goddess of the Sea and protector of fisherfolk, and the annual Tin Hau Festival, which falls in April or May is by far the most colorful and dramatic of all the territory's spiritual events. There are Tin Hau Temples all over Hong Kong, but the most popular mecca of the festival is the **Ta Miu (Green Temple)** in Joss House Bay. Huge armadas of colorfully decorated

OPPOSITE A lavish fireworks display in mid-harbor is part of the festivities. ABOVE Dragon Boats prepare for international heats near Tsimshatsui East promenade. OVERLEAF Softly glowing paper lanterns add romance to Moon Festival in Sung Dynasty Village in Laichikok.

junks, launches, cargo lighters, ferries and even harbor tugs flood across the harbor waters to crowd the foreshores below the temple, tom-toms beating, gongs clanging and maybe firecrackers exploding over the decks and bows.

Lions and dragons prance, leap and twist across gangplanks to the shore, and behind them come spectacular, lavishly decorated paper altars loaded with offerings of food, wine, tea, "lucky" money and even toys. And then come the worshippers themselves, carrying giant wrist-thick joss sticks and more offerings of fruit, pastries and even whole roasted piglets. One after another, the cavalcades stream ashore and up through the temple doorways, cramming into the prayer halls and chambers in a murky bedlam of billowing joss smoke, in the thick mists of which hundreds of figures kneel, *kowtow* and pray to the looming, impassive images, others haul the garish paper altars up the walls to hang on display in the temple rafters, others shake canisters of bamboo tapers, inscribed with numbers, taking the sticks that slide out of the tight clusters to nearby soothsayers to have their fortunes read for the coming year. And over it all, the drums boom and the gongs clash and whine, and engines grumble and roar as wave after wave of fishing junks and harbor craft pull into the crowded bay.

The Birthday of Lord Buddha
This inherent exuberance and excitement of the Cantonese somehow complements, rather than shatters, the more placid, reflective character of Buddhism in Hong Kong. Its major Buddhist monastery and temple, **Po Lin (Precious Lotus)** on Lantau Island, offers retreat, meditation and escape from the urban clamor for most of the year, but during the most important observance, the Birthday of Lord Buddha, held in May, peace and tranquillity give way to pandemonium as thousands of worshipers flock across to the island to fill the sanctified air once again with clouds of joss, the blood-stirring thunder of drums and the massed murmur and chorus of prayer. Similar spiritual explosions take place at the Buddhist **Castle Peak Monastery, Miu Fat Monastery** and the celebrated **Ten Thousand**

Buddhas Monastery in the New Territories, while at the **Tam Kung Temple** in Shau-kei-wan, Taoism and Buddhism put on one of their spiritual "double features" in which homage is paid to Tam Kung, the latter-day second patron saint of Hong Kong boat people, and honor is given to the other Great Teaching with a spectacular Washing the Buddha ceremony at the harbor foreshores — with more drums and gongs, more extravagant altars and offerings, and dancing, writhing lions and dragons.

WORLD OF THE LIVING DEAD

Alongside the fear of spirits and worship of gods, there lies the most vital of all the spiritual impulses and disciplines of the Chinese — ancestor-worship. Its importance in Chinese culture cannot be overstated — it is the bond, or thread of continuity, that ties their remarkable 5,000-year-old civilization together and has enabled them to keep it virtually intact, and its main traditions, customs, beliefs and rites unchanged, to the

OPPOSITE Tin Hau Festival — worshippers offer food, joss and prayers at Wong Tai Sin Temple.
ABOVE Dancing lion "walks the plank" at temple in Shaukeiwan.

present day. It is also the discipline that has maintained the ancient social codes of Confucius, keeping them firmly established as both the base and most powerful creed of the Three Teachings, setting the rules by which the society is structured and leaving individual matters like faith, hope and fortune to the two religions.

The essence of Confucianism, like many other basic Chinese traditions and beliefs, is the pursuit of social harmony. Its abiding principle is this: if people know their allotted place within a society, and are taught to

accept it, they'll achieve a measure of contentment; and contentment means peace. The broad picture of Confucianism is a vast pyramid — peasant or laboring masses at the base and the emperor or ruling elite at the topmost tip — with each teeming class or level in between submitting and kowtowing to the one above.

And there are levels within levels. Not only are wealth, birth and social role and status honored, but age is respected and even revered, filial piety elevates parents close to godliness and, most fascinating of all, ancestors are not only diligently recorded, honored and worshipped — they are placed in the realm of the living dead, an underworld which is the mirror-image of

the living society and in which their comforts and needs must be taken care of as if they were themselves alive.

This reverence for the dead adds its own color and somewhat bizarre ritual to the spiritual pageantry of Hong Kong. At any time in the city streets, people may be seen setting fire to paper replicas of jewelry, furniture, washing machines and, in the years to come, probably micro-computers too — the flames consigning these comforts and luxuries to needy ancestral spirits in the underworld.

In China, a recent edition of the *Shandong Law Journal* reported the sudden re-emergence of the ancient practice of arranging "marriages" for dead relatives. Incredible as it may seem, the corpses of unmarried women were being sold at high prices in Shandong to parents whose sons had died unwed, the journal said. In one particular case, the body of a girl killed in a road accident had been sold for nearly US$1,000 to a family whose son had died before an arranged married could take place. More than 10 other cases had been reported in one area of the province.

In each instance, symbolic "weddings" had been conducted, in keeping with the Chinese belief that it would provide a marriage partner in the wonder world for a male soul who would otherwise face a lonely afterlife.

The Festival of Hungry Ghosts

There are ritual occasions in Hong Kong when the full ceremony of ancestor-worship can be seen. The Festival of Hungry Ghosts, for instance, held on the 15th day of the seventh moon (August), is the day on which vast symbolic fortunes in gifts and provisions are consigned by ritual fire to the awaiting dead. Hungry ghosts mean underworld spirits who are financially down on their luck, whose homes have leaking roofs, whose TV set has blown a fuse, who need a car, bicycle or maybe even a horse and carriage to get around, and hungry or discontented spirits can mean trouble for the living. So, on this festive day all over Hong Kong, the urban pavements, temple forecourts, ancestral halls and grave sites blaze with paper offerings.

Ching Ming Festival

In April and July an even more astonishing ritual takes place. On this, the Ching Ming Festival, thousands upon thousands of people flock to the graves of their forebears to pay homage by sweeping, cleaning and repairing the tombs and sites, making offerings of food and, in some cases, actually taking out the skulls and bones and polishing them. Bizarre as it sounds, it's actually a rather tender event — it's a family communion and transaction with the dead in which their wishes and needs are anticipated and their blessings sought for the future course of the living. A similar ceremony is held in October during the Chung Yeung Festival.

The Bun Festival

There's one other major festival in Hong Kong that began as an observance but has now become more of an extravagant seven-day mardis gras. The Bun Festival on the island of **Cheung Chau,** held each May on dates that are not announced until about three weeks beforehand, was originally held to placate the spirits, so the story goes, of people murdered by a ruthless pirate who used the island as a base before the colonial British appeared on the scene.

Now, it's a huge fiesta that features religious ceremonies, Chinese opera performances and various other cultural displays and, on the third day, a tumultuous parade of lions and dragons, traditional drum, pipe and gong bands, costumed stilt-walkers and ornately decorated floats with tableaux depicting moral themes — and, riding majestically above the whole procession, children dressed in theatrical and historical costumes and suspended on the tips of poles with hidden harnesses and metal rods so that they appear to be levitating amidst the banners and flags.

Throughout the week-long celebration, mammoth images of three deities — the Gods of the Earth, Good Luck and Hell — preside over the festivities. But all the feasting and fun is really focused on the central symbol of the festival, three big bamboo towers literally covered with bread buns. These small round loaves are there as offerings to the dead, but at the climax of the festival they are taken down and distributed to the revelers — the idea being to grab as many as possible for good luck in the coming year. Until a few years ago, it was the tradition at each Bun Festival to make a massed scramble up the towers for the buns, but the free-for-all was abandoned when it got out of hand and one of the towers collapsed, injuring several revelers

THE GOD OF FOOLS AND HORSES

Given the extraordinary religious fervor and exuberance of the Cantonese, and, by comparison, the orderly, reserved and almost self-conscious character of the British and their fellow-Westerners, it's not surprising that while the two cultures lie quite peacefully alongside each other in Hong Kong they very rarely touch. Most direct contact between the Chinese and *gweilo* takes place in the business arena, and out-

OPPOSITE Filial piety at graves of ancestors in Chung Yeung Festival at Wo Hop Shek Cemetery. LEFT Beautifully dressed doll-like young girl at Cheung Chau Bun Festival.

side office hours they generally both tend to go their own ways. East and West may indeed meet in Hong Kong, but when it comes to actually mingling, East is still East and West is still very much West.

There are some obvious reasons for this. First of all, for most Westerners Hong Kong is a transitory place, and for most Hong Kong Chinese it's a sanctuary beyond which there's no place else they can really go. There's also a history of British and Western social and economic supremacy — and a colonial superiority often expressed

in the most racist terms over the years — that the Chinese have no real inclination to forget or forgive now that they are taking over the reins of power. And when it comes to superiority, there's no civilization on earth that can quite match that of the Chinese when it comes to belief in its own pre-eminence.

In the main, business is their common language and profit their common religion. And if there's a god that embraces both cultures it is a strange Taoist deity called Wong Tai Sin, the guardian namesake of the Wong Tai Sin Temple in Kowloon City — and the patron saint of racing punters!

It says a great deal about Taoism and the Chinese perspective on religion generally

that a new god could be created, only as recently as 1973 in fact, to preside over the fortunes of fools and horses. But then, Hong Kong's racing industry is no ordinary one — it is a mammoth business institution that provides the right mix of luck, leisure and profit that gives both the Lion and Dragon cultures an arena in which to meet and mingle. And it is extremely profitable, with its wealth spilling down the sides of its coffers and into various huge community projects to benefit society at large.

THE JOCKEY CLUB'S DOMAIN

The whole industry is operated exclusively by the Royal Hong Kong Jockey Club, which is the largest private employer in Hong Kong. Membership of it is probably more fiercely sought and highly prized than an award or mention in the annual Queen's Honors List. To win the right in the Jockey Club's annual ballot to buy, train and race a horse is to know that you have been decorated with full honors for your distinguished service to Hong Kong Inc.

The Race Tracks
Everything about the Jockey Club's vast domain is bigger, richer and more streamlined than anything like it anywhere else in the world. It operates only two racecourses, one at **Happy Valley** on Hong Kong Island and the other at **Shatin** in the New Territories, but the US$7.6-million Shatin course covers an area of 100 hectares (250 acres) — all of it reclaimed land — and has a capacity of 83,000, the biggest on earth. The equipment and facilities at both tracks are pure state-of-the-art, featuring fully computerized betting, closed-circuit television and huge infield video screens which flash late information for punters on the condition of the track, jockey changes and anything else that could possibly shave a half a nose off the anticipated outcome of a race.

Betting
Outside the tracks the club operates 125 off-course betting shops and a telephone betting system that covers 536,000 accounts. There are so many betting combinations available that anyone putting money on a

straight win place would be recognized immediately as a rank outsider. There are about 69 race meetings a year — the horses are stood down in the summer months because of the heat, humidity, rainstorms and the threat of typhoons — but the turnover is enormous. In 1993 for example, punters laid HK$60.8 billion in bets with more than 48,000 attending each meeting. An average of HK$871.6 million is bet on each race meeting and HK$60,143 million per race — a record HK$1.36 billion was bet on one day.

It is this frantic pursuit of luck that has created the huge racing revenues that, year by year, make an absolute mockery of a report once issued by the Hong Kong Government claiming that gambling was "not conducive to the basic Chinese character." The comment still triggers howls of laughter as the bulging, straining breadths of the racing industry continue to spread.

Among the Jockey Club's current expansion schemes there's a plan to greatly increase the number of telephone accounts, then to introduce accounts to anyone who

Of course, the mainstay of all this wealth is the Hong Kong Chinese — no less than one million of whom are dedicated and devout gamblers who would bet on two flies walking up a wall, and go for the quinella. And this passion for gambling is, in effect, simply an extension of their peculiar interpretation of the term "religion," in which the various gods and goddesses of Taoism and Buddhism and the mystic codes of folklore are thrown in with incense, ancestor-worship, fortune-sticks, calendars, geomancy, drums and gongs to conjure up blessings that are not so much spiritual as purely down to earth — health, happiness and good luck, with the accent on luck.

wants one — all they'll need is a bank guarantee to cover defaults, something like a personal loan account, a banking concept that would probably have you thrown out on your ear if you suggested it to your friendly branch manager back home. The club has introduced a service that just about translates the whole cultural impetus of Hong Kong into one symbolic form — automatic hole-in-the-wall betting machines, very much like banking cash dispensers, into which punters feed their account cards, key in their wager, and then go have a

OPPOSITE in Central District, on-course crowd ABOVE at Shatin race-track, and OVERLEAF night racing at Happy Valley.

The Lion and The Dragon

coffee and await the result without actually ever setting foot on the hallowed turf of the Sport of Kings.

Seals and Supernovas

The profits that the Jockey Club makes are so embarrassingly high that millions upon millions of surplus dollars are fed back into the community in the form of leisure, sporting and cultural facilities. It's another testament to Hong Kong's new awareness of its social role that instead of all the betting losses being blatantly creamed off, as they

A Cultural Balancing Act

While the brightly costumed emperors, mandarins and courtesans of traditional Cantonese Opera glide and pirouette about the stage to the accompanying howl and crash of traditional Chinese music, a Beethoven sonata or Bach suite provides the cultural counterpoint in the **Hong Kong Cultural Centre** complex in Tsimshatsui and at City Hall, the **Arts Centre** and the **Hong Kong Academy for Performing Arts**

would have been in the bad old days of laissez-faire, the money now pays for seals and supernovas, symphonies and sports meets and a lot of other things that spell the difference between a society and a ledger sheet. Among the major amenities that the Jockey Club has given Hong Kong are the magnificent Ocean Park complex between Aberdeen and Deep Water Bay, the Olympic standard Jubilee Sports Centre near the Shatin Racecourse, the Space Museum on the Tsimshatsui waterfront and the highly successful Academy for Performing Arts at Wanchai. And, without a doubt, endowments like these have added a new richness and variety to Hong Kong's cultural life.

on Hong Kong Island — and all are freely available for visitors' enjoyment.

For every Chinese folk-dancing display, a whirl of traditional costume and billowing silk, there's a Western ballet performance. For every Chinese puppet show or display of traditional martial arts there's a Western-style cabaret or theatrical drama, the latest Western movie (with Chinese sub-titles) and, occasionally, a locally produced revue sending up the more amusing and bizarre aspects of Hong Kong life and its expatriate community — and the encompassing clash of the Lion and Dragon cultures.

There are Western art and photographic exhibitions, displays by local expatriate batik designers, potters and weavers, Crufts-style dog and cat shows, pseudo-English pubs, cricket and rugby football matches, bone china, sterling silver and Home Counties twin-sets in the almost institutionalized Lane Crawford department stores, Government House garden parties, an annual pilgrimage to view the Governor's prized azaleas and many other instances in which the British upper lip, and those of their European and American fellow-expatriates, have remained dutifully stiffened amid the sweeping, boisterous,

Shiatsu massage to concerts and theater shows, as well as reviews of restaurants.

THE SPORTING LIFE

The point at which the two cultures really meet and mingle is in the wide range of leisure sports that are available in Hong Kong — most of them modern and Western and therefore pursuits that have no real link with traditional Chinese life. Hong Kong's teeming beach life, for example, is a Western form of leisure and sun-worship that

multicolored wash of Hong Kong Chinese life.

The energetic and very efficient Hong Kong Tourist Association (HKTA) puts out regular guides to cultural events in Hong Kong, and for easy day-by-day reference there's the "What's On" section in the *South China Morning Post* and HKTA's *Hong Kong Diary* and Hong Kong *This Week*, free of charge at their Information and Gift Centres. You can also try the fortnightly *Hong Kong Magazine*, distributed free at outlets such as book stores, restaurants in Lan Kwai Fong, Loft department store in Central, Pacific Place, the Arts Centre and the Hong Kong Cultural Centre, which lists anything from belly-dance classes and

the Cantonese citizenry have taken to in their many thousands — turning away from their own long-standing tradition in which it was considered quite base and "coolie-class" to be exposed to the sun long enough to get a tan.

The territory's 50,000 or so pleasure craft, ranging from luxury ocean-going yachts and cabin cruisers to small pleasure junks and power boats, are another popular leisure activity to which middle and upper range executive families of both cultures

OPPOSITE Scenic gondolas glide past ornamental pagoda at Ocean Park on Hong Kong's southside. ABOVE compelling character make-up of a Chinese Opera singer.

have taken like ducks to water. From there, the main cross-cultural fun-and-sun pursuits are water skiing, sailing, wind-surfing, snorkeling and skin-diving — all of which are available for the tourist or short-time visitor. Wind-surfing, for instance, the new boom sport in Hong Kong, can be arranged by hire at most beach resorts.

Tennis, squash and badminton are other Western sports which have become almost a status symbol among the emerging legions of executive-class Chinese and are therefore easily available to visitors.

Despite the heat and urban jungle, Hong Kong has its joggers, and a number of good jogging routes, particularly along the waterfront of Tsimshatsui East, in Victoria Park near Causeway Bay and along Bowen Road and other paths of the island's Mid-levels. There's an organization called the Hash House Harriers who sally forth on a hue and cry each week and are remarkable, aside from their stamina, for the considerable amounts of liquid replenishment that they take after each run. Amateur runners are also welcome to take part in Hong Kong's two annual marathons, the Coast of China Marathon on the first Sunday of each March, and the International Marathon in January.

For golfers, Hong Kong has a number of courses including the 18-hole international-class Royal Hong Kong Golf Club at Fanling in the New Territories. For details of these and other special interest activities see OFF THE BEATEN TRACK, page 183.

So, as with its people, Hong Kong manages to pack a vast amount of culture, leisure and sport into a relatively minuscule area. For the visitor, it means variety, excitement and interest — all the more fascinating for the fact that it all goes on in the shadow of a huge high-tech high-rise metropolis. For the people of Hong Kong themselves, it is another testimonial to the governing spirit of their society: it is living proof that even the Lion and the Dragon can lie side by side if there's profit in it for both of them.

Repulse Bay and its high cost condominiums which overlook Hong Kong's most popular beach.

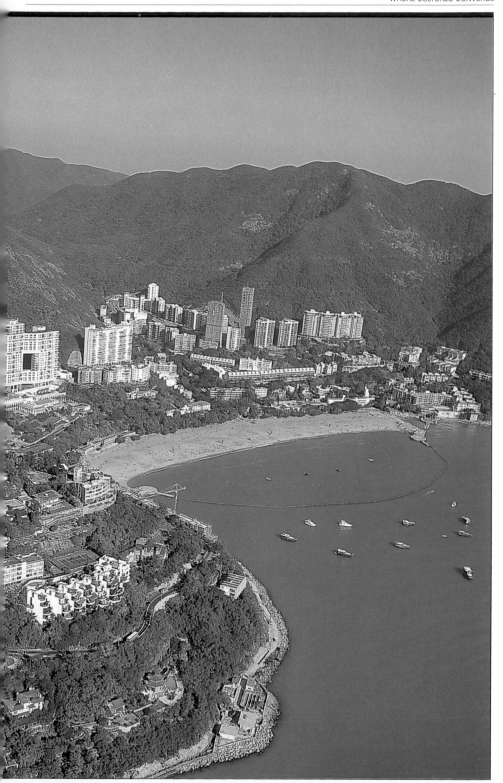

The Pleasure Path

THE CULINARY LANDSCAPE

Eating out in Hong Kong is not just a culinary experience, it's a taste of high adventure. With no fewer than 19,000 restaurants, noodle shops, snack and fast-food outlets throughout the territory, simple choice is the big biggest challenge — the culinary landscape crowded with thousands of neon signs, all beckoning the taste buds and promising ecstasy.

The choice is vast and complicated

diately recognizable route — the broad sweep of Chinese cuisine. Every other cuisine and national taste, and there are dozens of them in Hong Kong ranging from French, German, Swiss and Italian to Indian, Malaysian, Indonesian, Japanese, Korean, Thai, Mexican and many more, are wayside stopovers, chosen for their particular excellence and the reputation of their restaurants but purely complementary to Chinese fare.

It is Chinese food that reigns above all others in this teeming high-tech "China-

enough even for the Hong Kong resident with all the time in the world for leisurely exploration. For the average visitor, with not more than three or four days in which to find the best that there is on offer, the variety is so overwhelming that it can paralyze the decision-making processes, turning a once-in-a-lifetime culinary challenge into a retreat into the safe sanctuary of hotel restaurants. With a little courage and a reliable route-map, what lies before you is not so much a bewildering neon-lit maze but one of the world's biggest and most celebrated food bazaars.

Running right through the peaks, pinnacles and myriad path ways of the gastronomic jungle is one paramount and imme-

town." It packs the restaurants, dim-sum dining halls and food stalls each lunch time in the fading echo of the Noon-Day Gun, and it awaits the immense, scurrying flood of growling bellies that pours out of the air-conditioned discipline of the office blocks each evening, into the muggy heat and exhaust and clamor of the packed streets, into the dying fires of the sun and the soaring neon-decorated shadows and silhouettes of the urban jungle, where most of the glowing trail-markers point to one thing: food.

THE "SEEFOOD" TEST

To most Chinese, food is more than just simple taste or sustenance — it is a religion. Its creed is more than just sensation or indulgence, it is part of a general worship of the body and soul in which diet and certain health-promoting ingredients and tonics are combined with traditional herbal medicine, massage and acupuncture and muscular and breathing exercises to establish a regimen that goes back several thousand years into Chinese history but which we in the West are only now recognizing as the "whole treatment" of the physical and mental condition.

If its creed is health, its gospel is variety.

then boiled or stewed legs and haunches of meat. But while Western man continued to roast his food over fires, and developed the knife and fork to spear and slice the meat from the bone, the Chinese refined the stewing process — casting heavy three-legged bronze pots and cauldrons called *ings* in which to do it — and arrived at meat that was so tender that it virtually fell away from the bone, requiring only two twigs and nimble fingers to pick it away. Hence the origin of those most unlikely and somewhat have become the most infuriat-

It is generally acknowledged that Chinese food is a famine cuisine, its origins going back to the nation's perennial experimentation with all things animal, vegetable and even mineral in the search for enough for its many millions to eat. This gospel, according to the Hong Kong Cantonese, goes like this: "If its back points to heaven, you can eat it." Put a little less reverently, it is the proverbial "seafood" diet: everything you see, you eat.

ing of all Chinese eating implements, the chopsticks.

While the nets of the food-gatherers were cast wide for more and more ingredients, the cuisine was gradually refined by experimentation in the kitchens. If it was possible to eat a snail or a seaslug, it was another thing altogether to actually make it enjoyable, and the cuisine's characteristic refinement of textures, sauces and condiments evolved. The imperial courts and wealthy aristocracy added their important

FROM BRONZE *TING* STEWS TO DRUNKEN PRAWN CAULDRONS

The very earliest preparation of food in China was very much like that of the fur-clad cave-dwelling West — first roasted and

Faces of Cantonese culinary extravaganza — the traditional Chinese hotpot OPPOSITE; a variety of fresh fish CENTER and live offering from snake shop in back-street market. OVERLEAF The ornate floating seafood restaurants at Aberdeen.

culinary stamp too, encouraging their master chefs to perform great feats of creativity and ingenuity to keep their tastebuds quivering and their senses wallowing in indulgence.

As the cuisine expanded, the harsh limits of the Chinese environment added their say to the way in which it developed. The country's chronic shortage of cooking fuel, for instance, led to the process of speedy stir-frying. It also meant that food had to be cooked in small, fuel-efficient bite-sized portions, which made the use of chopsticks mas of the Chinese Central Market off Queen's Road Central, right across from the Chinese Merchandise Emporium, you'll see the ultimate in fresh-food preservation — live fish laid out on display for the discerning shoppers, skillfully, surgically scaled, skinned and filleted, with their hearts still beating to prove that as far as fresh goes, there's nothing fresher.

Creatures Great and Small

In all the distinctive cuisines of the world, the tastes and demands of the aristocracy

all the more inevitable. The generally hot summer climate, and the all-round heat in the south, meant that food could not be kept for long without going bad and perishing, and that meant that the first consideration of the Chinese cook was that the ingredients should be as fresh as the new day. Despite modern-day refrigeration, deep-freezing and chemical preservatives, that principle is still so sacrosanct among the Chinese that it is essentially why fish are kept alive in tanks in the Hong Kong restaurants, right up until it's time for the wok, why tortoises, eels, shrimps and prawns also huddle and twitch in baths until the moment of truth. And if you venture into the incredible hullabaloo and pungent aromas elevated the food from the kitchen to the realm of the gourmet and connoisseur by keeping the best chefs hard at work dreaming up new and more exotic ingredients and more extravagant ways of cooking and serving them. But what was honeyed larks' tongues to the French and Italians was kid's stuff to the Chinese. In China, the exceptionally jaded tastes of the emperors and their courts, and the abiding search for new things to eat, took the cuisine way beyond the normal borders of culinary courage and discretion and deep into the wild and wonderful animal world about us that television networks spend millions nowadays to present in all its natural, fascinating and endangered glory.

Snakes, eels, civet cats, pangolins (a type of ant-eater), bears, mice, sharks, lizards, rice-birds, sparrows, pigeons, sea-slugs, monkeys, dogs, cockroaches, even elephants — they all filed into the enormous ark of doom of Chinese cuisine. Some were prepared and eaten entirely, others contributed certain organs and appendages to particular dishes — the shark its distinctive fin, the elephant's trunk and the hapless bear's paw. In one renowned dish, now strictly banned in Hong Kong and unlikely to be found even in China, the brains of monkeys were

food and traditional medicine, a vast zoology of other animal life contributed to tonics, restoratives and aphrodisiacs aimed at the essential principle of both diet and medicine — balancing deficiencies in the vital yin and yang, or aggressive-passive male-female influences within the physical constitution. Fox's bezoar, deer horn and powdered rhinoceros horn are among the more well known ingredients of traditional medicine, not only for their use but for the toll they've taken of wildlife around the world. Even among the more acceptable,

spooned straight from their opened skulls in a particularly uninviting repast that was supposed to boost, among other things, the sexual potency of the banqueters.

This distinctive Chinese passion for all things wild and wonderful reached such outlandish proportions that at one latter-day stage a Chinese professor in the United States satirized it with a list of eight ultimate delicacies without which no gourmet banquet of ancient times was worth the tablecloth it was served upon. He came up with deer's tail, ape's lips, unborn baby jaguar, camel's hump, bear's paw, elephant's trunk, fish tail and monkey head.

In the close bonding that developed from their earliest days between Chinese

domesticated food-giving animals, the organs were treasured as much as the meat itself for their health-giving properties. The bull's heart helped promote cardiac strength, for instance. Its testicles were said to do wonders for the flagging virility. The bile duct of the snake, taken warm from the newly slaughtered body and emptied into a glass of wine or brandy, is said to help cure eye disorders and improve vision.

Traditional herbal medicine shop OPPOSITE offers tonics and cures that call upon thousands of years of medical research. ABOVE: Dried sea horses feature among range of traditional products of herbal medicine store.

The snake is among certain creatures whose flesh is said to have "hot" as opposed to "cooling" properties, and is still eaten in winter-time in Hong Kong as an invigorating tonic food. It's among a considerable number of meat-giving creatures that are shunned by the more fastidious, and traditionally better-fed Westerners, who tend to regard it as the sustenance of savages. Dog-meat is also a warming food and can be found on market-stalls throughout southern China. Here in Hong Kong, the British and European community, in-

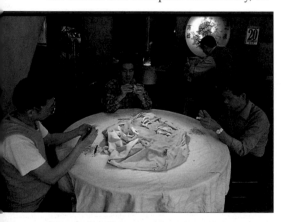

fatuated with "man's best friend" and staggering under the weight of their heavy beef roasts, have strictly forbidden this outrageous practice, but it goes on in secrecy all the same.

To give the Chinese chefs their due, creativity and experimentation have not atrophied in this age of chain restaurants and fast-food fads. Every once in a while, a new culinary technique or dish appears on the tables somewhere, is quickly copied throughout the restaurant world and adds to the vast 5,000-year-old compendium of the Chinese cuisine. In the 1970s, the new culinary craze was "sizzling" dishes — both Chinese and Western recipes served up spitting and spluttering on super-hot iron pans, with the diners lifting the skirts of the tablecloth all around the table to screen themselves from the flying oil and fat. In the 1980s, another new culinary delight called "drunken" prawns hit the scene, and one that embraces the most cherished principles of Chinese food — absolute freshness, taste sensation and a touch of the bizarre.

The prawns, huge ones, are brought to the table live and twitching in a lidded glass bowl. A bottle of Chinese dark rice wine is poured in through a hole in the lid. The prawns cavort about in it, getting riotously sozzled and then monstrously so — leaping and threshing so violently that you fear they're going to smash their way right out of the bowl. Finally, they succumb, as all hopelessly inebriated drinkers do, to supine unconsciousness, and are then lifted out one by one and dropped into boiling soup stock. If your nerves have been sturdy enough to follow the process to its end, the result is a juicy, deliciously marinated taste.

GOD LOVES A GOURMET

If food is a religion to the Chinese, restaurants are more than just an occasional place of worship, they are a devotional way of life. The Hong Kong Cantonese spend nearly as much on eating as they do on housing, and this in a relatively confined property market in which the lack of space keeps apartment rents and prices at an astronomical level, possibly the highest in the world outside New York's Manhattan. More than that, they spend most of their money eating out.

The restaurant satisfies many distinctive Chinese needs. It is the cathedral wherein the great cuisine is paid homage — and, naturally, there's a Chinese saying that sums up this point: "Heaven loves the man who eats well." It is also a community meeting place in which another of their racial characteristics is taken care of: if you ask a Chinese to define loneliness, he'll tell you it's when there's simply no-one else around. In Hong Kong it performs yet another very important social function — with living space so limited, and most Chinese apartments so cramped, the restaurant is the obvious place in which to entertain family and friends. With business the other major religion, it's inevitable that the restaurant will provide the main entertaining and even negotiating forum.

Cuisine includes traditional delicacies like bird's nests ABOVE being prepared in a Western District restaurant. Ornate brass urns OPPOSITE offer herbal teas that are taken as much for restorative as stimulative effects.

Compared with most Western restaurants and the Western etiquette for dining out, all but the most high-priced Chinese eating places are a natural extension of the home. Most Western establishments are for adults only — the average Hong Kong Chinese restaurant is for the whole family. On Sundays, particularly, when most Cantonese businessmen and office workers shrug off their suits and ties and devote their entire attention to family life, their grandparents and their smallest children crowd with them into the casual carefree bedlam of a

dim sum dining hall or a full-blown multi-storey eating palace. While most Western restaurants follow the bistro style of quiet dignity and taste, in keeping with the characteristic Western need for social privacy, the Chinese restaurant is a place in which the ambiance is measured in terms of the number of people who can be packed in at any one time, the noise they make, the gusto with which the food is consumed, the number of children darting and laughing between the tables, the mess that's made and the number of staff who are worn off their feet trying to keep up with the clamor.

Amid the pandemonium, the most sober and conscientious decisions are made, for no Chinese worth his birthright will order a

dish without first discussing it with everyone around him, then the waiter, then the manager if need be, and even the chef if it comes to that. No dish is ordered without consideration for the others that are to go with it, for while the cardinal feature of the Chinese cuisine is its variety, the cardinal rule is the right combination of foods, recipes, tastes, textures and even colors that make up a perfectly composed meal.

Tea is the main beverage, with myriad tastes and blends of its own that have evolved over some 5,000 years — a history as long as that of the food itself. Again, Chinese tea has medicinal origins; the stimulative properties of the "lusty leaf" were first regarded as a tonic. It was centuries after its discovery that experimentation began, developing three main categories of the beverage — plain unfermented green tea, semi-fermented and "fruity" olongs and stronger, Indian-style black tea. Add to these the various herbal blends — jasmine, chrysanthemum etcetera — and the range is as wide and exotic as that of wine and liquor.

As for hard drink, the Chinese prefer beer, rice wine and cognac with their meals, and they observe a fairly strict control and etiquette in which alcohol complements a meal but very rarely becomes the main course. Although Chinese history celebrates the inebriated poet and writer, and the artist's propensity for strong drink as something quite understandable, extreme drunkenness is frowned upon and you will not often see a Hong Kong Cantonese in his or her cups.

You'll know they've had a drink — their faces usually go blood-red on two glasses. But the drinking is done in concert with the food, glasses raised in toast in a dozen different celebrative excuses as each course reaches the table, the food effectively absorbing and neutralizing much of the alcohol intake. Boisterous drinking games are sometimes played, but they rarely go beyond the happy-go-lucky upswing of drinking. When the meal is finished the

The lavish creativity of Hong Kong's nightlife — string duo and piano perform amid the huge atrium of Royal Garden Hotel in Tsimshatsui East.

evening is over. The games cease, the laughter ends and everyone almost abruptly gets up and goes home.

THE REGIONAL TASTES

The main contributions to Chinese cuisine have come from the imperial courts and the country's principal ethnic groups and regions. The emperors themselves had immense kitchens manned by anything up to 4,000 chefs, assistants and service staff to feed and banquet their legions of retainers, courtiers, administrators and advisors, extended families and concubines. "Pony express" teams rushed fresh seasonal fruits and delicacies from all parts of the country. Occasionally, the imperial whim added new recipes to the burgeoning compendium of the cuisine: the infamous Empress Dowager, Ci Xi, the last effective imperial ruler of China, is said to have dreamed one night of steamed buns filled with pork. They appeared on the imperial menu the next day and have been popular ever since. As the expanding Moslem empire pushed the Islamic faith down the Silk Road into northwest China, destroying the idolatry face of Buddhism as it went, the Moslem cuisine of lamb and beef kebabs and its flat, unleavened bread, joined the Chinese table. The Mongolians, sweeping down through the Great Wall to wreak the most terrifying destruction and wholesale slaughter that China has ever known, introduced the hotpot dishes that have also been part of China's regional tastes since the reign of the powerful but short-lived Yuan dynasty.

But it is the culinary customs and creativity of the various regions, based on distinctive regional foodstuffs and local climates, that has contributed the most character to the vast variety of the cuisine. Nowadays, the cuisine has been categorized under four main regions or schools — the North (Hebei, Shandong and Henan), the East (Jiangsu and Zhejiang), the South (largely Cantonese) and the West (Sichuan and Yunnan).

RIGHT Hong Kong's Cantonese restaurants are packed at mealtimes — some of them so crowded that people wait alongside diners for a place to sit and eat.

The Northern, or Beijing style is based largely on wheat-flour breads, dumplings and noodles, the staple of the comparatively austere temperate-frigid climate, and features the "barbarian" foods of the northern and northwestern tribes — the mutton, lamb and beef of the Moslems and Mongolians, served with scallions, leeks, pickled cabbage and cucumbers. But against this rather mundane culinary backdrop, the richness and variety of Shandong cooking adds regional splendor. The Shandong chefs were the maestros of the

juices, and so rich that at one stage in its history its leading chefs were accused of preparing "unnecessarily elaborate dishes and overly opulent banquets." Although Shanghai itself was only a small, nondescript fishing port until the British forced it open as a trading concession, Hangzhou had a far more illustrious history as the capital of the hard-pressed but culturally glorious Southern Song dynasty, and its contribution to the Eastern cuisine has been aristocratic and quite considerable. Nanjing (Nanking), west along the Yangtze River,

imperial courts in Beijing, famous for their delicate sauces and ingredients stir-fried with vegetables, crab, shrimp, chicken or meatballs. Of all the ingredients, none rank in stature or popularity with that abiding star of the Northern cuisine, the Beijing duck, with its golden brown crispy-thin basted slices of skin and flesh wrapped in unleavened pancakes with salty plum sauce and fresh scallions.

Eastern, or Shanghai cuisine is noted for its chicken and seafood dishes, especially fish, shrimp and crab, its rich tastes and its extravagant use of garlic and sesame oil. In fact, it's the richest and oiliest of the regional culinary styles, so oily that steamed bread is served instead of rice to soak up the

has added its famous smoked meats. As for Shanghai, it has contributed an annual culinary fever, triggered in the autumn months, when gourmets and common diners go wild over seasonal Shanghai hairy crab.

The Western cuisine, originating from the mountainous, misty Sichuan province, is the spiciest of all the regional types, reflecting both the need for "heating" foods in the damp and comparatively chilly climate and the character of the people. The citizens of Chongqing and Chengdu like to describe themselves as the fiery "Latins" of China. The cuisine is certainly hot — as one noted expert on Chinese food described it, "the poor sister of the lot, but one with a slightly vicious tongue." Green and red chilies, garlic, ginger and peppers are liberally used to spice up the food. A lot of oil is used too. The effect with most dishes, Sichuan prawns and pork and wind-dried beef recipes for example, is a reasonably mellow jolt to the senses. But anyone who's had the courage to try the province's common *pièce de résistance*, Sichuan Hotpot, will tell you that for much of the meal you can only nod your appreciation (or shock) — you're too speechless and tear-stricken to do anything else.

It is Southern, or Cantonese food that is the widely known, most popular and undoubtedly the supreme regional cuisine of China. It is born of the crowded, richly fertile sub-tropical lands and waterways of the south-eastern provinces, and it offers an absolute wealth of foodstuffs and ingredients — chickens, ducks, pork, geese, pigeons, prawns, crabs, lobsters, along with a similar variety of vegetables, tropical fruits and melons. It is recognized as the lightest of the regional cuisines, with particularly wide use of the stir-fry technique; and it's also noted for its combinations of meat and fish and other seafood, and meat dishes pepped up with oyster or lobster sauces. Another specialty is red roast pork, comparable with the finest and tastiest cold cut recipes of the West. But its most renowned specialty, a sub-cuisine of its own, is its *dim sum,* or "touch the heart" delicacies, mainly light bite-sized steamed or fried pork, prawn, beef or squid recipes usually cooked in pasta jackets or bean-curd skin and taken with tea from breakfast time, through lunch and into the early afternoon. *Dim sum* tea-houses are among the biggest, most ornate, most popular and most packed of all the restaurants in Hong Kong. To lunch at one of them you have to get there very early — not long after 11:00 am — otherwise you'll join crowds of hopefuls standing around in the raucous dining rooms pressing against the crowded tables and waiting for the lucky ones to finish their meals and leave. When you finally manage to grab a table, the various delicacies are brought around on trolleys, many of them in bamboo steaming baskets. You choose whatever catches your fancy and when the meal is over the check is calculated from the number of empty baskets. In

some more modern *dim sum* palaces the dishes are ticked off a card.

THE CULINARY TRAIL

With such a huge selection of restaurants in Hong Kong, the only reliable guide or route-map is one that breaks it down into the four main tourist districts — Central and Wanchai-Causeway Bay on the island and the central and eastern sections of Tsimshatsui in Kowloon. Of course, there

are other top-class restaurants and seafood spots further afield, in Aberdeen and Stanley, in the New Territories and on the islands of Lamma and Cheung Chau, and the best of these are mentioned later in this section of the guide.

In all the restaurants highlighted in this book, the standard of cuisine is high. Most of them are also recommended by the Hong Kong Tourist Association, which has a department staffed by some 30 people keeping a constant check on restaurants and

OPPOSITE Chinese food is a religion worshipped in the vast majority of some 19,000 restaurants and other food outlets in Hong Kong. Winter melon soup ABOVE, a popular light soup served in summer.

nightclubs and promoting only those that show a consistent determination to please. Most places have a menu printed in English, and restaurants recommended in this guide certainly do unless otherwise stated.

CENTRAL DISTRICT

This, the crowded business and banking center of Hong Kong, spins like a human treadmill during the day and then winds down into a quiet, almost serene backwater with a few ripples of activity at night — the towering office blocks lighted up but empty and the nightlife scattered around the neighborhood. But nightlife there certainly is. The main action is in a wedge of neon signs and strolling crowds bounded by **Lan Kwai Fong** and **Wellington** and **D'Aguilar Streets.** Lan Kwai Fong itself is a cluster of streets that has lately become a distinct neighborhood of bistro-style eating places, bars and discos, particularly popular with the *gweilo* community, especially the trendy young from The Peak, the Mid-Levels and middle-class apartment and tract housing developments like Discovery Bay on Lantau Island.

CHINESE CUISINE

Cantonese
The imperial courts of the Chinese Cuisine in this district are the **Yung Kee Restaurant** © 2522 1624, a multi-storey gaudily decorated Cantonese eating place in Wellington Street, and the famous **Luk Yu TeaHouse** © 2523 2973, in nearby Stanley Street, which is such a popular *dim sum* establishment and restaurant that you virtually need to camp outside overnight to get a table. The Yung Kee is noted for its Cantonese roast duck and pork and its wide selection of Cantonese and Shanghainese specialties, while the Luk Yu is worth a visit not only for its food but also its fairly faithful re-creation of the bustling tea-house atmosphere of bygone years.

But for an absolutely superb *dim sum* and a memorable experience of the multistorey pandemonium of tea-house life, you

can go no better than the **Blue Heaven** © 2524 3608, at 38 Queen's Road Central, right on the intersection with Wyndham Street — but again, you need to be quick off the mark and determined to beat the hordes of office workers that pour into it at lunchtime. You'll also have to make an advance booking or move pretty swiftly on your feet to get a table at the **City Hall Chinese Restaurant** © 2521 1303, in the City Hall on the waterfront side of Connaught Road near the Star Ferry, which combines the best traditions of the tea-house with splendid harbor views.

For some other good-value eating places for both lunchtime *dim sum* and evening meals there's the award-winning **Tai Woo Seafood Restaurant** © 2524 5618, 15-19 Wellington Street, for seafood hotpots, steamed garoupa, garlic prawns, sautéed scallops, beef in taro's nest and mango pudding. Tai Woo has other branches on Hong Kong Island as well as a number of outlets in Kowloon and the New Territories. Or you can try the **Jade Garden** restaurants: Basement, Jardine House, 1 Connaught Place © 2524 5098 and 1/F Swire House, 11 Chater Road © 2526 3031 — where specialties include double-boiled duck with parsley and pan-fried stuffed beancurd.

Well worth a visit is **Tsui Hang Village** © 2524 2012, New World Tower, 16-18 Queen's Road Central. The restaurant is purportedly a place of homage to the home village of Dr. Sun Yatsen, founder of the Republic of China, and is well known for both classic and modern Cantonese dishes such as succulent pigeon and chicken, tasty thick soups and fried milk fritters.

A more unique establishment is the **Yat Chau Health Restaurant** © 2545 8688, 1-3/F Yat Chau Building, 262 Des Voeux Road Central, which "caters for the health-conscious foodies of the '90s" from a "variety of medicinal foods derived from secret court recipes in old China but prepared with modern, scientific methods." The menu, which changes with the seasons, gives a short description of each item along with an analysis of its medicinal properties and it's benefits. Whether you should be replenishing the Yin or Yang, the lungs, "Five Viscera" or the "Six Bowels" is something that resident Chinese herbalists and waiters can advise you on in table-side consultations. If you don't speak Chinese, it helps to have someone with you who does, otherwise you may find your constipation being treated with a herbal dish for "coughing blood." Specialties include quail eggs with tremella, shrimp and chicken soup with sea horse and sea dragon and duck with tangerine peel and pilosa asiabell root.

At the hotels you can expect to pay more. Highly recommended is the popular rooftop **Eagle's Nest** © 2523 3111, Hong-

with camphor, ducks' tongues, bean curd with minced beef in a pungent sauce and scallops with hot garlic sauce.

Hunan

Another restaurant which will put fire in your belly with lots of chilies and garlic is **Hunan Garden** © 2868 2880, 3/F The Forum, Exchange Square, where many dishes are served in the traditional way, in bamboo stems or earthen pots. Levels of hotness are clearly, and mercifully, and thankfully indicated on the menu.

kong Hilton, 2 Queen's Road, which offers creative Cantonese cuisine and vegetarian specialties, and the elegant **Man Wah** © 2522 0111 at the Mandarin Oriental, with its spectacular views of the harbor. In Pacific Place, restaurants noted for the quality of their cuisine are the **Golden Leaf** © 2521 3838 at the Hotel Conrad; **Man Ho** © 2810 8366, J.W. Marriott Hotel; and the **Summer Palace** © 2820 8520 at Island Shangri-La.

Sichuan

The Sichuan Garden © 2521 4433, 3/F Gloucester Tower (in the Landmark shopping complex) and at Shop 4, The Mall, Pacific Place, specializes in smoked duck

Chiu Chow

This cuisine comes from the coastal region around the Swatow district of eastern Guangdong and is similar to Cantonese food, but a little heavier and spicier. It features its own variations of duck, goose and pigeon dishes, along with oysters fried in egg batter and clams in a biting chili and black bean sauce. Chiu Chow restaurants are also noted for their shark's fin and bird's nest soups — the disgorged linings of sea swallow nests reputed to do wonders for rejuvenation and a particularly sturdy

ABOVE Typical *dim sum* restaurant in Central District.

tea called "Iron Maiden," drunk from tiny thimble-sized cups before and after the meal. The best place to go is the **Chiu Chow Garden Restaurant** ℂ 2525 8246, Basement, Jardine House, 1 Connaught Place, or to their branch near Admiralty MTR ℂ 2845 1323, G/F Lippo Centre, Queensway.

Shanghainese & Peking

The Shanghai Garden Restaurant ℂ 2524 8181, Hutchison House, 10 Harcourt Road, is a popular venue for dishes such as "drunken" chicken, fried Shanghai noodles

and sweet black sesame dumplings. A good place to try for Peking food — Peking duck, beggar's chicken clay-breaking ceremonies and nightly noodle-making shows — is **Peking Garden** ℂ 2526 6456, Basement, Alexandra House, 6 Ice House Street, or it's branches at the Excelsior Hotel in Causeway Bay, Cityplaza in Taikoo Shing and in the Mall at Pacific Place. Or you can try **Noble House** ℂ 2877 3993, Basement, Standard Chartered Bank Building, 4 Des Voeux Road Central.

INTERNATIONAL FARE

Indian & Sri Lankan

An establishment that has earned a reputation for good food and friendliness over the years is the **Ashoka** ℂ 2524 9623 at 57 Wyndham Street. You won't be disappointed. Also, **Tandoor** ℂ 2521 8363, 3/F On Hing Building, On Hing Terrace, **Shalimar** ℂ 2522 8489, 2/F 28A Stanley Street, and **Koh-I-Noor** ℂ 2877 9706,

34 D'Aguilar Street, Lan Kwai Fong, where Halal food is always available. For Sri Lankan, the homey **Club Sri Lanka** ℂ 2526 6559, Basement, 17 Hollywood Road, offers very reasonably priced buffet dining.

Japanese

Japanese food is very popular in Hong Kong and, as with Western cuisine, the prices vary radically. In Lan Kwai Fong, the **Yorohachi** ℂ 2524 1251, 5-6 Lan Kwai Fong, and the **Hanagushi** ℂ 2521 0868, 34-36 D'Aguilar Street, offer set dinner courses, tempura and beef sukiyaki, soya noodles and other traditional fare at reasonable prices. If you don't mind paying more, **The Benkay** ℂ 2521 3344, 1st Basement, Gloucester Tower (in The Landmark), **Genji** ℂ 2523 3111 at the Hilton Hotel and the **Nadaman** ℂ 2820 8570, 7/F Island Shangri-La Hotel, Pacific Place.

Thai

For such favorites as spicy tom yum soups and red and green curries, king prawns and Thai beer, the very popular **Supatra's Thai Gourmet** ℂ 2522 5073, 50 D'Aguilar Street, Lan Kwai Fong, and the trendy **Phukets Seafood Grill** ℂ 2868 9672 on Mosque Junction in the Mid-Levels above Lan Kwai Fong — the new escalator will take you nearly there — are two of many excellent Thai restaurants to open in Hong Kong in recent years.

Western

Central District offers some of the best restaurants around, probably because it is also the territory's business and banking citadel. The menus range from hamburgers and fried chicken to French and Italian haute cuisine, and the decor from trendy high-tech to homespun. Fast-food and take-away restaurants such as **Hardie's, Kentucky Fried Chicken, Wendy's, McDonald's, Domino's, Marco Polo Pizza, Pizza Hut, Spaghetti House** and **Oliver's Super Sandwiches** abound not only in Central but throughout Hong Kong.

From the beginning of the day, there are several reputable breakfast spots in Central, headed by **The Landmark's** mezzanine **La Terrazza** ℂ 2526 4200, and the ground-floor

Fountainside Restaurant ℃ 2526 4018. Both feature fairly hearty American and Continental breakfasts and good coffee. For value, **Jim's Eurodiner** would be hard to beat fruit, two eggs, hash browns, baked tomato and a choice of sausage, ham or bacon will cost you as little as US$5. You'll find Jim's in the Basement, Paks Building, 5-11 Stanley Street ℃ 2868 6886. Or you can try the **DeliFrance** fast-food restaurants in Queensway Plaza, 20-22 Queen's Road Central, and in World-Wide Plaza on the corner of Des Voeux Road Central and

fying array of hamburgers, open sandwiches and chili dishes, but the food is pricey. At night, the chrome and sunset and the in-house video monitors wink and flash on supper club diners, and at weekends the dance floor is thrown open to writhing disco dancers and blazing lasers. Around the corner in 38 D'Aguilar Street, **Graffiti** ℃ 2521 2202 offers a distinctly creative lunch — each table is issued with crayons, and diners are invited to doodle and even compose complex sketches on the blank art-paper tablecloths.

Pedder Street. For a good hearty English breakfast, try the **Bull & Bear** ℃ 2525 7436, G/F Hutchison House.

Going up-market, head for the **Mandarin Oriental's Coffee Shop** ℃ 2522 0111, or **Brown's** ℃ 2523 7003 in the bowels of Exchange Square, where young stockbrokers tend to gather. The Hilton Hotel's ℃ 2523 3111, **Skettis** and **Cat Street** restaurants are both well-worth trying not only for breakfast but for lunch and dinner.

In Central's mad lunch-time scramble, it's not so much where to eat but where you can grab a table.

In the Lan Kwai Fong neighborhood, the **California** ℃ 2521 1345, G/F California Tower, 30-32 Lan Kwai Fong, serves a satis-

Among some of the other Lan Kwai Fong and nearby establishments that offer good value for lunch and dinner, or to just simply sit back with a drink and watch the Lan Kwai Fong scene, take your pick from the following:

The three popular adjacent venues for dining and nightlife are **Club 1997**, **Post 97** and **Mecca 97**, 8-11 Lan Kwai Fong ℃ 2810 9333. Open 24 hours over the weekend, Club 1997 is a disco and bar, Post 97 a cafe-restaurant and Mecca 97 a Middle Eastern restaurant.

OPPOSITE Sanpans, divers and floating kitchen in the Causeway Bay Typhoon Shelter.
ABOVE Alfresco food stalls in Western District.

For a bit of French colonial nostalgia and Vietnamese food there's the very up-market **Indochine** ✆ 2869 7399, 2/F California Tower, 30-32 Lan Kwai Fong. For a modern-day setting and French cuisine **Papillon** ✆ 2526 5965, 1/F 8-13 Wo On Lane, and the pricier, more formal, **Cafe de Paris** ✆ 2524 7521, 30-32 D'Aguilar Street. Well worth a visit for Lebanese food is the aptly named **Beirut** ✆ 2804 6611, 27 D'Aguilar Street, and for those hankering after sauerkraut and draft pils, the **Schnurrbart** ✆ 2537 1677, next door offers a relaxed and informal bar-restaurant setting, with a menu that's more on the snack side than a full meal.

For good Italian food, try **Ristorante Il Mercato** ✆ 2868 3068, Basement, 34-36 D'Aguilar Street, and **Va Bene "stile vene-ziano"** ✆ 2845 5577, 58-62 D'Aguilar Street. Around the corner at 24-30 Ice House Street, **La Taverna** ✆ 2522 8904, is packed with the usual Chianti bottles and features a good menu with a particularly well-prepared range of antipastas. In Pacific Place, **Grappa's Ristorante** ✆ 2521 4028, at Shop 132, Level 1, is popular with business and media trendies.

If you're lusting for downhome American food, **Trios** ✆ 2877 9773, 9B Wo On Lane, specializes in Maine lobster and US steaks, and **Al's Diner** ✆ 2869 1869, 27-39 D'Aguilar Street, US prime sirloin, root beer floats and golden oldies juke-box music. For a cheap hamburger, fries and apple pie, there's a small **McDonald's** across the road. In Pacific Place, the very American **Dan Ryan's Chicago Grill** ✆ 2845 4600, for extra large portions of such dishes as Maryland crab, barbecued ribs, charcoal-grilled Swordfish and salads. The **La Cafe** ✆ 2526 6863, G/F, Lippo Centre (opposite Pacific Place) has American "nouvelle cuisine," and in the Sports Bar you can watch US and international football, baseball and basketball on a giant 40-inch screen.

A short walk from Lan Kwai Fong you'll find the cozy **Mozart Stub'n** ✆ 2522 1763 at 8 Glenealy (at the top of steps), which has great Wiener schnitzel, veal goulash, bread dumplings and Austrian souffles. Next door, **Cafe Afrikan** ✆ 2868 9299, will surprise anyone who considers there's no such thing as distinctive African cuisine. At the

bottom of Glenealy, in the old colonial building — you can't possibly miss it — **Michelle's at the Fringe** ✆ 2877 4000, 1/F South Block, 2 Lower Albert Road, has an impressive Mediterranean menu. Along the top end of Wyndham Street, **La Bodega** ✆ 2877 3101 offers paella and a tasty selection of tapas. Nearby, **Le Tire Bouchon** ✆ 2523 5459, 9 Old Bailey Street, is noted for its excellent French provincial cooking, wines and cheese board at reasonable prices. For bistro-style dining and a very fine selection of wines, try **Pomeroy's Wine Bar and Restaurant** ✆ 2810 1162, G/F On Hing Building, On Hing Terrace (off Wyndham Street), and at **Pacific Place** ✆ 2523 4772, Shop 349, Level 3.

In Prince's Building, next to Statue Square, you'll find Creole and Cajun fare at **Prince's Tavern** ✆ 2523 9352, on the mezzanine floor and excellent, but not cheap, seafood at **Bentley's Seafood Restaurant and Oyster Bar** ✆ 2868 0881, in the basement.

But for those who can't really enjoy themselves without a bit of "Hurry on now, gents" nostalgia you can try two traditional British pub-style haunts: **Mad Dogs in the Basement**, Regent Centre, 1-13 D'Aguilar Street, with its ale, Trivial Pursuit nights, Scottish football, live music and no-nonsense culinary fare, and the **Bull & Bear** ✆ 2525 7436, at G/F Hutchison House, 10 Harcourt Road.

There are several distinguished restaurants that have built abiding reputations from their lunch and supper menus. On the lower end of Wyndham Street in the basement of the South China Building, the family-owned **Jimmy's Kitchen** ✆ 2526 5293, has been operating for more than 60 years and is one of the most popular and most reputable of all Hong Kong restaurants. Its menu is varied — Western, Cantonese and Indian — and unless you're on a tight budget, affordable. At the Mandarin Oriental Hotel, **The Pierrot** offers superb French cuisine, and for perhaps the most sumptuous and meticulously prepared Western food in Hong Kong, the **Mandarin Grill** is in a class of its own. For reservations for both restaurants call 2522 0111. The other hotels, the Hilton, Ritz Carlton, Furama, Conrad, Island Shangri-La and Marriott also have fine restaurants that certainly will not prove disappointing.

Further west along the waterfront the Victoria Hotel in the Shun Tak Centre, 200 Connaught Road Central, is flexing its culinary muscle with a high-class range of Western, Chinese and buffet restaurants such as **Bocarinos Grill, Cafe Terrace, Dynasty Restaurant and Interlude**. For reservations ✆ 2540 7228.

At night, the two most romantic spots to my mind, both offering bird's-eye views of Central and across the harbor to Kowloon, are **La Ronda** ✆ 2525 5111 in the revolving restaurant of the Furama for International cuisine, and the **Eagle's Nest** ✆ 2523 3111 in the Hilton, offering Chinese fare with a distinctly Western decor and very accomplished Filipino live band.

Other than the major restaurants there are various tourist attractions and services that present movable feasts on night-time harbor cruises, or the adventure of eating out alfresco style from the thousands of open-air food stalls that are found throughout Hong Kong.

The Pearl of Hong Kong, a converted vehicular ferry, and the Pearl of the Orient, have evening harbor cruises along with Chinese and Western cuisine, dancing and a cabaret. Contact **Hong Kong Harbour Tour Night Club** ✆ 2541 6026. The Hilton Hotel's famous converted sailing barque, the **Wan Fu**, sails through the harbor to either Aberdeen or both Aberdeen and Repulse Bay. Depending on the cruise, hors d'oeuvres or a barbecue dinner is served on board. For more information ✆ 2523 3111.

WANCHAI–CAUSEWAY BAY

While Central District breathes a kind of weary sigh of relief in the evening, a financial powerhouse at rest, Wanchai and Causeway Bay come into their own as teeming neon-lit centers of food, shopping and entertainment. In Wanchai, the blazing, beckoning signs of its old Suzy Wong scene, the "girlie" bars and big hostess clubs, now seem slightly tacky and against the district's rising reputation as one of Hong Kong's best dining out domains. In Causeway Bay, the lure of bargain clothing boutiques, even better bargains on the hawker stalls that line the sidewalks, and the huge Japanese department stores — Daimaru, Matsuzakaya and Sogo — that have chosen the district as their own, have turned the area into a restaurant and nightlife center so packed with people that it's often difficult to find space to stroll on some streets.

Causeway Bay, its main attractions centered on Times Square with its impressive food floor, the Excelsior Hotel and the Japanese emporiums, is to my mind a

glimpse of the East Asian urban giants of the future. If you can recall the futuristic Harrison Ford movie, *Bladerunner,* and add the stunning visual effect of virtual wall-to-wall neon, you have the color, drama and excitement of Causeway Bay.

CHINESE CUISINE

The two most outstanding restaurants are undoubtedly the **Tao Yuan** ✆ 2573 8080 and **Forum**, ✆ 2892 0248 both in the Wanchai

ABOVE Grades and brands of rice are offered in graceful polished casks in typical Hong Kong rice store.

area. The Tao Yuan, which you'll find in the Great Eagle Centre in Wanchai North, near the Hong Kong Exhibition and Convention Centre, is an up-market new-style Cantonese establishment with harbor views and a pleasant peach decor, and a menu which features the novel "nouvelle cuisine," drunk prawns. Already well noted for its seafood dishes, it also offers succulent baby lobster, stuffed scallops, baked crab, baked oysters in port wine and satay sauce, sautéed sea welks, and a range of more exotic recipes that include braised civet cat fillet, sautéed

Harbour Centre, 25 Harbour Road; and the **Chrysanthemum Chinese Restaurant** Ⓒ 2838 2222, Basement, China Harbour View Hotel, for chrysanthemum blossom dishes and tea.

For panoramic views of Victoria Harbour (but be prepared to pay for it), you can try **One Harbour Road** Ⓒ 2588 1234, in the Grand Hyatt Hotel, and for even more spectacular views at more reasonable prices, the **Round Dragon Chinese Restaurant** Ⓒ 2861 1668, 60/F Hopewell Centre, 183 Queen's Road East. For those not counting

tender tortoise, snake soup and stuffed bamboo fungus with vegetables.

As for the **Forum** Ⓒ 2892 0248, at 485 Lockhart Road, one dish reigns above all the others — braised abalone. The rubbery ear-shaped mollusk is braised for a full 15 hours in a stock of ham, chicken and beef, and the result (and the price) is truly sensational.

Elsewhere, for the most popular Cantonese restaurants take your pick, in Wanchai: **Canton Room** Ⓒ 2866 2166, in the Luk Kwok Hotel, 72 Gloucester Road; **Harbour View Tsui Hang Village Restaurant** Ⓒ 2827 5755, 2/F Great Eagle Centre, 23 Harbour Road; **East Ocean Seafood Restaurant**, Ⓒ 2827 8887, 3/F

every penny or cent, **Fook Lam Moon** Ⓒ 2866 0663, 35-45 Johnston Road, serves such delicacies as shark's fin and bird's nest soups, bird's nest in bamboo pith and abalone. Also, you might take a look at **Sun Tung Lok Shark's Fin Restaurant** Ⓒ 2574 8261, 376-382 Lockhart Road, where waiters will explain the shark's fin grading and price differences before you order.

In Causeway Bay: the **Tin Tin Hot Pot** restaurants at 78-84 Percival Street Ⓒ 2895 3883 and 1 Great George Street Ⓒ 2890 9966 offer such dishes as sautéed oysters with port wine, prawns fried with chili and pungent preserved bean curd sauce and Thaistyle curry-fried crab. **Sunning Unicorn** Ⓒ 2577 6620, 1 Sunning Road, serves interesting nouvelle Chinoise on Wedgwood tableware and its menu covers are said to be threaded with real gold.

For home-style dishes, health-enhancing casseroles and "male" and "female" soups, try the renowned **Ah Yee Leng Tong,** which has eight outlets in Kowloon, three in the New Territories and four in Wanchai Causeway Bay at 13 Fleming Road © 2573 0402; 503-505 Lockhart Road © 2834 3480; Basement, Hang Lung Centre, 2-20 Paterson Street © 2576 8385, and 42 Leighton Road 2895 0192.

Restaurant © 2577 3391, Hennessy Centre, 500 Hennessy Road, and the **Carriana** © 2511 1282, 151 Gloucester Road. For Shanghainese, the **Shanghai Grand Restaurant,** 4/F Island Shopping Centre, 1 Great George Street.

Peking

The most popular venue is the rather unimaginatively named but by no means disappointing **New American Restaurant** © 2575 0458 at G/F 177-179 Wanchai Road in Wanchai. This restaurant has been around

Sichuan

The top choices are all located in Causeway Bay and include the family-run **Red Pepper** © 2577 3811, 7 Lan Fong Road, for "strange taste" spiced shredded chicken and sizzling prawns. At **Sze Chuen Lau** © 2891 9027, 466 Lockhart Road, house favorites include spiced perfumed chicken, kumquat beef and chili and camphor-flavored tea-smoked duck. Or you can try **Cleveland Szechuen Restaurant** © 2576 3876, New Town Mansion, 6 Cleveland Street, and in Happy Valley, the ever-popular **Pep'n Chilli** © 2573 8251, 12-22 Blue Pool Road.

Chiu Chow/Shanghai

In Causeway Bay, the **Chiuchow Garden**

for decades and is a favorite haunt for expatriates and visiting dignitaries. Reservations are always necessary. In Causeway Bay, **Hong Kong Chung Chuk Lau** © 2577 4914, 30 Leighton Road, specializes in Mongolian hotpots and you do the cooking yourself — during the winter months.

Vegetarian

For some traditional Buddhist culinary artistry in which mushroom and beancurd

OPPOSITE Wanchai and other districts of Hong Kong abound with fresh fruit and vegetable markets. ABOVE Dried seafoods and spiced meats on sale in closed market — traditional preserved foods that have survived the modern-day development of home refrigeration.

The Pleasure Path

recipes have the shape, texture and even the taste of chicken, pork or beef, try the **Wishful Cottage** ℂ 2573 5645, 336-340 Lockhart Road, **Vegi Food Kitchen** ℂ 2890 6660, 8 Cleveland Street, and **Kung Tak Lam** ℂ 2890 3127, 35 Tung Lo Wan Road, which specializes in chili-flavored Shanghainese dishes. All three are located in Causeway Bay.

INTERNATIONAL FARE

Japanese
Because of the big multi-storey Japanese department stores in Causeway Bay, the area abounds with Japanese restaurants. At the top of the range you'll find the **Kanetanaka** ℂ 2833 6018, 22/F East Point Centre, 545-563 Hennessy Road, **Sui Sha Ya** ℂ 2838 1808, 1/F Lockhart House, 440 Jaffe Road, **Ichiban** ℂ 2890 7580, 21 Lan Fong Road, and Tomokazu at two locations: 17-19 Percival Street ℂ 2891 2898 and Shop B, Lockhart House, 441 Lockhart Road ℂ 2833 6339.

But for something a little different, and certainly more exciting, try the department stores themselves. The giant **Sogo,** for example, has a vast basement food stall which is divided into various Japanese and Cantonese kitchens and informal eating areas where you can enjoy full à la carte meals or just pick snacks from various stalls and counters.

Korean
For pungent peppery kim chi, or assorted vegetables pickled and spiced and then fermented (they're buried in the ground for several months), tabletop barbecues and hotpots, try **Arirang** ℂ 2572 3027, 76 Morrison Hill Road, Happy Valley, and **Koreana** ℂ 2577 5145 at 55 Paterson Street, Causeway Bay.

Indian & Burmese
The Viceroy of India ℂ 2827 7777 at 2/F Sun Hung Kai Centre, 30 Harbour Road, Wanchai, has built up an enviable reputation for its curries. It's also noted for its marvelous harbor views, fountain-decked outdoor terrace and its Saturday night entertainment — come 10:30 pm the tables

disappear, a live band or DJ sets up and the trendies pour in to dance and drink the night away. Otherwise, the **Maharaja I** ℂ 2574 9838, 222 Wanchai Road. For milder Burmese food, the **Rangoon** ℂ 2892 1182, 265 Gloucester Road in Causeway Bay.

Indonesian
The Shinta ℂ 2527 8780, 2/F Kar Yau Building, 36-44 Queen's Road East (not far from Pacific Place), offers excellent Indonesian fare such as spicy beef rendang, satay (charcoal-grilled meat with spicy peanut sauce), gado (vegetable salad) and curries, and on Saturday nights a sumptuous buffet. For a mixture of Indonesian and Filipino, the **Cinta** 2527 1199, Basement, Hotel New Harbour, 6 Fenwick Street, **Wanchai**, and for Indo-Malaysian, **Banana Leaf** ℂ 2573 8187, 440 Jaffe Road, Causeway Bay. This restaurant is always very busy so it would be best to reserve a table to avoid waiting around.

Thai
Baan Thai ℂ 2831 9155, 4/F Causeway Bay Plaza I, 489 Hennessy Road, and in Wanchai, the very popular **Chili Club** ℂ 2527 2872, 1/F 88 Lockhart Road, and the **Golden Poppy** ℂ 2528 3278, 5/F 18 Lockhart Road.

Vietnamese
Since the advent of the "boat people" and their desperate refugee voyages across the South China Sea, Vietnamese cuisine has taken root and flourished in Hong Kong. In ingredients, preparation and style it's probably closest to the Cantonese school of cooking, with the addition of crisp lettuce and fresh mint and an assortment of condiments based on fiery red and green peppers. It features a particularly savory spring roll, eaten in jackets of lettuce and mint, a delicious barbecued prawn with sugar cane, an interesting variety of beef dishes and a range of fragrant meat and noodle-based soups. In Causeway Bay you can't miss the **Paterson (Vietnamese) Restaurant**

OPPOSITE Many Chinese restaurants in Hong Kong offer not only food but fun too — foursome ponders *mahjong* game in Kowloon eating house.

© 2890 6146 at 10 Cleveland Street, east of the Excelsior Hotel — it's a big boisterous eating house, as packed and as noisy as any large Cantonese restaurant, and it has a wide-ranging menu that does particular wonders with deep-fried and spicy crab.

Western

Landau's © 2827 7901, 2/F Sun Hung Kai Centre, Wanchai, has dominated the traditional scene for some years, offering a range of hors d'oeuvres, pickled herrings, escargots and tasty whatnots like goose terrine to

go with it. The **Excelsior Hotel Coffee Shop** © 2894 8888 in Causeway Bay, is also highly recommended, for its harbor views as well as its food, and the **Amigo** © 2577 2202 at 79A Wongneichong Road in Happy Valley, is the place if you want good French cuisine in a romantic Spanish-style setting. For more romance, the **Revolving 66** © 2862 6166, 62/F Hopewell Centre, 183 Queen's Road East, offers a la carte candle-lit dinners, seafood and steaks, afternoon tea and magnificent views of Hong Kong.

For Mexican specialties, US steaks and seafood, margaritas and nightly entertainment with Ben Abellaneosa and Los Mexicanos, try **Casa Mexicana** © 2566 5560, G/F Victoria Centre, 15 Watson Road,

North Point. However, be warned that halfway through the evening the waiters shove wide-brimmed hats on your head and everyone goes completely wild: it is definitely not a place for a pleasant, peaceful evening out. On the same premises, **Texas Rib House & Lounge** dishes up the finest spare ribs this side of the Panhandle.

In Wanchai, some Italian restaurants of note include "the friendliest Italian restaurant in town," **La Bella Donna** © 2802 9970, 1/F Shui On Centre, 8 Harbour Road, the Rigoletto © 2527 7144, U-G/F East Town Building, 16 Fenwick Street, and the up-market **Grissini** © 2861 1234 in the Grand Hyatt Hotel, which has an extensive all-Italian wine list. In Causeway Bay, **Bologna** © 2574 7282, G/F Elizabeth House, 250 Gloucester Road, and, further along the road, on the first floor of the Excelsior Hotel, **Cammino** © 2837 6780.

Also in Wanchai, **Harry Ramsden's** © 2832 9626, at 213 Queen's Road East, next to the Hopewell Centre, has brought real English fish and chips to Hong Kong. **Brett's Seafood Restaurant** © 2866 6608, 72-86B Lockhart Road, has an excellent selection of seafood, flown in from Australia, along with your basic fish and chips. The restaurant is open practically round the clock, from 7:30 am to 3:00 am.

TSIMSHATSUI

Tsimshatsui and the Kowloon peninsula were once known as the "other side" of Hong Kong, linked only by the Star Ferry with the island and providing a huge urban dormitory for the territory's Cantonese industrial work force. But the district was also the conduit for arrivals at Kai Tak Airport and, being at the very southern tip of China and the strategic Kowloon-Canton Railway, it had a tourist district centered on the Peninsula Hotel and Nathan Road, the main thoroughfare into the Kowloon hinterland down which, it was often half-jok-

ABOVE The skill required to make Chinese noodles is featured in a fascinating demonstration presented during the evening at the Peking Garden Restaurant. Noodle stall OPPOSITE and hot-pot snacks.

The Pleasure Path

ingly predicted, Mao Zedong's occupation forces would one day march.

In the past two decades, the tourist development in Tsimshatsui has been phenomenal, with major new hotels soaring up around the Peninsula and along Nathan Road's so-called Golden Mile, and, more recently, a whole new district, Tsimshatsui East, springing up on largely reclaimed land to add a series of gigantic new hotels, shopping plazas, restaurants and nightclubs to the Hong Kong extravaganza.

In many respects, the district offers Hong Kong's best variety of restaurants, largely because its tourist facilities and amenities have been concentrated into the Tsimshatsui East area and the Golden Mile. Certainly, for Chinese cuisine, you can take your pick of dozens of establishments, and many regional tastes, which have a high, proven reputation.

CHINESE CUISINE

You can choose the opulence and glitter of several palatial restaurant/nightclubs. Among them, **Ocean City** ℂ 2369 9688, Level 3, New World Centre, 18 Salisbury Road, is one of Hong Kong's largest dinner-dance venues with entertainment by some of Hong Kong's more well-known cabaret performers. **Ocean Palace** ℂ 2730 7111, 4/F Ocean Centre, Harbour City, Canton Road, has a Chinese classical dance performance every evening, followed by cabaret shows and dancing.

Alternatively you can choose from the hundreds of smaller restaurants in the area — take your pick:

For "drunken" prawns, Peking duck, game dishes and roast pigeon, the **Flower Lounge** restaurants at 11 Canton Road ℂ 2730 2200, 3 Peace Avenue ℂ 2715 6557 and Basement 2, Royal Garden Hotel ℂ 2722 1592, and Orchard Court ℂ 2317 5111, 1/F Ma's Mansion, 37 Hankow Road. For gourmet favorites such as shark's fin soup with crab and fish roe and roasted pigeon with cheese sauce, **Heichinrou** ℂ 2375 7123, 2/F Lippo Sun Plaza, 28 Canton Road.

The following group also have branches on Hong Kong Island: **Ah Yee Leng Tong**

ℂ 2721 3460, 29A Granville Road, is very popular with the local community for health-enhancing casseroles and "male" and "female" soups. **Tai Woo Seafood Restaurant** ℂ 2369 9773, 14-16 Hillwood Road, offers reasonably priced seafood dishes such as hotpots, steamed garoupa, sautéed scallops and garlic prawns. For home-style cooking, "drunken" prawns and seasonal specialties, **Tao Yuan** ℂ 2736 1688, 1/F, Departure Level, China Hong Kong City, 33 Canton Road, is highly recommended.

For those not watching their budgets, two excellent restaurants you can try for shark's fin soup, other seafood and game dishes are **Sun Tung Lok Shark's Fin Restaurant** ℂ 2730 0288, G/F Harbour City, 17-19 Canton Road, and Fook Lam Moon ℂ 2366 0286, 1/F 53-59 Kimberley Road.

All the hotels in Kowloon have excellent Chinese restaurants and here are a few of the more well-known ones, in the lower price range:

Dynasty ℂ 2369 4111 at the New World Hotel; **Celestial Court** ℂ 2369 1111, 2/F Sheraton Hotel ℂ Towers; **Loong Yuen** ℂ 2369 3111, 1st Basement, Holiday Inn Golden Mile. At the higher end: the **Chinese Restaurant** ℂ 2311 1234, 2/F Hyatt Regency; **Golden Unicorn** ℂ 2730 6565, 6/F Omni The Hongkong Hotel; the waterfront **Lai Ching Heen** ℂ 2721 1211, Regent Hotel, which has splendid views of the harbor and Hong Kong Island; **Spring Moon Chinese Restaurant** ℂ 2366 6251, The Peninsula; and **T'ang Court** ℂ 2375 1133, Renaissance.

Sichuan
Fung Lum's ℂ 2367 8686, 1/F Polly Commercial Bldg, 21-23 Prat Avenue, specialties include tea-flavored smoked duck, boneless chicken and prawns with chili and garlic sauce. You can also try **Lotus Pond Szechuen** ℂ 2730 8688, G/F, Phase IV, Harbour City, 15 Canton Road.

Chiu Chow
ChuiChow Garden Restaurant ℂ 2368 7266, 2/F Tsimshatsui Centre, 66 Mody Road, Tsimshatsui East, and **Golden Island Bird's Nest Chiu Chau Restaurant** ℂ 2736 6288, 2/F, East Half, Star House, 3 Salisbury

Road or at 3/F, BCC Building, 25-31 Carnarvon Road © 2369 5211.

Shanghai & Peking
Tien Heung Lau © 2368 9660, G/F 18C Austin Avenue — this restaurant is small so reservations are necessary — and **Wu Kong Shanghai Restaurant** © 2366 7244, Basement, Alpha House, 27 Nathan Road. For Peking food, the **Peking Garden** restaurants at two locations: © 2735 8211 3/F Star House, 3 Salisbury Road and © 2721 8868, 1/F Empire Centre, 68 Mody Road, Tsim-

where you can watch breads and kebabs being prepared for clay-oven baking. The **Koh-I-Noor** © 2368 3065, 1/F 3-4 Peninsula Apartments, 16C Mody Road, and **Maharaja II** © 2366 6671, G/F, 1-3A Granville Circuit, are also worth trying. Both have branches on Hong Kong Island. For vegetarian only, **Woodlands** © 2369 3718, 8 Minden Avenue.

Japanese
One novel establishment to try is **Ah-So** © 2730 3392, 159 World Finance Centre,

shatsui East. You can also try the long-established, modestly priced **Spring Deer** © 2723 3673, 1/F 42 Mody Road.

Vegetarian
One of my favorite vegetarian restaurants is **Bodhi** © 2366 8283, 1/F 32-34 Lock Road, which has a wonderful selection of beancurd, fungi and bamboo shoot dishes.

INTERNATIONAL FARE

Indian
Curry lovers are well taken care of at the famed **Gaylord Indian Restaurant** © 2376 1001, 1/F Ashley Centre, 23-25 Ashley Road, where tandooris are a speciality and

South Tower, Harbour City, Canton Road, which calls itself "Hong Kong's Only Floating Sushi Bar" — the food being served from floating "boats." If you'd prefer a place with its feet a little more firmly on dry land, there's **Kotobuki** © 2368 2711, Flat A & B, 1/F Good Result Building, 176 Nathan Road, or **Sui Sha Ya** © 2722 5001, G/F 9 Chatham Road.

Korean and Vietnamese
For Korean, **Arirang** © 2735 2281, G/F Sutton Court, Harbour City, 19 Canton Road, and for Vietnamese, two branches of

The Lan Kwai Fong neighborhood above Central District features French bistros and American hamburger restaurants.

The Pleasure Path

the **Golden Bull**: ✆ 2730 4866, 101 Ocean Centre, Harbour City, 5 Canton Road, and at ✆ 2369 4617, L1, 17, New World Centre, 18 Salisbury Road.

Indonesian

Java Rijsttafel ✆ 2367 1230, 38 Hankow Road, and, like its counterpart on Hong Kong Island, the busy, fast-food style **Banana Leaf** ✆ 2382 8189, 3/F 438-442 Prince Edward Road for Indo-Malaysian food.

Thai

The Golden Elephant ✆ 2735 0733, G/F, Phase I, Harbour City, Canton Road, and the **Thai Restaurant**, ✆ 2735 9181, Bangkok Royal Hotel, 2-12 Pilkem Street, Yaumatei.

Western

When it comes to Western food, Tsimshatsui outshines Hong Kong and once again it's difficult to know where to start.

For years the **Au Trou Normand** ✆ 2366 8754, 6 Carnarvon Road has been rated the finest French restaurant in town, and its classic recipes, its variety of wines and decor are still five-star. Its main competition traditionally coming from the Peninsula Hotel's ✆ 2366 6251 excellent European restaurants — **Gaddi's**, the Swiss-style **Chesa** and the **Verandah Grill**, with the mainland branch of **Jimmy's Kitchen** ✆ 2376 0327, 29 Ashley Road, up among them too.

But new competition is now rising among the many hotels that have sprung up in the last decade or so, and at most you'll usually find a classy French, Italian or Continental restaurant. A list of a few of the best follows:

For French cuisine, **Le Restaurant de France** ✆ 2722 1818, 3/F Regal Kowloon Hotel, **Les Celebrites**, ✆ 2739 1111, Hotel Nikko, and **Margaux** ✆ 2721 2111, at M/F Kowloon Shangri-La. For Continental, **Hugo's** ✆ 2311 1234, 2/F Hyatt Regency, **Plume** ✆ 2721 1211, Regent Hotel, **Tai Pan Grill** ✆ 2736 0088, 6/F Omni The Hongkong Hotel, and **Baron's Table** ✆ 2369 3111, 1/F Holiday Inn Golden Mile. And for Italian, **Sabatini's** ✆ 2721 2111 at the Royal Garden Hotel and **Capriccio** ✆ 2375 1133 at the Ramada Renaissance.

Moving out of the hotels, the Kowloon branch of **Grappa's** ✆ 2317 0288, Shop 1058, 1/F Ocean Centre in Harbour City offers home-style Italian pastas, sausages, breads and desserts at reasonable prices. For Australian tucker and a cold Foster's, **Kangaroo Pub** ✆ 2376 0083, 1/F 25 Haiphong Road, and for large helpings of British pub food, along with a good selection of vegetarian dishes, **Mad Dogs** ✆ 2301 2222, Basement, 32 Nathan Road.

There's an endless number of American restaurants in this area at the moment and you can take your pick of a few of the more popular ones: **Dan Ryan's Chicago Grill** ✆ 2735 6111, Shop 200, Ocean Terminal, Harbour City, Canton Road; **Beverly Hills Deli** ✆ 2369 8695, New World Centre, 18 Salisbury Road, also offers kosher meals; and the **San Francisco Steak House** ✆ 2735 7576, 101 Barnton Court, Harbour City, for US beef and seafood, salad bar and burgers. Also, **Planet Hollywood,** 3 Canton Road, owned by movie stars Arnold Schwarzenegger, Bruce Willis and Sylvester Stallone, features Californian cuisine and trendy Hollywood decor.

Another venue worth mentioning, though not especially for its food, is **Someplace Else** ✆ 2369 1111 in the basement of the Sheraton Hotel on Nathan Road. Its a crowded watering hole for young executive types, especially on Friday and Saturday nights, with American-style Victorian bric-a-brac decor, Mexican food, exotic cocktails and live entertainment.

For Harbour City shoppers, **The Boulevarde** ✆ 2730 3377, Shop 3283, Ocean Terminal, 3 Canton Road is a welcome break for afternoon tea. The restaurant also serves breakfast, lunch and buffet dinner.

OTHER CULINARY TRAILS

Eating out in Hong Kong needn't be confined to Central District, Wanchai-Causeway Bay and Tsimshatsui, especially if you have a weekend, or even if it's only a day or night, to spare. Hong Kong is a very compact city, with an efficient transportation service, and reaching the areas outside the

Lavish display of specialities including Peking Duck as the centerpiece at a Central District restaurant.

normal tourist beat is not as difficult as you might think.

HONG KONG ISLAND

Anyone who saw *Love is a Many Splendored Thing* is familiar with the much-publicized gastronomic symbols of Hong Kong, the palatial floating restaurants in Aberdeen, and they can be visited directly or by organized tour, or by way of harbor cruises from Central District or Tsimshatsui. The most well known is the **Jumbo** © 2553 9111, which

is moored beside its sister ships the **Jumbo Floating Palace** © 2554 0513 and **Tai Pak** © 2552 5953. All are excellent for *dim sum*, seafood (you can select your own from tanks) and the usual Cantonese fare. Closeby, the **Blue Ocean Restaurant** © 2555 9415, 9/F Aberdeen Marina Tower, 8 Shum Wan Road, offers more seafood and views of Aberdeen Harbour, it's fishing junks and marina moorings.

At the Peak, the very classy **Cafe Deco Bar and Grill** © 2849 5111, in the Peak Galleria features a mixture of Asian and Western cuisine and about HK$8 million

worth of original deco items such as a restored 1939 Wurlitzer juke box, a 1930s' bronze canopy from a hotel in Miami, toilet basins from the 1920s, an old porcelain and nickel ice box from a New York City church kitchen, a 1920 oyster bar with zinc top, 1925 wall sconces and old brass doors. And this, of course, is another location from where you'll get absolutely fantastic views of Hong Kong and Victoria Harbour. Opposite, the old **Peak Cafe** © 2849 7868, serves a mixture of Asian and American cuisine. During the weekends barbecue dinners are served in the pleasant garden area. A short walk from the cafe, **Peak 100** © 2849 7788, 100 Peak Road, offers Mediterranean meals and, weather permitting, outdoor dining on its large terrace.

Repulse Bay may have lost its graceful time-honored landmark, the Repulse Bay Hotel, but a replica of the romantic **Verandah** © 2812 2722 has been built into the high-rise luxury apartment block that now occupies the site. The restaurant serves excellent Continental cuisine, or you can just go for afternoon tea. Also in this complex, choose from the Euro-Japanese **Kagiya** © 2812 2120 at Shop 202, **Hei Fung Terrace Chinese Restaurant** © 2812 2622 on the 1st floor and for a variety of Asian dishes, **Spices** © 2812 2711 on the ground floor.

Down on the beach in the Lido complex near the huge Tin Hau and Kwun Yum statues, you'll find a **McDonald's** © 2812 1544, **Kentucky Fried Chicken** © 2812 0230 and some other fast-food restaurants. At the other end, the popular **Seaview** © 2812 2803, offers alfresco dining with a good Cantonese menu and, as its name suggests, pleasant views of the bay.

At Stanley you can spend the day browsing through the cut-price boutiques and stalls of the open market and lunch or dine in one of the many restaurants or pubs scattered about the town. These include **Beaches** © 2813 7313 at 92B Stanley Street, an open-fronted cafe-disco serving mainly Western food, and on Stanley Main Street, **Lord Stanley's Bistro & Bar** © 2813 8562, and **Ristorante Il Mercato** © 2813 9090.

Also in Stanley Main Street, the elegant **Stanley's French Restaurant** © 2813 8873, was the first Western establishment to open

---

ABOVE Beautifully painted screen and OPPOSITE pseudo-traditional decor of Hollywood Road above Central District.

there, and more than a decade later is still one of the best restaurants in the southern island area. Located in an old village house, Stanley's French features two glassed-in verandahs which offer fine views of the bay, and at night you can enjoy rooftop dining. In much the same vein is **Stanley's Oriental** ✆ 2813 9988, whose menu is a mixture of Asian and Western dishes, served either inside or on the verandah. During the day and at weekends both restaurants are quite casual but in the evenings, when the candles come out, more formal attire is expected.

Over at Hung Shing Yeh Beach, about a 30-minute walk away, the **Han Lok Yuen (Pigeon Restaurant)** ✆ 2982 0608 at 16 Hung Shing Yeh Road, is one of my favorite spots on the island. To reach it: just before you arrive at the beach, walk up the steps on your left and near the top on the left you'll see a large terrace with tables and umbrellas. It's a bit of a climb but worth the effort for the baked pigeon, minced quail served with lettuce, fried pepper prawns, cold beer and seaviews.

OUTLYING ISLANDS

Lamma and Cheung Chau are both famous for their seafront Cantonese seafood restaurants, so many that they stand virtually cheek by jowl. In Yung Shue Wan, Lamma's main village, recommended restaurants include **Lung Wah Sea Food** ✆ 2982 0281 at 20 Main Street, which also serves Western-style fish and chips, the **Man Fung Seafood (Lamma Seaview)** ✆ 2982 1112 on 5 Main Street and **Lamcombe Seafood** ✆ 2982 0881 at 47 Main Street. Other places to look out for are the **Waterfront Bar & Restaurant**, the **Capital** for fondues and the **Sampan**, which has a sitting out area.

On the other side of the island the small fishing village of So Kwu Wan, or Picnic Bay, is a popular destination for expatriates, who flock there in junkloads during the weekends and evenings to drink and gorge on peppered prawns, chili crab and baked lobster in the many open-air, waterfront restaurants. Recommended are the **Lamma Mandarin** ✆ 2982 8128 (no relation of the Mandarin Oriental), **Peach Garden** ✆ 2982 8581 and the **Rainbow Seafood Restaurant** ✆ 2982 8100.

On Cheung Chau, the **Warwick Hotel** ✆ 2981 0081 on the east side of the island serves Western and Chinese food. But if you'd rather not be in an air-conditioned environment there are plenty of open-air Chinese restaurants along the waterfront promenade and at Tung Wan Beach. You can also try the **Garden Cafe** at 84 Tung Wan Road, **Pontus Cafe** on Tai Sun Street and an Indian restaurant called the **Cartoon Club**, located on Pak She Street near the Pak Tai Temple.

If you really want to get away from the crowds, take a sampan from Cheung Chau to Tai Long Wan on Lantau island to the **Frog and Toad** ✆ 2989 2300. The restaurant is about a half-mile walk from the beach along a concrete path that takes you through farms (and patches of cow dung).

For those with less time to spare, Lantau's largest residential area, Discovery Bay (or Disco Bay as it's locally referred to) is only about 30 minutes by high-speed ferry from Star Ferry in Central and can be a pleasant interlude either during the day or at night. The restaurants, all located in the shopping complex by the ferry terminal, are casual and reasonably priced: **Siam Palace Thai Restaurant** ✆ 2987 9191, **Jo Jo Indian Restaurant** ✆ 2987 0122, and the **Seoul Garden Korean Restaurant** ✆ 2987 0073. But if you'd rather just sit on the

chicken blood 正 鷄 血

Open from 1:00 to 9:00 pm, it's best visited for lunch but let them know you're coming. If you're going for dinner make it an early one you don't want to miss the last boat back to Hong Kong.

For those touring around Lantau, **Charlie's Restaurant and Bar** ✆ 2984 8329, 13-14 Law Uk Village, Poi O, is a welcome stopoff point for lunch. The Australian-operated alfresco restaurant offers Cantonese, Indian and Western cuisine, as well as afternoon tea, and has an extensive wine list. Visa, Master Card and Amex credit cards are accepted. If you've ventured as far Tai O fishing village, **Ho King Restaurant** ✆ 2985 5115, 15 Wing On Street, is another good place for lunch.

beach, takeaways include **McDonald's** and **Cajun Chicken**.

LEI YUE MUN AND THE NEW TERRITORIES

For adventurous seafood lovers, the village of Lei Yue Mun, on Kowloon's eastern tip of the harbor, shouldn't be missed. Here you select your own seafood from rows and rows of tanks that line the alleyways and if you can decide whether it's to be scallops, prawns and snapper or abalone, crabs and lobster or all six, you take your catch to a nearby restaurant which will gladly cook the food for you. Great views of the harbor from a different perspective, along with close-ups of jets flying in and out of Kai

Tak— an experience in itself. To get there, take MTR to Kwun Tong and from there either a Kowloon Motor Bus (KMB) No. 14C or minibus to the Sam Ka Tsuen terminus.

Out in the New Territories, Shatin offers some reputable restaurants. Firmly docked on the Shing Mun River Channel, the three-decked marbled concrete **Treasure Floating Restaurant** offers *dim sum* and seafood. At the night the restaurant is a blaze of lights and quite an amazing sight. A good place to eat after a day at the races. It's land address is 55 Tai Chung Kiu Road ✆ 2637 7000. On the same road you can try the **Regal Riverside Hotel** ✆ 2649 7878, which has Thai, Western and seafood restaurants along with a disco and karaoke rooms. Another good spot is the 50-year-old **Lung Wah Hotel Restaurant**, ✆ 2691 1594, 22 Ha Wo Che, which is famous for its pigeon and beancurd dishes.

If you've taken time out to explore Sai Kung Country Park, its beaches and surrounding islands, the picturesque fishing port of Sai Kung is a convenient stopoff point for lunch and dinner, or even breakfast. The town has a number of streetside cafes, nothing fancy, as well as excellent Cantonese seafood restaurants such as **San Shui** ✆ 2792 1828, G/F 7-15 Siu Yat Building, Lot 941, New Town, which has some interesting dishes on its menu — barbecued fish in bamboo stems, fried clams with black beans and chilies and stuffed cuttlefish. On Fook Man Road, the **Duke of York Pub** ✆ 2792 8435 offers pub fare and plenty of cold beer, and friendly **Susanna's** ✆ 2792 7163, at 76 Po Tung Road, very spicy seafood.

For a more serene setting, the **Sampan Thai Seafood Restaurant** ✆ 2719 3238 at Hebe Haven — a boating center southwest of Sai Kung — offers delicious food and, in the summer months, outdoor dining.

SHOP TILL YOU DROP

THE GUCCI TRAIL

Whether a bargain-packed "Emporium of the East" or a latter-day showplace of the latest fashions and consumer electronics, Hong Kong has always been an exciting but hard-nosed shopping center — the great Oriental emporium that the early China traders envisioned it as being, and something that must be making the ghost of Lord Palmerston chew on his top hat.

And Hong Kong is a place where you won't find toilet paper advertised on TV, or mouth-wash, or any other of the mass-marketed household essentials that crowd the commercials channels of the West. Hong Kong's English-language ATV World and TVB Pearl programming pushes Swiss watches, French perfumes, high-class

jewelry, up-market Japanese electronic consumer products, the target and tone of its commercials reflecting the same tone of its mainstream shopping — Gucci, not anything as crass as the morning gargle.

This up-market trend makes shopping a covetous experience, and the Hong Kong version of a window-browsing far more than just a stroll in the streets. Since the beginning of the eighties, huge self-contained, climate-controlled, luxury-packed shopping malls have sprung up all over the place to revolutionize the retail indus-

OPPOSITE Hong Kong's traditional arts — ornately sculptured marble and jade chops in Man Wa Street store, Western District. ABOVE Calligrapher works in open-air studio in Kowloon.

The Pleasure Path

try, many of them featuring multi-storey atriums, decorative fountains and regular cultural exhibitions and performances — anything from police brass bands to string quartets or Chinese acrobats — to attract the crowds. Just as the ultra-modern infrastructure of Hong Kong has made the place something of a capitalist funland, these great retail palaces have made shopping an adventure playground.

Like some kind of living, growing organism, they've also gradually linked up in certain districts, providing environments in which you can browse in air-conditioned comfort for hours, crossing from mall to mall, without actually exposing yourself to the outside air — a blessed relief in the sweltering and humid high-summer months.

In **Central District**, for example, you can stroll from Star Ferry to the converted pedestrian overpass between Jardine House and Exchange Square that gives you the choice of either continuing along the waterfront towards the **Shun Tak Centre** shopping arcades and going across another overpass to the **Wing On** and **Sincere** department stores, giving blissful shelter from rain and the fierce summer heat, not to mention the traffic. Or you can go straight ahead into the bargain outlets of World-Wide Plaza on your right or to the high-class boutiques in **Swire House** on your left, with access to more shopping floors in St George's Building and the **Mandarin Hotel** and, via other pedestrian crossovers, **Prince's Building, The Landmark** and the posh **Galleria.**

This is the start of the Gucci Trail — alongside Gucci you'll find Chanel, Christian Dior, Lanvin, Hermes, Giorgio Armani, Nina Ricci, Issey Miyake and Salvatore Ferragamo. You'll find Rolex, Seiko, Girard Peregaux and Cartier watches. You'll drool over heavy 22-carat gold necklaces, bracelets and other high-fashion jewelry, Italian pig-skin shoes and silk ties, French perfumes, fine porcelain, the latest in American and Japanese sports equipment and fashions, Burmese jade, crystal glassware and antique fine arts — and you'll feel strangely avid and perhaps a little embarrassed at the long-suppressed instinct for the luxuries of life that is rising out of your soul.

From here, the trail extends to **Lane Crawford** on Queen's Road Central, the traditional home of Harrod's-style upper-drawer British shopping, to dozens of watch and gold-jewelry shops and to another **Wing On** in Melbourne Plaza. Continue along Queen's Road to the Hilton Hotel arcade and then take the pedestrian overpass into the walk-through of Queensway shopping plaza that runs between the Far East Finance Centre and Admiralty Towers, above the Admiralty MTR station, from where another pedestrian bridge takes you into the glistening shopping mall of Pacific Place.

This vast complex houses a wide range of up-market boutiques, a **Marks and Spencer, Seibu** (a Japanese department store with a range of trendy merchandise and prices that have to be seen to be believed), specialty shops, restaurants, cinemas and the **Marriott, Conrad** and **Island Shangri-La** hotels.

From there it runs down into Wanchai and Causeway Bay, where the accent changes from Western to Japanese high fashion and luxury accessories in the giant Tokyo-style department stores, **Mitsukoshi, Daimaru**, **Matsuzakaya** and **Sogo**. Just around the corner from Mitsukoshi, between Russell and Sharp streets, you'll find the spectacular Times Square with its inside scenic elevators, up-market boutiques, huge music store, restaurants and cinemas. There's also another branch of **Lane Crawford** in this district, and a range of boutiques and shops selling everything from silk scarves to cameras and electronics to Chinese antiques in the **Excelsior Hotel Shopping Arcade**.

Beyond Causeway Bay in the Taikoo Shing housing development at Quarry Bay, you'll find another enormous emporium, **Cityplaza,** which has four towers for up-market and bargain shopping and a variety of eating places. And if you feel like a little exercise in between window-browsing there's an ice-skating rink in one of the atriums. Cityplaza is easily accessible by

OPPOSITE Hong Kong's commercial extravaganza — the vast atrium of New Town Plaza shopping mall in Shatin.

MTR — just take the train to Taikoo station and one of the exits takes you right into Tower I.

The giants of the shopping world are clustered over the harbor in Tsimshatsui and Tsimshatsui East. From the moment you get off the Star Ferry, in fact, you're drawn into the luxury vortex of shopping plazas, all interlinked **Star House, Harbour City (Ocean Terminal, Ocean Centre** and **Ocean Galleries)** and **China Hong Kong City,** containing no less than five hotels and hundreds of shops. It's such a mammoth place

pick of a half-dozen shopping plazas around the Royal Garden, Regal Meridien Holiday Inn Crowne Plaza Harbour View hotels.

Finally, for jewelry lovers Hong Kong offers high-quality diamonds and other gems, all of which are exempt from tax and duty charges, at reasonable prices. Gold and platinum are also competitively priced. As with other shopping, where to go for the best buys is always a problem and before rushing into the first shop you see, please consult HKTA's *Shopping Guide to Jewellery,* which tells you what you need to look for in

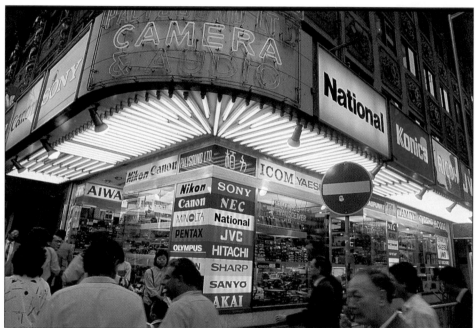

that an information desk in the Ocean Terminal, staffed by English-speaking guides, will provide you with maps and even a computer print-out of suitable shops to help you find your way through the retail maze.

Some other malls in Tsimshatsui include **Park Lane Shopper's Boulevarde** on the Nathan Road side of Kowloon Park and opposite, Park Lane Square. Also, the **New World Centre,** across Salisbury Road on the southern fringe of the Tsimshatsui reclamation. For the discerning buyer there are smaller shopping arcades in the Peninsula, Hyatt Regency, Sheraton, Holiday Inn Golden Mile and Regent hotels.

From there you can wend your way into the heart of Tsimshatsui East and take your

a stone, and their Shopping booklet for reputable retailers. (For more on jade, see THE BARGAIN TRAIL, p117.)

CUSTOM TAILORS OR WHATEVER

Gone are the days when you could walk into any tailor shop in Hong Kong and have a man's or woman's suit or dress shirt made in 24 hours at ridiculously cheap prices. A lot of the 24-hour tailors are no longer around, and the conventional ones are now charging prices comparable with designer-label fashion off the hook. However, one tailor who's still keeping the tradition alive is the famous and long-established **Sam's**

Tailor ✆ 2721 8375, Burlington Arcade, K, 92-94 Nathan Road, Tsimshatsui, whose prices, depending on the material, range from around HK$1,800 to HK$6,000.

THE SPACE-AGE BAZAAR

For the latest in high-tech consumer products Hong Kong has them all, in the thousands of shops and plazas that make up this city. With the help of the territory's free-port status, as fast as they come off the space-age assembly lines in Japan, South Korea, Taiwan and China they're usually available here — months before they appear in most other countries. And at competitive prices.

But with a combination of spiraling shop rents, increasingly slim profit margins, the deteriorating caliber of retail employees and sheer greed, shopping for these goods can be an unpleasant experience. Particular consumer complaints in recent years have been over "bait-and-switch" tactics, where what you get is not what you were shown. Also, components or accessories are often removed from the product boxes and, when the deal is done, the shop assistant claims that these are optional extras — which you must have or the product itself won't work properly, and which he'll sell you at a 50 percent discount because you're such a nice customer. Don't rush into a deal — prices can vary from shop to shop, sometimes considerably. For example, in one store I was quoted HK$1,800 for a portable compact disc player which was selling for HK$1,300 in another.

The Tsimshatsui district is famous for its bargains (and unscrupulous deals) in cameras and consumer electronics, especially in the honeycomb of brightly lit, fixed ghetto blasters that are the cutthroat stores on Nathan Road and back-streets either side. Like most of the smaller stores in Hong Kong, these places operate on the principle of high turnover, which means that some of them have profit margins on their most popular lines shaved down to as little as HK$40 to HK$80. On Hong Kong Island, you can try the row of shops running along Queen Victoria and Stanley streets in Central. In Wanchai, Johnston and Hennessy

roads and in Causeway Bay, Cannon Street (which leads to the **Excelsior Hotel**) and along **Ye Wo Street**.

But if you're concerned about getting ripped off, or just don't want to deal with the frequently rude assistants, some reputable dealers recommended by HKTA follow:

Hong Kong Island
The Sony Service Centre's Chung Yuen Electrical Co stores at Shop 104-105 Prince's Building, Chater Road ✆ 2524 8066 and 105 Des Voeux Road ✆ 2544 5188 in Central and

at 525 Lockhart Road ✆ 2893 3358 in Causeway Bay; **Crown Photo Supplies** ✆ 2868 4343, Shop 111, 1/F Swire House, 11 Chater Road, Central; **Fortress** ✆ 2544 1665, 107-111 Des Voeux Road, Central; and **Universal Audio & Video Centre** ✆ 2801 6422 in Shop 135 at The Mall in Pacific Place. For cameras only, **Photo Scientific Appliances** ✆ 2522 1903, 6 Stanley Street, Central.

Tsimshatsui
Crown Photo Supplies ✆ 2376 1836, 27 Hankow Road; Fortress ✆ 2735 8628, Shop 281, Ocean Terminal; and **Wood's**

Cameras, tailor-made clothes and silks shown OPPOSITE and ABOVE are among the top items of the Hong Kong tourist's shopping list.

Photo Supplies ℭ 2736 8128, Room 1004, 10/F Silvercord, Tower 2, 30 Canton Road. For cameras only, the **Camera Shop** ℭ 2730 9227 in Shop 121, Ocean Terminal.

For computer buffs, I recommend the following two shopping complexes in Tsimshatsui: **Silvercord**, 30 Canton Road, and Star Computer City, 2/F Star House, 3 Salisbury Road. Also, **A-1 Electronic Co** ℭ 2366 6552, at Shop B 117A in the Holiday Inn Golden Mile Hotel arcade or their branch on Hong Kong Island ℭ 2861 3218 at 48 Lockhart Road, Wanchai.

Lastly, and not mentioned in any of HKTA shopping guides, you'll find a multi-level computer bazaar in Shamshuipo called the **Golden Shopping Arcade** where you can gèt hardware, software, accessories and spare parts for just about any brand you can name. You can also get software (and the possibility of viruses) that you'd swear could not be offered at the prices you're being quoted, if you know what I mean. It's a "freelance" establishment in the truest sense of the word and you'll find that matters like warranties and guarantees have to be treated with something of a wink and a nod — so be careful, and if you feel unsettled about the equipment or the price, take the prudent route and don't buy. If you know all about computers, and know exactly what you want, you should come out satisfied.

The Bargain Trail

Outside the big plazas, there are literally thousands of department stores and smaller shops to choose from, offering just about anything your heart desires. Their prices are cheaper because their rents are lower, the competition between them is fierce, and, as already mentioned, they operate on the basis of a swift turnover. Many of thèm also cater more for the domestic Chinese buyer, which in some cases means better prices and, in the case of clothing, means some very good deals if you can fit into the generally smaller Chinese sizes.

Starting in the western area of Central District, the **Shun Tak Centre** in the Macau Ferry Terminal offers several levels of shops selling the latest in fashion and informal gear. Nearby, the **Wing On** and **Sincere** department stores not only offer high fashion but reasonable bargains in clothing, luggage, shoes and body-care products, particularly when there's a sale on.

For watches and jewelry, there are dozens of stores running virtually parallel with each other on Des Voeux and Queen's roads. For really good value, the City Chain watch shops — there are around 70 branches scattered throughout Hong Kong — have permanent 30 to 50 percent discounts.

A relatively cheap place for quality men's shirts, suits and casual ensembles is **Crocodile**, which has a number of outlets in Central, Pacific Place, Causeway Bay and Kowloon.

Elsewhere in Central, you'll find haberdashery items on the steps on Pottinger Street, and across Queen's Road in "The Lanes," or Li Yuen Streets East and West, which run down to Des Voeux Road, cheap clothing, underwear, shoes, silkwear, make-up, jewelry and Gucci lookalike handbags. Nearby on Des Voeux Road, **World-Wide Plaza** has lots of small shops selling much of what's to be found in the lanes.

For mainly Chinese products, the five floors of the **Chinese Merchandise Emporium** at 92-104 Queen's Road, just past Pottinger Street. The prices are good and style and quality are steadily improving as the society modernizes. Style is still one of its major drawbacks though — as you make your way from floor to floor you can see where the clock stopped in China, with radios, fans and clothes still quaintly fifties-design. But it's still a treasure house of interesting souvenirs — herbal medicines, Chinese teas, mahjong sets, jewelry, carpets and antiques, silk embroidery, fine linenware, carved marble and soapstone figures, jade and nephrite jewelry and sculptures, intricate cloisonné and bamboo ware, traditional kites in the form of hawks and ducks, mouth organs, ping-pong sets, calligraphy and painting sets, ornate old-fashioned treadle-style sewing machines, kung fu swords and tom-toms, dragon masks and even the sturdy Phoenix and Swallow bicycles of China, modeled on the old British workhorse, The Raleigh Roadster.

In Wanchai around the Wanchai Road and Spring Garden Lane area there are stalls and shops selling designer jeans, children's clothes and casual wear for both men and women. Further along in Causeway Bay, the bargain shopping is more concentrated, largely in the area between Hysan Avenue and the Excelsior Hotel. Again, there's just about everything you'd want to know on sale in the myriad stores and boutiques that absolutely throng with shoppers. The area is particularly rich in women's clothing and shoes and a popular place you can try is **Jardine's Bazaar**, which is similar to the lanes in Central. Also in the vicinity is another huge Chinese emporium, **China Products.**

No shopping visit to Hong Kong is really complete without a browse through the open market and bargain boutiques at Stanley, which you can reach by taking bus No 6 or the air-conditioned 260 from the Exchange Square terminal in Central. Famous for years for its cut-price clothing and arts and crafts, the market has become a mainstream tourist attraction these days, with tour coaches thundering out there every day. At weekends the place is packed, and if you want my advice, go there during the week. Stanley isn't as cheap as it used to be and bargaining doesn't seem to be the thing to do anymore. But you won't be disappointed, it's still a good place to shop, and a lot of fun.

In Tsimshatsui, the most interesting place for browsing and buying both day and night is along the "Golden Mile" of Nathan Road, checking out the side streets if you have the time. One area off Nathan Road that shouldn't be missed is Granville Road, which is noted for its cheap clothes. Most of the shops are outlets selling factory "seconds" and production overruns and if you've got the patience to sort through the endless racks and piles of clothes you'll find some amazing bargains.

Other locations for more overruns of designer brand clothes as well as electronics, carpets, lamps and porcelain, etc are the factories themselves. Personally, the last

place I'd want to shop in Hong Kong is at the factory, but if the discounts appeal to you I suggest you obtain *The Complete Guide to Hong Kong Factory Bargains* — a handy pocket-sized book found in most book shops — for tips and the best and most reliable places to go. Also, HKTA's Factory Outlets/Locally Made Fashion Outlets brochure, which lists all HKTA members dealing in the manufacturing and retailing of ready-to-wear.

OPPOSITE Jewelry shops abound on and off the Golden Mile on Nathan Road — the main tourist shopping mecca of Kowloon. ABOVE Shopper admires decorated vase in Ocean Terminal, part of the extensive Harbour City complex of shops and hotels.

For Chinese products, **Chinese Arts & Crafts** in Star House, by Star Ferry, sells happy coats, silk dressing gowns, embroidered linen, inexpensive to very pricey jewelry and jade items, porcelain and antiques, along with rosewood furniture and beautiful Chinese carpets. Good for souvenirs and gifts and like its competitor in Central, prices are very reasonable.

For more browsing and buying, **Temple Street** is Hong Kong's most popular night market and can be reached by MTR, alighting at Jordan station. From the Jordan Road entrance you make your way through block after block of stalls and shops selling fake Rolex, Dunhill and Cartier watches and designer clothes, more cheap watches, sunglasses, silk ties, trousers, shirts, sweaters, jackets, suits, men's underpants at HK$10 for three pairs and T-shirts for HK$10 to $15. You can pick-up electronic keyrings that beep, solar calculators the size of credit cards (which also double as FM radios), or FM radios the size of cigarette lighters, or cigarette lighters that double as FM radios. You'll find Nepalese hawkers sitting on the sidewalk selling Nepalese jewelry, masks and colorful bags. You'll see street dentists, Chinese opera ,and for HK$50 you can have some of your fortune told — the full story will cost more.

Where Temple Street caters mainly to men, Tung Choi Street in Mongkok is the "Ladies' Market" selling bright sweaters, scarves, jeans, underwear and makeup.

Back in Yaumatei, another of Hong Kong's traditional open-air bargain centers, the **Jade Market**, under the flyover near Kansu Street, offers a range of jade, and prices. But be careful, if you know nothing about the stone, don't spend a lot of money unless you have an expert with you.

East of Tsimshatsui East in **Hung Hom, Whampoa Garden** is another place for value for money. When you arrive, if you think you see a large ship in the middle of the shopping area you're not mistaken. The Whampoa hasn't run aground and was, in fact, especially built as a shopping mall — inside, a Japanese department store, Chinese restaurant and a coffee shop. Nearby, the **Hong Kong Place** arcade stages a Musical Fountain Show. To get there from Kowloon, take a taxi and if you're coming from Hong Kong Island, Star Ferries will take you directly there.

Not forgetting the children, apart from the department stores, these days about the only place specializing in toys is the massive **Toys "R" Us** in the basement of Ocean Centre.

Out in the New Territories the shopping plazas in the New Towns at Shatin, Tsuen Wan and Tuen Mun — all conveniently accessible via the MTR/KCR — have added to the bargain market, forced by their locations to undercut the prices in the central tourist districts. If you have the time, they're definitely worth visiting.

THE ANTIQUE/ARTS & CRAFTS TRAIL

For Chinese and Asian antiques there's really only one place to go, the area in Central starting from the upper end of Wyndham Street, continuing all the way along Hollywood Road until you reach "Cat Street," just by the Man Mo Temple.

Here you'll find a wide range of high-priced boutique-style stores offering everything from Chinese and Thai carved Buddhas to Indonesian masks and batiks, Persian and Indian carpets, rosewood furniture, Thai and Himalayan artwork and a fascinating array of snuff bottles, porcelain, silver jewelry, Korean and Japanese wooden chests and traditional Chinese silk paintings and scrolls.

If the prices frighten you off, there's an irresistible junk shop on the corner of Hollywood Road and Lyndhurst Terrace laden with an incredible assortment of second-hand Western and Chinese collectibles Mao paraphernalia, watches, cameras, Chinese coins, black and white photos of old Hong Kong and China and books and magazines. For much the same thing, but on a larger scale, hawkers at "Cat Street" display their "antiques" along the pavements of two narrow streets.

Another interesting place for Asian arts and crafts is the **Amazing Grace Elephant Company** in Ocean Centre, at the Excelsior

OPPOSITE A Rolls Royce replica and hostesses await customers at Club Bboss.

Hotel Shopping Arcade and at Cityplaza in Taikoo Shing. They also have a discount warehouse in Tuen Mun in Flat A, Yeu Shing Industrial Building, 4 Kin Fung Circus. For inquiries ✆ 2463 8156.

THE SAFETY TRAIL

Being the frenetic open market that Hong Kong is, the trading rules and practices naturally get a little twisted and bent here and there, and there are certain precautions that should be taken before buying anything of technical or financial value. The first rule is this: don't go shopping until you've obtained a copy of the HKTA's three guides: *Shopping, Shopping Guide to Jewellery and Shopping Guide to Consumer Electronics*.

They're handy little booklets packed with information on where to go and who to trust on your shopping spree, and it offers the added guarantee of its own membership system — every retail outlet in the book has the HKTA stamp of approval. If you have any complaints or queries about a member, you can contact the Membership Department ✆ 2801 7278

When you're shopping outside the major retail plazas, take cash and not plastic. Such is the low-profit turnover in most shops, especially the clothing, camera and electronics places, that the retailers put a five percent "handling" charge on the cost to discourage credit cards. If this happens to you, suggest you report the shop to your credit card company.

Always shop around and compare prices before making any decision, and even then make sure that the best bargain price you get includes not only the camera or stereo unit you want to buy but the standard accessories that go with it. For complaints or advice call the Consumer Council ✆ 2304 1234

Again, outside the major plazas, the question of a warranty on cameras and electrical goods is a constant problem. The best way to tackle it is to shop only where you see the HKTA sign, meaning the establishment has been vetted for good customer service and honesty, and insist that a warranty be provided and stamped with the dealer's chop before you hand over the money.

Don't be timid. Bargain where you feel you can. Go for whatever discount you can get, it's accepted practice in most "freelance" outlets in Hong Kong. But then again, don't lose your cool if you get cold-shouldered. Try at all times to make shopping a fun experience, not a cultural collision — remembering that, with the vast variety of stores throughout Hong Kong, and the fierce competition, if one shop won't give you the price you want you'll get it somewhere else.

Don't let touts physically drag you into their shops. It means you're stepping into a tourist trap. When you're buying ivory

Laser-lashed dance floor of Club Bboss, one of the biggest and most astonishing entertainment centers in the world.

or jade, shop only at an HKTA-recommended establishment and go there armed with HKTA advice. There are some very clever bone and plastic imitations of ivory around Hong Kong, and plastic and ordinary stone "jade". Remember also that some countries have now banned the import of ivory, so check on that with your consulate or trade commission before you bother to look around.

If you're buying Chinese or Asian furniture to ship home, make sure you get all receipts from the retailer, the total price,

shipping information and check requirement for disinfestation before or after importation to the destination country. The HKTA advises that on major purchases you take out All Risk Insurance as well to cover the possibility of in-transit damage. Remember also that rattan and certain other Asian woods and materials dry out and become brittle or even crack when they're shipped from constant humidity to centrally heated homes.

Lastly, be careful about the amount of luggage you try to hand-carry on to your plane at Kai Tak Airport. For most airlines, United States carriers excluded, there's a size limit to cabin luggage, and there's a team of female inspectors inside the depar-

ture barrier which is so zealous you'd swear it trained with Delta Force or the SAS. Anything beyond a reasonably sized hold-all will not get through, and you'll leave Hong Kong in anger when you should have a contented, perhaps over-stimulated and exhausted smile on your face.

THE GLITTER CITY

ONE THOUSAND AND ONE NIGHTS

Hong Kong's nightlife operates at the same tempo as the business of the day — fast, furious and in a constant boom. It follows the same pattern as the business world too — every few years it bursts beyond its own conventions and attempts the impossible, or at least the decidedly improbable. And within no time at all another improbable dream is just another convention.

The latest nightlife triumph is to after-dark entertainment what the Jumbo 747 was to the airline industry when the monster airliner first nosed its way out of Boeing's assembly plant in Seattle. You'll find it in Tsimshatsui East — three huge hostess clubs called the **Club Bboss** ℂ 2369 2883, LG/F New Mandarin Plaza, 14 Science Museum Road, **Club Metropolitan** ℂ 2311 1111, LG/F Chinachem Golden Plaza, 77 Mody Road, **China City Night Club** ℂ 2723 3278, 4/F Peninsula Centre, 67 Mody Road, the biggest and most astonishing entertainment centers anywhere in the world.

When you stroll into the Club Bboss, for example, you enter a vast 6,510 sq m (70,000 sq ft) luxuriously appointed dance-lounge and are driven to your plush, discreetly positioned personal "relaxation zone" in a full-sized battery-powered replica of an antique Rolls-Royce — gliding down a long glass-smooth boardwalk which glitters and twinkles with overhead lighting and, as it streaks into the distance before you, looks like the main runway of an international airport at night, turned upside down.

Both Bboss and China City have huge laser-lashed dance floors, non-stop big-band entertainment and teams of Cantonese and Filipino rock and soul singers, romantically lighted hospitality lounges and nooks as far as the eye can see, and absolute regiments of hostesses and service staff. Bboss boasts no fewer than 1,000 hostesses on its books, up to 400 of whom will be on duty any night of the week. Specially selected for their looks, poise and their conversational skills and costumed in elegant thigh-split traditional silk cheongsams they're supervised by a legion of *mama-sans* who carry walkie-talkie radios to keep in touch with customer requests.

Different sector managers carry special goes beyond that, companionship, conversation and reasonably restrained flirtation will cost an extra HK$53, strictly for 15 minutes. For a full night outside on the town the fee is a flat HK$1,500 — reasonable by any standards for the beauty and intellect of the girls, and certainly a much more attractive proposition than the high-priced hustle of the "hostess" bars of Wanchai and Tsimshatsui.

Both complexes have special segregated areas for Japanese visitors — quiet, private and almost Zen-like in mood. While the

pager beepers which show a digital code that corresponds with a particular request or area of the huge nightspot. The waitresses, selected again for their looks and poise, wear black bow ties and tails, kneel at your table to serve drinks and snacks and are so well tuned in to customer service that they'll have a cigarette lighter poised before you while the cigarette is still on its way to your lips.

In both Bboss and China City entertainment palaces, digital clocks over the seating areas begin operating the moment a tall, slim, raven-haired hostess is led like a vestal virgin to your divan by a radio-equipped *mama-san*. There is a minimum HK$450 charge for a drink and snacks. If your desire

Club Bboss has the most imaginative decor, the style and tone of a kind of high-class Star Wars bordello, the China City offers a lush and romantic patio garden with an aviary full of lovebirds. Club Metropole is an elaborately decorated hostess club with an XO tunnel of cognac and whisky bottles.

These huge nightspots have to be seen simply to be believed (and such is the level of discretion on which they operate that you don't necessarily have to contract a hostess to visit one). They are a forward

OPPOSITE Ornate lanterns await buyers in Happy Valley store. ABOVE Draught beer and pint glasses at Kowloon pub — a legacy of the British administration and commercial presence in Hong Kong.

glimpse of the twenty-first century, a promise of the extravagant style of entertainment to come in the great Asiatic cities of the future. As one manager described it: "Compared with us, every other nightclub in Hong Kong is just a small store. We're the supermarkets of the nightlife business."

There are lots more cheaper and less palatial hostess clubs around. Most of them have big-band entertainment and non-stop Filipino and Cantonese singers, legions of pretty, well-groomed hostesses and, like Bboss, Metropole and China City, all sorts

of extravagant and bizarre gimmicks to make the visitor feel pampered.

The giant **New Tonnochy Night Club** ✆ 2511 1383, 1-5 Tonnochy Road, Wanchai, for example, greets its visitors with a turbaned honor guard, and violins play guests to their seats. While the bands crash from one swing number to the next, 200 hostesses chat and dance with their clients at HK$200 plus an hour, drinks not included. The same goes for Tonnochy's main rival, **Mandarin Palace Night Club** ✆ 2575 6551 at 24-28 Marsh Road.

Over in Tsimshatsui, there's a much wider range to choose from, but you'd be well-advised to check in detail first about the prices of drinks, companionship and

cover charge before you enter. The management won't mind being questioned; they prefer to discourage Western customers rather than end up with dissatisfied and possibly troublesome guests. For the best and most reputable, try two establishments in the **New World Centre** on Salisbury Road — **Club Cabaret** ✆ 2369 8432 and **Club Deluxe** ✆ 2721 0277.

THE NIGHT TRAIL

Not all nightlife in Hong Kong is as awe-

some and futuristic, and as male-oriented, as Club Bboss, China City and Metropole. Like eating out, stepping out on the town is to face a myriad of different nightspots and an almost impossible variety of choices of entertainment. Most bars offer Happy Hour (two drinks for the price of one) from around 5:00 to 9:00 pm and at the bigger venues which offer music and dancing, you'll probably have to pay a cover charge which, depending on where you are, can vary from HK$30 to $150. During the week, nightlife usually ends around 2:30 am but at weekends you can party till 5:00 or 6:00 am.

On Hong Kong Island's Central District, the fashionable **Lan Kwai Fong** bars and restaurants are often so busy at weekends that finding even elbowroom may not be easy, especially after 10:00 pm.

For starters you can try the three affiliated venues of **Nineteen 97** ℂ 2810 9333, 8-11 Lan Kwai Fong — drinks upstairs at **Post 97,** dinner downstairs in Mecca 97 and then dance the night away in **Club 1997**. Across the road, the **Jazz Club** ℂ 2845 8477, frequently features top international performers, along with their regular, first-rate house band.

Around the corner, **California** ℂ 2521 1345 and Graffiti 2521 2202 restaurants turn

bar, brothel and nightclub district of Hong Kong but has now become a respectable business and restaurant area with a surviving core of fairly tame topless bars and nightclubs along with karaoke lounges, discos and bars. For live rock and roll, Suzy Wong and old Hong Kong memorabilia, try **The Wanch** ℂ 2861 1621, at 54 Jaffe Road. **Joe Bananas** ℂ 2529 1811, which is also a restaurant, at 23 Luard Road, has a resident DJ, extra loud disco music and dance floor — but if you're wearing fur, shorts or a shirt without a collar, you won't be allowed in,

into thumping discos in the late evening, **DD II** ℂ 2524 8809, has more lasers and videos and Yelts Inn loud music and plenty of Sol. Across the road at **Hardy's** ℂ 2526 7184, you can listen to folk music or even get up on stage yourself and sing. Just around the corner from there, up the lane on your left, the popular **Club 64** ℂ 2523 2801, offers alfresco drinking on hard stools and the occasional rat scampering by, and at the top of the steps **Le Jardin** ℂ 2526 2717, has friendly waiters and a pleasant outdoor area with comfortable chairs. Elsewhere there are plenty of other places to choose from — just wander around and go with the flow.

From there you can head to Wanchai which used to be the notorious **Suzy Wong**

company policy. During the weekends the place is packed, so get there early. Nearby, the dark and drab, but friendly and informal discos, **Neptune** ℂ 2865 1883, Basement, 98-108 Jaffe Road, and **Pussycat** ℂ 2527 7415, 17 Fenwick Street, are a home away from home for Filipina housemaids working in Hong Kong, and can be a lot of fun. On the edge of Wanchai, one of the hottest nightspots in town is **JJ's** ℂ 2588 1234, in the Grand Hyatt Hotel, which features live rhythm and blues, disco dancing, videos and excellent bar food. In Causeway

OPPOSITE Night spots like Bloom Bar LEFT and Discos like Rick's Cafe RIGHT and Hot Gossip ABOVE are among a wide range of venues for a convivial night out.

Bay, the **Jump Bar & Restaurant** ✆ 2832 9007, 7/F Causeway Bay Plaza, Phase II, 463 Lockhart Road, has the latest in pop music and a disco from 11:00 pm.

Over in Tsimshatsui, the **Bar City** nightlife complex, ✆ 2369 8571, in Basement 2 of the New World Centre, offers hi-tech disco in the **Zodiac**, cabaret in the **Country & Western** and live bands in the **Crazy Horse Saloon.** Also in the center, the chic **Catwalk** ✆ 2369 4111, on the 18th floor of the New World Hotel has a resident six-piece salsa band, disco floor, video wall, karaoke lounge area and private karaoke rooms. For just disco, the long-standing **Rick's Cafe** ✆ 2367, 2939 at 4 Hart Avenue.

"TIME GENTLEMEN, PLEASE!"

For those who yearn for the relaxed conviviality of the British or Australian pub, the trail begins in Central at **Mad Dogs**, 1-13 D'Aguilar Street and then down to the **Jockey** ✆ 2 526 1478 in Swire House. From there wander along to Hutchison House on Harcourt Road to the Tudor-style English "Free House" **Bull & Bear** ✆ 2525 7436, then over to Admiralty Station to the long-established **Godown** ✆ 2866 1166, which still has its Wednesday night jazz session and 60s' music. After that, head into the neon-struck depths of Wanchai, where you'll find the **Old China Hand** ✆ 2527 9174, at 104 Lockhart Road and the nearby **Horse & Groom** ✆ 2507 2517, staunchly pulling pints in the midst of the touts and topless hustle of the girlie and hostess bars. For a pub atmosphere combined with a rustic club decor, a lot of enthusiastic clientele and the prospect of a sing-song or two, the Excelsior Hotel in Causeway Bay offers the **Dickens Bar** ✆ 2837 6782.

From there the trail switches to the "other side" and slips simultaneously Down Under — the **Kangaroo Pub** ✆ 2376 0083, 1/F 35 Hai Phong Road, **Waltzing Matilda** ✆ 2368 8046, G/F 12-14 Hart Avenue, and the long-standing doyen of them all, **Ned Kelly's Last Stand** ✆ 2376 0562 at 11A Ashley Road, with a decor

Girlie bars, RIGHT and OVERLEAF, await the U.S. fleet.

celebrating the modern-day folk hero of the bush-ranging era who challenged the Victorian state constabulary in a bullet-proof iron mask and breast-plate, and got shot in the legs. The roof of the place is blasted off in the evenings by a traditional Dixieland jazz band.

For more sedate English drinking, with food to go with it, the Tsimshatsui branch of **Mad Dogs** ✆ 2301 2222, on 32 Nathan Road and **Blacksmith's Arms** ✆ 2369 6696 at 16 Minden Avenue. And if you want to extend your pub-crawl you can sally

which has been around since the early heady 70s and was Hong Kong's first top-less bar. Nowadays it has become as much a cultural landmark as a den of titillation and welcomes wives and girlfriend. It even has HKTA's stamp of approval. But from there, the topless scene really plunges into tacky and even sleazy joints in which the girls tend to sag with boredom and are in-vigorated only by the prospect of proving that a fool and his money are soon parted.

Wanchai, once the thumping heart of all bar-life in Hong Kong, is now a pale,

as far as Stanley and find among others the rustic **Smuggler's Inn** ✆ 2813 8852, 90A Stanley Main Street.

THE TOPLESS TRAIL

For the gentleman with no jacket, Hong Kong abounds with hostess and girlie bars, most of them aimed specifically at the lonesome wolf or the much-awaited high light of any Hong Kong bar-girl's life, the day the US Seventh Fleet hits town. In other words, they are nearly all devoted to vacuuming your wallet as fast as it can be done.

Top of the bill is **Bottoms Up** ✆ 2721 4509, 14-16 Hankow Road, Tsimshatsui,

tired shadow of its old self. Its bars have been renovated and chromed up, and the neon signs still blaze right along the Lockhart Road entertainment strip, but the touts work the sidewalks with almost inde-cent determination, and wherever there are touts in Hong Kong you can be sure there's also trouble.

Club Suzie Wong ✆ 2527 7461, 21 Fen-wick Street, is a money-grabbing travesty of the relative erotic nobility that Suzie Wong herself stood for, and so too is the **An-An** ✆ 2528 1280, 15 Fenwick Street, and, indeed at most of the girlie bars throughout the "Wanch" you pay very little for your beer in any one of them but you pay through the nose for "girlie" drinks — HK$101 to $330 for each thimble-sized glass of cold tea, and if you don't pay attention they'll be slammed in front of you as fast as the girls knock them back. If you can trust the honest advice of a Wanchai veteran, stay out of them.

Go instead to the bars that offer a little class and entertainment for the money — **Popeye Bar**, 127 Lockhart Road, for instance, features Filipina go-go dancers and disco dancing. And no "hostesses."

On the Tsimshatsui side, follow the same advice and pick only those bars which offer and early evening, or the revolving **La Ronda Restaurant and Lounge** ℂ 2525 5111, at the Furama Hotel. In Wanchai, the **Champagne Bar** ℂ 2588 1234, at the Grand Hyatt Hotel, and in Causeway Bay, **Talk of the Town Cocktail Lounge** ℂ 2837 6786, at the Excelsior Hotel and **Gallery Bar & Lounge** ℂ 2890 3355 at the Park Lane Hotel.

In Tsimshatsui, **Mezzanine Lounge** ℂ 2721 1211, Regent Hotel; **Sky Lounge** ℂ 2369 1111, Sheraton Hotel; and **Gripps** ℂ 2736 0088, at Omni The Hong Kong Hotel.

dancing and entertainment along with the companionable hustle.

THE OLD -FASHIONED WAY

In the background to the disco blast, Hong Kong's nightlife trail is dotted with more traditional cocktail joints and supper clubs, mostly at the hotels, which offer live music, and sometimes dancing, to go with the menu.

In Central District you can try **Mandarin Oriental's** ℂ 2522 0111 somewhat renowned mezzanine Clipper Lounge in which the seating is plush, the clientele drip with Rolexes and 22-carat gold and there's unobtrusive live music each afternoon

THE CULTURAL TRAIL

If your nightlife tastes run strictly to highbrow, or just rock, Hong Kong has certainly graduated from its old reputation as a cultural desert — theater, films, ballet, Chinese opera and orchestral concerts and performances by the highly regarded Hong Kong Philharmonic Orchestra are now held on a regular basis. Also, in January and February each year Hong Kong puts its growing

The topless and bottom line of Hong Kong's nightlife in Tsimshatsui's Bottoms Up OPPOSITE. ABOVE One of Wanchai's strip of hostess bars and discos.

cultural reputation bravely on the line with the Hong Kong Arts Festival and Fringe Festival, drawing top-class orchestras, soloists, dance troupes, theater companies, movies and fringe events from all over Asia and the West.

The main venues are, in Wanchai, the **Hong Kong Arts Centre** ✆ 2582 0200, 2 Harbour Road and, next door, the **Hong Kong Academy for Performing Arts** ✆ 2584 1500. In Central, **City Hall** ✆ 2922 12840, 7 Edinburgh Place, and near Lan Kwai Fong, the **Fringe Club** ✆ 2521 7251, on 2 Lower Albert Road, which stages more offbeat theater shows.

In Tsimshatsui, the **Hong Kong Cultural Centre** ✆ 2734 2009, next to Star Ferry, offers a gigantic 2,100-seat Concert Hall with a 93-stop pipe organ, a Grand Theatre with a revolving stage and seating for 1,750, a studio theater for smaller performances and six exhibition galleries, along with restaurants and bars. Recent performers have included such international stars as soprano Dame Kiri Te Kanawa.

In Hung Hom, the 12,500-seat **Hong Kong Coliseum** ✆ 2765 9234, 9 Cheong Wan Road, regularly stages massive spectator events — sports meets, ice shows, ballet and pop and rock concerts. Also in Hung Hom, the 2,600-seat amphitheater at the **Ko Shan Theatre** ✆ 2334 2331, on Ko Shan Road, is the main venue for pop concerts by local underground, and sometimes international, bands. Cantonese opera performances are held at least once a month. For more pop shows and opera, as well as foreign and Chinese films, you can also try the **Academic Community Hall** ✆ 2338 6121, at the Baptist College, near the Kowloon Tong MTR station.

For other venues along with a weekly rundown of events, consult HKTA's *Hong Kong Diary* and *Hong Kong This Week*, or the *South China Morning Post* newspaper.

The riot of coloured neon that competes for attraction along Nathan Road, Kowloon.

The Broad Highway

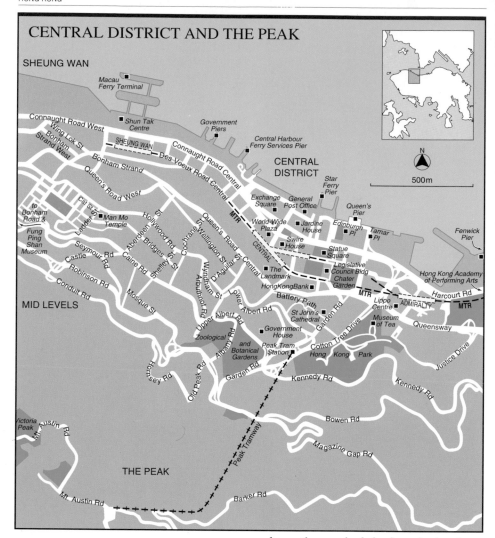

CENTRAL DISTRICT AND THE PEAK

SHEUNG WAN

Macau Ferry Terminal
Shun Tak Centre
Government Piers
Connaught Road West
Wing Lok St
Bonham Strand West
SHEUNG WAN
Connaught Road Central
Central Harbour Ferry Services Pier
Des Voeux Road Central
CENTRAL DISTRICT
Bonham Strand
Queen's Road West
Star Ferry Pier
Exchange Square
General Post Office
Queen's Pier
to Bonham Road &
Man Mo Temple
Cat St
Ladder St
Hollywood Rd
Wellington St
Queen's Road Central
World-Wide Plaza
Jardine House
Edinburgh Pl
Tamar Pl
Fenwick Pier
Fung Ping Shan Museum
Aberdeen St
Bridges St
D'Aguilar St
Cochrane St
CENTRAL
Swire House
Seymour Rd
Castle Rd
Shelley St
Wyndham St
Statue Square
Hong Kong Academy of Performing Arts
Robinson Rd
Caine Rd
Arbuthnot Rd
Lower Albert Rd
The Landmark
HongKongBank
Legislative Council Bldg
Chater Garden
Conduit Rd
Mosque St
Upper Albert Rd
Battery Path
St John's Cathedral
Garden Rd
MTR
Harcourt Rd
MID LEVELS
Lippo Centre
ADMIRALTY
MTR
Zoological
Albany Rd
Government House
Museum of Tea
Queensway
and Botanical Gardens
Peak Tram Station
Cotton Tree Drive
Hong Kong Park
Homsey Rd
Old Peak Rd
Garden Rd
Kennedy Rd
Justice Drive
Victoria Peak
Mt. Austin Rd
Kennedy Rd
Bowen Rd
THE PEAK
Peak Tramway
Magazine Gap Rd
Mt. Austin Rd
Barker Rd

N
500m

CENTRAL DISTRICT AND THE PEAK

All roads in Hong Kong lead from Central District, the financial and bureaucratic hub of the territory. All the important action takes place there, the major board rooms of the business world clustered around this humming powerhouse of key banks, the combined stock exchanges, the huge office blocks and the most established of the big business hotels.

Central District begins on its waterfront, at the foot of its high-rise office skyline, at the Star Ferry Terminal from where the packed harbor ferries have labored faithfully for nearly fifty years to and from the "other side." Since the Cross-Harbour Tunnel and MTR went into operation, the harbor ferries have become more of a sedate and scenic short harbor-cruise than a vital transport link, but they're still packed on each trip and they give visitors and residents alike a chance to relax and catch their breath in the constant urban clamor. And a first-class trip still costs only HK$1.50 the cheapest scenic cruise in the world.

Alongside the ferry terminal stands the General Post Office, a huge edifice that is nonetheless dwarfed by the towering Jardine House, Hong Kong's pioneer sky-

scraper which, when it was first built, sank slightly on its reclaimed harbor foundations, and with startling results — the minute shift made thousands of small tiles decorating the building's façade pop off and end anger pedestrians below. Protective nets had to be strung around the tower to avoid people being brained. It has since been safely reclad.

Adjacent to Jardine House, **Exchange Square**, home of the nerve-center of Hong Kong's business world, the Stock Exchange of Hong Kong, soars up in a spectacular cliff-face of curved glass — and here you can start your tour of Central District, which is compact enough to be explored on foot.

As already mentioned, the covered pedestrian overpass alongside Exchange Square will take you in two directions — one going straight ahead across the roaring stream of traffic on Connaught Road into **World-Wide Plaza** and **Swire House** and to the temperature-controlled shopping atrium of **The Landmark**, and the other west along the harborfront side of Connaught Road passing the outlying islands ferry piers and ending at the twin silver towers of the **Shun Tak Centre**, home of the **Victoria Hotel** and **Macau Ferry Terminal,** and the beginning of Western District.

Before Victoria Hotel, another walkway crosses Connaught Road into the **Hang Seng Bank Building** and continues over Des Voeux Road to the top floor of Central Market. At the end of that walkway you'll find the world's longest escalator (800-meters) — well, so we're told running above street level up Cochrane Street, across Hollywood Road, up Shelley Street to Robinson Road in the Mid-Levels, then making its final ascent to Conduit Road. The escalator is only one-way though, going down in the mornings until around 10:00 to 10:30 then up until 10:00 pm. Travel time is around 20 minutes.

Chinatown

Veteran residents of Hong Kong still chuckle now and then over an American visitor who once hit town for the first time and immediately asked: "Where's the Chinatown?" But there is, in fact, a "Chi-

nese" neighborhood, Western District, beyond the Victoria Hotel, known as that not for its particularly traditional Chinese character but because very few foreigners have moved into it over the years.

Hong Kong's earliest land surveys and maps named it "Chinatown" because it was where the first hordes of immigrant Cantonese, flooding across from the mainland, set up their mat shed homes and shops. Although the burgeoning office development in Central is now pushing into it, with more and more companies attracted by the

lower rents, it is still a district in which much of the old Chinese character has survived.

Its stores are strictly Chinese, many of them selling Chinese provisions, rice, tea, herbal medicines, clothing and textiles and practical arts and crafts that are definitely not on sale just for tourist mantel-pieces, and they've retained a great deal of their traditional style and decor — old swishing ceiling fans and inner gloom while the modernized boutiques of Central glitter with decorative chrome and plate glass.

OPPOSITE Junk passes Exchange Square providing a contrast with Central District's newest architectural wonder. Waterfalls and escalators ABOVE lead to the main entrance of the building.

Of all the retail and residential districts of Hong Kong Island it is the most inscrutable, and well worth exploring. The open, heaped wooden barrels of its rice stores and strange and odorous dried animal organs and vegetation of its herbal medicine shops squat below packed tenements from which pet finches twitter and sing from rattan cages hung outside the windows. In the provisions stores, amid a planned chaos of dried foodstuffs and mounds of fresh fruit, you can still see fresh eggs being checked against naked light bulbs to ensure they're

not fertilized, and "Thousand Year Eggs" being unearthed from their chemical burial mounds where they've been cured in alkaline ash for not a thousand years but maybe a few hundred days, turning their whites brown and yolks green and their taste slightly metallic and very tart.

The residents of Western District reflect the character of the area itself — conservative, traditional in pursuit and taste, clinging with great dignity to that which the heady and progressive pace of change in Hong Kong has allowed them to salvage from their 5,000-year-old culture. But it won't remain that way forever. Already, the district's skyline is sprouting commercial offices, and along its harborfront one of the newest major reclamation schemes is about to mushroom with new development, matching the growth of the remarkable **Macau Ferry Terminal,** with its shopping mall and huge jetfoil pens — looking for all the world like a space age German U-boat depot. Opposite here, on the corner of Connaught Road and Morrison Street you'll

find **Western Market,** a reconstructed 1858 Edwardian building, selling mainly souvenirs and fabrics, along with a Chinese restaurant on the top floor. Nearby in Man Wa Lane there are rows of stalls selling traditional soapstone chops, or seals. If you want them to, the craftsmen will translate your name into Chinese characters and engrave it on the seal. They make interesting souvenirs and are not expensive. From there wend your way through the streets and alleys of shops selling anything from batteries, electrical products and cheap clothing to funeral offerings, snakes, herbal medicines and teas and one-man printer stalls — where a business card or the like can be set up quickly in movable type and printed on a hand-operated platen press — until you reach "Cat Street" flea-market and antique shops and Man Mo Temple at the end of Hollywood Road.

Man and Mo

The 1840s **Man Mo Temple,** with its ornate green tiled roof, bell tower, smoke tower and main hall of prayer, is dedicated to the God of Civil Servants, Man Cheong, and a famous second century warrior, Kwan Kung, or Mo, since deified as the God of War, and guardian deity of pawnshops and curio dealers for good measure.

In typical Chinese fashion, the temple celebrates war, peace and commerce, and is a sacred place for Buddhists and Taoists alike — a prime example of the cultural exchange, or mutual "borrowing" of each other's gods, that made it possible for both religions to exist in harmony rather than confront each other in China. Being on the edge of Western District, Man Mo is a "working" place of worship, not a tourist attraction, and this has to be kept in mind when you're visiting.

In the main palace, you'll find huge incense coils hanging from the ceiling, each one donated by a worshiper and, as they smolder and smoke for anything up to two weeks, symbolically broadcasting prayers and pleas to the gods. As for the deities themselves, garish, richly costumed and blackened images of Man and Mo sit together on the main altar, and in front of them their tools of trade — a pen for **Man,** the scholarly deity, and an executioner's sword for Kwan Kung, symbolic of his own execution in the fierce intrigues of his time. "Years ago, the sword of every public executioner used to be kept in the local Kwan Kung temple," says *Temples,* by Joyce Savidge (Hong Kong Government Publications), one of the most informative and brightly illustrated guides to the territory's temple trail. "After an execution the presiding magistrate would always call at the temple to worship—and to make sure that the ghost of the criminal didn't follow him home."

lator, take the last stretch to Conduit Road.

At this point you have two choices — walk directly back down the steps running alongside the escalator to Central, or walk east to the start of Conduit Road to a path that will take you straight into the Zoological and Botanical Gardens, with its elegant pink flamingos, Mandarin ducks, peacocks and other exotic birds, along with Orangutans, gibbons and other animals. In the early mornings the gardens are a popular meeting place for people practicing tai chi, the ancient, disciplined ballet-like series of

From Man Mo Temple, continue up Hollywood Road for more antiques and curios. Here you can either break your journey and go back down to the shops in Queen's Road Central or hop on the escalator for a Mid-Levels tour. If you decide on the latter, as you go up the stretch from Caine Road to Mosque Street you'll see on your left the old **Jamia Mosque** with its striking green-and-white minaret. Reaching Robinson Road, a short walk west takes you to **Ohel Leah Synagogue**, now integrated into a massive high-rise residential development. Built in 1902, it's the only surviving synagogue in Hong Kong, and China. Services are held daily, and for more information © 2801 5442. Back on the esca-

martial and breathing exercises that tone up the mental and physical constitution. From the gardens you'll get a good view of Government House directly below. The official residence of the Governor, the building was erected in 1855 and features an interesting tile-roofed tower added for observation by the Japanese occupation forces when they seized Hong Kong in World War II.

Exiting out of the gardens, walk down Garden Road to **St John's Cathedral**, a beautiful old church built in the late 1840s and constructed in the shape of a cross from

OPPOSITE Decorative lanterns in Buddhist temple. ABOVE Sleek office towers dominate Central District, Hong Kong's financial center.

The Broad Highway

bricks brought from Canton (Guangzhou). It combines early English, Gothic and Norman architecture. Services are held daily, ✆ 2523 4157 for information. Through the church grounds, Battery Path leads you back down to Queen's Road Central where you're within easy striking distance of shops, hotels, Lan Kwai Fong, the trams and the MTR, and Statue Square. Around this roughly ornamental pedestrian mall stand the two most striking contrasts of tradition and the twenty-first century Hong Kong — the **HongKongBank** and the **Legislative Council Building.**

"Beam me up, Scottie" ...

On one side of Statue Square, the arched colonial stone architecture of the **Legisla-** **tive Council Building** (formerly the Supreme Court) recalls the days of drum tattoos and musketry, cabin trunks and tuxedos, the reign of the great ocean liners and flying boats, gin slings and fox-trots and all the other trappings and trimmings of the "white man's burden." And right across Chater Road, parked like a visitor from outer space between the headquarters of Standard Chartered Bank and the old Bank of China, stands the incredible, futuristic new headquarters of the HongkongBank (more popularly known by its traditional name, the Hongkong and Shanghai Banking Corporation.

There's nothing quite like this astonishing edifice of high-tech industrial architecture anywhere in Asia, and probably

anywhere else in the world, and nothing else has aroused the sort of passions that still reverberate through the Hong Kong business community. Some people consider it aesthetically imprudent and even downright ugly, and certainly not the sort of image that a banking institution as traditional as the Hongkong and Shanghai should project. Personally, I take my hat off to the HongKongBank for breaking so radically with tradition. It's a courageous design, and every bit as brilliant as that other most controversial post-war architectural project, the Sydney Opera House in Australia. Every time I look at it, I'm reminded of the creative ingenuity that went into the sets of the industrial space colonies in Sean Connery's thrilling science fiction movie, *Outland*.

As you stand and study it, or beam yourself up the escalators into its glassed bowels, you can almost imagine the stairways retracting behind you — the rocket engines whining and dust swirling prior to T-minus 00.00.00 and lift-off. It then takes only a slight further stretch of the mind to consider that all this radicalism is simply a supreme act of prudence on the HongKongBank's part, and quite in keeping with the Hong Kong tradition of hedging all bets — it's obviously designed to pack up and blast off to another safe tax haven should there be any real threat to free profit-making when Beijing takes over in 1997. Next door to the bank, on the 11th floor of the old Bank of

ABOVE The Hong Kong shoreline at night.

China Building you'll find the **Tsui Museum of Art** ✆ 2868 2688, displaying more than 2,000 pieces of Chinese antiquities including ceramics, bronze and carved wood and ivory furniture. Heading east to the meeting point of Queensway and Garden Road, you can study China's answer to the symbolic power of the HongKongBank's headquarters — the **Bank of China's** own gigantic 70-storey 315 m (1,033 ft)-high landmark with a soaring cubist-style design close to the existing limit of science fiction imagination. Nearby, the collonaded façade of the **Lippo Centre** and the sheer gargantuan size of **Pacific Place** are there to remind us all that Hong Kong is an international financial hub, whatever 1997 may bring.

Down on the waterfront, **Edinburgh Place** and **HMS Tamar,** the headquarters of the British Forces in Hong Kong, look almost dumpy and mundane in comparison with the HongKongBank. In between Tamar and Edinburgh Place, near Star Ferry you'll find the **City Hall,** the venue for much of Hong Kong's regular cultural activity.

Tea and Tapestry

In Hong Kong Park on Cotton Tree Drive you'll find **Flagstaff House,** a renovated 1940s' colonial building with a distinct Greek neoclassic-style to it. Formerly home of the Commander of the British Forces, the building now houses the **Museum of Teaware** ✆ 2869 0690, featuring exhibitions of Chinese tea, porcelain and pots and much of the tea-making equipage from the latter centuries of this 5,000-year-old culture.

For more Chinese relics, the Hong Kong University's **Fung Ping Shan Museum** 2859 2114 on Bonham Road, has an interesting exhibition of Yuan dynasty bronzeware, artifacts from the Warring States and Indian Buddhist sculptures. To get there take bus No. 3 from Edinburgh Place, or Nos 23 or 103 from Causeway Bay.

For more walking jaunts, HKTA sells an excellent booklet called *Central and Western District Walking Tour.* It tells you where to go to find the best shopping and eating, most interesting streets, main tourist attractions and facilities and has accompanying illustrations and a map.

To the Peak

A short stroll up Garden Road to Lower Albert Road — just past St John's Cathedral — will take you to **St John's Building** on the other side of the road where, at its base, you'll find the lower terminal of what is quaintly referred to as the "funicular railway" the cable-operated Peak Tram. (Alternatively, you can take the free, topless double-decker bus from Star Ferry.) Climbing smoothly up a rather disturbingly sheer series of hillsides, so sheer in some places that you have to stand at a 45-degree angle to move from your seat, it'll take you 397 meters up the 552-meter **Victoria Peak** that dominates Hong Kong Island — and to one of the most breathtaking views anywhere in the world.

In the more official colonial days gone by, the Peak was strictly for the folks who lived on the hill, the measure of one's business or bureaucratic success being how close you could reside to the top. It's still Hong Kong's paramount status symbol, and so too are the fine, comparatively sprawling mansions and homes that nestle in the folds of the upper slopes and right along its highest ridges — despite the simply beastly spring and early summer weather when the humidity blankets much of it in impenetrable cloud.

At the time of writing, the Peak Tower had just been torn down and a somewhat controversial, HK$400 million seven-storey complex about to be built. Scheduled for completion in 1995, the building will include a new tram terminus, retail outlets and restaurants. Adjacent, the ultramodern **Peak Galleria**, housing the chic **Cafe Deco Bar & Grill,** up-market shops, an indoor fountain and an underground car park, has just opened. Miraculously, **Peak Cafe**, which was originally built as a sedan chair shelter in 1901, still stands, but only because there was such a public protest against developers' plans to replace it.

From the terminus a pathway (Lugard and Harlech roads) circles the peak like a collar, and a one-hour stroll gives you dramatic panoramic views of the entire harbor

OPPOSITE Kowloon's new Cultural Centre and the preserved clock tower of the old railway terminus.

and its twin urban beehives, along with the islands of Lantau, Cheung Chau and Lamma. Another path (Mt Austin Road) takes you right up to the summit for an even more dramatic 360-degree view, and on a clear day you'll be able to see the islands in the south and the mountains in the New Territories.

WANCHAI AND CAUSEWAY BAY

This crowded, high-rise tourist corridor begins on the eastern side of the Admiralty

rumbling double-decker antiques shuttle back and forth all day and late into the night right along the northern corridor of Hong Kong Island, linking its western and eastern extremities from Kennedy Town in the west, through Central, Wanchai, Causeway Bay and Taikoo Shing and Shaukeiwan in the east. While they labor and clang their way through the dense urban traffic above ground, the MTR streaks along virtually the same route below. A few years ago the 83-year-old system was earmarked for the chop, but they're such faithful work

and Pacific Place complexes where the glassed edges of the business citadel soften into the glowing crimson and gold of Wanchai's neon-packed entertainment district. As with all other urban areas of Hong Kong, getting there is easy — you can take the MTR from Central or Admiralty, and take a look at the world's biggest and most crowded connecting underground concourse at the same time, or you can take a taxi from the Star Ferry, approaching Wanchai along the harborfront motorway, Harcourt Road, or you can allow yourself another of Hong Kong's traditional and slightly more sedate experiences and go there by tram.

For a flat fee of HK$1.20 these grinding,

horses, still carrying many thousands of passengers a day, and they're such an abiding symbol of Hong Kong, that the planners backed down in the face of the fierce public protest that was bound to follow.

Starting at Wanchai's waterfront, at the beginning of Harbour Road, you'll find the **Hong Kong Academy for Performing Arts** and the **Hong Kong Arts Centre.** Most cultural events are held in the evenings, but during the day the Arts Centre in particular has regular art exhibitions. Opposite, an entire block houses the integrated **Hong Kong Convention Centre,** the **Grand Hyatt Hotel** and the **New World Hotel,** and across the street from there you can't miss Asia's tallest building, the massive 78-storey **Central Plaza.** Further along **Harbour Road** you can call in to **Causeway Centre** to the **Museum of Chinese Historical Relics** ✆ 2827 4692, which has a collection of Chinese paintings and handicrafts; and if you have time to sit down for a few hours, there are two movie theaters in the vicinity, **Columbia Classic** and **Cine Art.**

From here several overpasses will take you across Gloucester Road and into Wanchai — to its nightclubs, bars, Chinese stores and restaurants, open markets and crowded alfresco food stalls and shops. At the beginning of Queen's Road East, just past Pacific Place, you'll find rows of shops that specialize in rosewood and mahogany furniture, along with carved camphor chests. Further along, of historical interest there's the **Hung Shing (Tai Wong) Temple,** where locals go to have their fortunes told, and the quaint **Wanchai Post Office**, which was built in 1912. Towering behind these two small images of Hong Kong's past life is the 66-storey **Hopewell Centre** with its breathtaking scenic elevator ride and eye-in-the sky revolving restaurant.

On your way to Causeway Bay, a nice detour is to take the tram around Happy Valley to view the district's prime attraction, the **Happy Valley Racecourse** which, like its bigger and more modern sister track over in Shatin, is the one of the most popular places in Hong Kong. For details on horseracing, see THE SPORTS TRAIL, p184.

The main reason for going to Causeway Bay is, of course, to shop, both day and night, in the boutiques and giant Japanese department stores. But, there are a few other attractions — on the waterfront in a small garden opposite the Excelsior Hotel and World Trade Centre, you can actually watch the firing of the famous Noon Day Gun, whose origin to this day is still being disputed. Nearby, the **Causeway Bay Typhoon Shelter** houses junks and sampans alongside the luxury craft of the Royal Hong Kong Yacht Club.

To the east of the Excelsior Hotel, Victoria Park will introduce you to legions of early morning tai chi devotees and, in the late afternoons and evenings, older residents taking their prized caged birds for walkies. During the Chinese New Year and Mid-Autumn festivals the place is packed with thousands of people celebrating the occasions. If you're in an energetic frame of mind, the park has a jogging track, swimming pools and tennis courts. To the east of the park, at the beginning of Tin Hau Temple Road, the seventeenth-century **Tin Hau Temple** is well worth a visit, along with the recently restored octagonal **Lin Fa Temple** on Lin Fa Street.

From here, go up to Tai Hang Road to where you'll see a large white pagoda standing in the shadow of monolithic housing estates. This is the famed **Tiger Balm Gardens,** now renovated and renamed **Aw Boon Haw Gardens** in memory of its 1935 founder, a flamboyant Chinese multimillionaire who came up with the recipe for the renowned balm that cures everything from a headache to a rattlesnake bite. The "garden" is grotesque but fascinating, full of grottoes, pagodas and colorful statues of mythical Chinese figures and animals. One particular tableau depicts Judgment and Hell, where saints and miscreants alike are judged on their earthly behavior. For the unlucky ones, the punishments are awful — tongues torn out, bodies sawn in half, and a host of other gruesome consequences.

Heading east from Causeway Bay, the MTR or trams will carry you to **Taikoo Shing** housing development in Quarry Bay, where the four Cityplaza towers offer bargain and up-market shopping in air-conditioned comfort and convenience, and a whirl or two around the ice-skating rink if you so desire. Further down the line you'll reach **Shaukeiwan,** once a pirate lair, now the home of one of Hong Kong's biggest fishing fleets. Here, at the end of Shaukeiwan Main Street by the waterfront, you'll find temples and monasteries;Tam Kung Temple, whose deity is a locally-inspired God of Weather and Good Health and which plays an extravagantly colorful central role in the annual Tam Kung, Tin Hau and Buddha's Birthday festivals.

What distinguishes Tam Kung from other gods is his age — he's said to have

OPPOSITE Looking across harbor to Causeway Bay and its giant Japanese department stores.

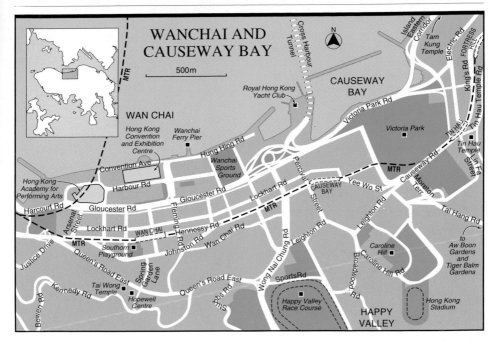

WANCHAI AND
CAUSEWAY BAY

500m

CAUSEWAY
BAY

WAN CHAI

Royal Hong Kong
Yacht Club

Hong Kong
Convention
and Exhibition
Centre

Wanchai
Ferry Pier

Victoria Park

Victoria Park Rd

Tam
Kung
Temple

Tin Hau
Temple

Hung Hing Rd

Convention Ave

Wanchai
Sports
Ground

Hong Kong
Academy for
Performing Arts

Harbour Rd

Harcourt Rd

Gloucester Rd

Gloucester Rd

Lockhart Rd

Yee Wo St

CAUSEWAY
BAY

Lockhart Rd

Fleming Rd

Hennessy Rd

WAN CHAI

MTR

Southorn
Playground

Johnston Rd

Wan Chai Rd

Leighton Rd

Caroline
Hill

to
Aw Boon
Gardens
and
Tiger Balm
Gardens

Tai Hang Rd

Justice Drive

Queen's Road East

Spring Garden Lane

Kennedy Rd

Bowen Rd

Tai Wong
Temple

Hopewell
Centre

Queen's Road East

Wong Nai Chung Rd

Sports Rd

Broadwood Rd

Caroline Hill Rd

Happy Valley
Race Course

HAPPY
VALLEY

Hong Kong
Stadium

been only 12 years old when people began worshipping him — and in a tradition that's quite quaint (though actually has nothing to do with his tender years) his crimson and gilded image is carried from the temple only for the opening of his birthday celebrations, then hustled back inside. Continuing on the MTR, two stops past Shaukeiwan will take you to the end of the line, Chaiwan, where an old Hakka village at 14 Kut Shing Street has been converted into the **Law Uk Folk Museum** © 2896 7006.

THE ISLAND TRAIL

From Central District, the main tourist route leads over or through the island's central mountain spine to Aberdeen, Repulse Bay and Stanley. They're easy to get to — if you're not on an organized hotel tour you can take the Nº 6 bus from the Central Terminal at Exchange Square to Repulse Bay and Stanley, crossing the mountain through Wongneichong Gap and passing the garden swathe of the Hong Kong Cricket Club along the way. Or you can take a more scenic route on the air-conditioned express bus, also from Exchange Square, via the Aberdeen Tunnel and Deep Water Bay. For Aberdeen itself, Nos 7 and 70.

Aberdeen is still the most fascinating fishing and boat-people haven in Hong Kong with thousands of fisherfolk still living on a small clutter of surviving junks and their successors, new-style bullet-nosed trawlers. Along the waterfront, you'll be approached by very aggressive old ladies wanting to give you a personal sampan tour through the junks and to the floating restaurants for an outrageous fee. If you say no to their HK$300 offer and walk away they'll quickly chase after you, haggling all the way until they reluctantly agree to HK$50 or less.

The town itself has been modernized, with new boutiques and shopping centers replacing much of the old Chinese retail and ship's chandler's sections, but there are still a few places of historical interest such as the 1851 **Tin Hau Temple** on Aberdeen Reservoir Road and the **Hung Hsing Shrine** on the corner of Aberdeen Old Main Street and Aberdeen Main Road.

The island of **Ap Lei Chau**, once a quiet fishing community reached by sampan, it is now connected to the mainland by a long soaring bridge and has been developed into

OPPOSITE The Star Ferry established in 1898 connects Hong Kong and Kowloon in eight minutes.

another enormous housing estate. But here and there you'll still find fishing families tending their nets, baskets of fresh fish being hauled and slopped ashore and, all the way along the waterfront, boats being built and repaired.

Just south of Aberdeen stands the pride of Hong Kong's cultural and recreational circuit, **Ocean Park/Middle Kingdom** ✆ 2552 0291 and **Water World** ✆ 2555 6055, a huge playground and marine entertainment complex built into a sharply rising coastal headland. Ocean Park was financed

with a trickle of funds from the spillover of the Royal Hong Kong Jockey Club's vast gambling profits and, like Hong Kong itself, it is in a constant state of growth.

At last count it included an outdoor escalator and cable car system linking its lowland and headland amenities, a roller coaster set dramatically on the edge of the headland, more funfair rides, a shark aquarium, a Wave Cove with simulated waves and a most contented population of seals and other ocean life, dolphin and killer whale shows, an aviary and a children's adventure playground.

Middle Kingdom takes you through 5,000 years of Chinese history, along with arts and crafts demonstrations, Cantonese

opera and the "world's longest dancing dragon."

Water World is adjacent to Ocean Park with its own entrance and features giant water slides, wave pool and more pools. It's open in summer from June to October.

All three are easily reached from Central by a special Citybus from Admiralty MTR station or, excluding Sunday and Public Holidays, a No. 6 minibus from Star Ferry.

From Ocean Park, the road winds through Deep Water Bay, one of Hong Kong's most attractive small beaches, and

to the nine hole **Royal Hong Kong Golf Club**. From there the route continues to **Repulse Bay** — its beach and high-cost luxury condominiums.

The most commanding view of Repulse Bay is from the restaurant and sweeping lawns of **The Verandah**, the elegant surviving relic of the old Repulse Bay Hotel. It's not just a place for afternoon tea and candle-lit suppers, though it's expensive, even by Hong Kong standards, but also a popular place for young newly weds to have their photos taken on their wedding day. But most of the action takes place on the beach — which has been extended to more than twice its original size and in high-summer is absolutely packed with bathers, especially at weekends — at the eastern-end complex which features two huge statues of **Kwun Yum** and **Tin Hau** standing protectively over the beach, children's playground, McDonald's and other fast-food outlets, barbecue facilities and a flea market selling souvenirs, sportswear, ladies' clothes and so on. Past the **Seaview Chinese Restaurant** at the other end of the beach, you can walk along the seafront to Deep Water Bay, though last time I was there the path was under repair, having been torn to bits by a typhoon.

THE HARBOR

The visual excitement of hundreds of ships of all sizes and shapes churning the water in every direction with the backdrop of Hong Kong's famous skyline is probably one of the most vivid of all the pleasant memories visitors have of Hong Kong.

The simplest way to enjoy the harbor is to take the relaxing seven minute ride on the famous **Star Ferry** between Hong Kong Island and Tsimshatsui on the Kowloon

Beyond Repulse Bay the road twists and turns southeast to Stanley, one of Hong Kong's oldest settlements but best known for its clamorous tourist market. Until quite recently, Stanley was a picturesque fishing village; today, Stanley Bay is being reclaimed, the tin-roofed fishermen's and squatter's shanties are being torn down to be replaced with yet more luxury highrises and the villagers will have to find somewhere else to live. For a reminder of what Stanley used to be you can visit the **Tin Hau Temple**, at the far end of the market, and the old colonial-style Police Station, now a historical monument. Also of interest, the military cemetery opposite St Stephen's Beach.

Peninsula. Organized, scheduled harbor cruises on gaily decorated Chinese junks, some taking in dinner cruises around Hong Kong Island, are operated by **Hong Kong Watertours**. © 2367 1970. Details of these cruises are available at HKTA, most hotel tour desks or from Water Tours boarding piers next to the Star Ferry on both sides of the harbor. **The Hong Kong Ferry Company** © 2542 3082 also operates a wide

Garish pavilions, sculptures and other attractions OPPOSITE at Aw Boon Haw (Tiger Balm) Gardens in Causeway Bay. A New Year welcome RIGHT at the Ocean Park/Middle Kingdom complex. ABOVE Buddhist and Taoist statues and tableaux draw thousands of visitors each weekend to the famous beach at Repulse Bay.

range of services, and the ones to the outlying islands in particular provide an inexpensive alternative to the organized harbor cruises. For dinner cruises see page 197.

MACAU

No visit to Hong Kong is really complete without a day-trip or overnighter comparing its fast-paced urban hustle with the relative permanent siesta that exists on its Portuguese-administered sister enclave to

the west, Macau and its two islands, Taipa and Coloane, which are linked to the city by a bridge and causeway. And no visit is really complete either without a fling or two at Macau's principal industry and source of income, its casinos.

Macau arose as a trading port for foreigners on the South China Coast long before Hong Kong, and was established by Portuguese traders and missionaries in 1557. Its trading power gave way to that of Canton (Guangzhou) and the other Treaty Ports opened up by the British in China, and was eventually eclipsed by the phenomenal growth of Hong Kong, leaving this tiny mainland enclave with a lot to show in the way of culture, especially its

Roman Catholic churches and cathedrals, but not much else. Nowadays it's a fascinating blend of Cantonese joss and quite seedy Portuguese colonial authority — along with the annual roar and high-octane odors of its most celebrated European contribution, the **Macau Grand Prix** and a burgeoning holiday resort, offering high-class hotels and a great deal of gambling and nightlife to go with them. It's also in a frenzy of development a very modern, much larger ferry terminal has already been built, office towers, apartment blocks, hotels and banks have sprouted up, an international airport on Taipa, along with a four-lane bridge into the city, will be ready for use in 1995. But most ambitious of all is the amazing reclamation going on in Praia Grande Bay where a city surrounding two artificial lakes, for a population of around 60,000, is about to emerge, increasing Macau's land space by 20 percent. The area will contain office and residential towers, hotels, parks and a tree-lined promenade.

GETTING THERE

To get there you can go by high-speed jetfoil or hydrofoil, jetcat or steamer from the Macau Ferry Terminal on the western harborfront of Hong Kong Island, near the Victoria Hotel, or from the China Ferry Terminal in Canton Road, Tsimshatsui. The trip by jetfoil takes about one hour and the fare is HK$100 one way (HK$108 at weekends). Helicopters also leave from the ferry terminal but will set you back HK$1,086 (one way) during the week and HK$1,189 at weekends. Macau's currency is patacas but Hong Kong money is freely circulated. HK$100 = $102.30 patacas, and about eight patacas = US$1. You're going "overseas," from British to Portuguese sovereignty, so don't forget your passport.

HOTELS

When you arrive in Macau you're left in no doubt as to why you've been attracted there — the double roofs of the giant **Hotel Lisboa** © (853) 577666, the biggest casino in town, are shaped like the hubs of roulette wheels. If you're there purely for gambling, the Lisboa is probably the place to stay — but it's one vast betting machine, with everything centered on its gaming floors, and there's very little charm or culture to go with it. If you stay there, the hotel bluntly demands a deposit, or your credit card, before they'll hand over the key, just in case you find yourself a little down on your luck the next day.

At the ✆ (853) 567888 **Mandarin Oriental,** the rooms are a little bigger and more comfortable, the whole atmosphere a little more relaxed and pleasant, and it has its own small casino on the first floor. Out on Taipa Island, the one that lies on the other end of the sweeping coathanger bridge from downtown Macau, the ✆ (853) 327000 **Hyatt Regency** is a family resort with swimming pool, squash and tennis courts and games room. On the southeastern end of Coloane island, overlooking Hac Sa beach, you'll find another resort, the luxurious eight-storey 208-room **Westin Resort,** stunningly terraced up the mountainside. Sports facilities include one heated indoor and two outdoor swimming pools, eight tennis courts, two squash courts, lawn bowling, health club and access to the **Macau Golf and Country Club**. Around the other side of the island, the **Pousada de Coloane** has a beautiful location near the beach, with some rooms with balconies overlooking the sea, but it's quite shabby and rundown, which is a shame.

One of my favorite hotels is the old colonial-style **Bela Vista**, which lies west above the Praia Grande waterfront. Once very run down, and the best deal in town, it's now been restored to its former glory and is now the most expensive hotel in Macau. If the price frightens you, at least pop in for a look and sit a while and have an early evening drink on its verandah — it's very romantic.

Not all hotels are five star, and accommodation such as Portuguese-style inns and villas are available. If you intend to go at the weekend rates are higher and a reservation is a must. During the week, most hotels will give a discount. A list of hotels, and by no means all that's available, follows. For more, the Macau Government Tourist Office produces a detailed hotel brochure with an indication of their rates and facilities.

Expensive (from US$125)
Bela Vista ✆ (853) 965 333, fax: (853) 965 588, Hong Kong booking ✆ 2881 1688.
Hyatt Regency ✆ (853) 831 234, fax: (853) 830 195, Hong Kong booking ✆ 2559 0168.
Mandarin Oriental ✆ (853) 567 8888, fax: (853) 594 589, Hong Kong booking ✆ 2881 1688.

Built within an old fort, **Pousada de Sao Tiago** ✆ (853) 378 111, fax: (853) 552 170, Hong Kong booking ✆ 2739 1216.
Pousada Ritz ✆ (853) 339 955, fax: (853) 317 826, Hong Kong booking office ✆ 2540 6333.

Westin Resort ✆ (853) 871 111, fax: (853) 871 122, Hong Kong booking ✆ 2803 2015.

Medium (from US$75)
Holiday Inn ✆ (853) 783 333, fax: (853) 782 321, Hong Kong booking ✆ 2736 6855, has its own, small casino.
Hotel Lisboa ✆ (853) 377 666, fax: (853) 567 193, Hong Kong booking ✆ 2559 1028.
New Century ✆ (853) 831 111, fax: (853) 832 222, Hong Kong booking office ✆ 2581 9863.
New World Emperor (853) 781 888, fax: (853) 782 287, Hong Kong booking ✆ 2724 4622.

OPPOSITE Buddhist statues draw hundreds of visitors each weekend. ABOVE The Casino Lisboa dominates the huge gambling industry in Portuguese-administered Macau.

MACAU

500m

N

CHINA

Barrier Gate

Istmo Ferreira Do Amaral

Aveida Do Conselheiro Borja

Canidrome

Rampa Dos Cavaleiros

Kun Iam Tong

Avenida Do Coronel Mesquita

Avenida Do Ouvidor Arriaga

Avenida De Horta E Costa

Almirant Lacerda

PORTO INTERIOR

Avenida Do

Rua Das Lorchas

Estrada Do Repouso

Museum

Old Protestant Cemetery

Loo Yim-Yok's Garden

Public Garden (Flora)

Reservato

Residence of Dr Sun Yat-sen

Old Moute Fortress

Avenida Do Conselheiro Ferreira De Almeida

Estrada Da Vitoria

Ruins of St Paul's

Macau Palace

Casino Jai Alai

Avenida Amizade

Passenger Ferr

Avenida Almeid Ribeiro

St Paul's Cathedral

Dr Rodrigo Rodrigues

Macau Grand Prix Start/Finish

Church of St Augustine

Avenida Do

Oriental Hotel

Rua Padre Antonio

Avenida Amizade

President Hotel

Passenger Ferry to Taipa/Coloane

Rua Do Almirante Sergio

Rua Da Praia Grande

Baia Da Praia Grande

Avenida Amizade

PORTO EXTERIOR

Hotel Lisboa

Penha Church

Bela Vista Hotel

A-Ma Monastery

Avenida Da Republica

Macau-Taipa Bridge

Hyatt Regency

Macau Race Course

TAIPA

Taipa-Coloane Bridge

COLOANE

Pousade De Coloane

Saludes

Presidente ✆ (853) 553 888, fax: (853) 552 735, Hong Kong booking office ✆ 2857 1533.

Inexpensive (below US$75)
Guia ✆ (853) 513 888, fax: (853) 559 822.
Mondial ✆ (853) 566 866, fax: (853) 514 083, Hong Kong booking office ✆ 2540 8180.
Pousada de Coloane ✆ (853) 28143, fax: (853) 328 251, Hong Kong booking ✆ 2540 8180.
Sintra ✆ (853) 710 111, fax: (853) 510 527, Hong Kong booking ✆ 2546 6944.

CASINOS

But of all that Macau has to offer, nothing stirs the blood more than its main tourist attraction, the casinos. And nothing can clean you out quicker if you catch the gambling fever. It's as well to accept and appreciate beforehand that the casinos are not there to make tourists happy. Their main customers, and overwhelmingly so, are the Hong Kong Chinese taxi drivers, amahs, laborers, office workers and largely working-class family groups that flood to Macau to engage in the strictly Chinese passion for betting on two flies strolling up a wall.

The Lisboa is the biggest, most popular and busiest casino, and the only place in Macau where roulette is still played; others are the **Macau Palace** floating casino, the **Avendia de Demetrio Cinatti**, the **Kam Pek** and, next to the ferry terminal, the Jai Alai.

You'll find the main Chinese games are roulette, fan tan, blackjack and big and small (dai-siu). The ranks of slot machines are left to the bread-and-butter punters, Japanese tour groups and other visiting foreigners. Unless you're an experienced gambler and know how to slide onto the tables and control your bets, stay out of it and just watch. If you want to take your chances with the slot machines, be prepared to blow a couple of hundred Hong Kong dollars and then withdraw. Their payouts are sparse, and even when you win big there's nothing like the promotional celebration you get in Atlantic City or Las Vegas.

A Hong Kong journalist and his wife hit an incredible HK$1.8 million jackpot in the Lisboa, and wouldn't have known it if they'd been distracted and hadn't actually watched the five red sirens fall into place. There were no bells, flashing lights or sirens. Then, before they'd even been given their check, members of a local triad, or underworld gang, approached them and told them it would cost them half the jackpot to leave Macau. They bravely refused, but ended up handing over HK$100,000 for "protection and security." The wife and children left for Hong Kong that night. The journalist crept quietly out of the hotel the next morning. "Here I was, a big winner,"

he told a friend later. "And I had to slink out of the Lisboa feeling like a thief!"

GREYHOUND AND HORSE RACING

For more gambling, Greyhound races are held year-round at the Canidrome ✆ (853) 574 413, Avenida General Castelo Branco, near the border, on Tuesdays, Thursdays and weekends from 8 pm, and horseracing at the **Macau Jockey Club** on Taipa island, mid-week and at weekends from June to September. For information ✆ (853) 321 888.

The mixture of Portuguese and Chinese architecture ABOVE give Macau its special cultural character.

RECREATION AND NIGHT LIFE

Aside from sports facilities at the hotels, you can go horse riding at the **Macau Horse Riding Centre** ✆ (853) 328 303, Hac Sa, Coloane, tenpin bowling and ice skating at the **Future Bright Amusement Park** ✆ (853) 989 2318, Praca de Luis Camoes, and windsurfing at **Cheoc Van** and **Hac Sa** beaches. Also at **Hac Sa**, a sports and recreation complex features an Olympic-size swimming pool, mini golf course, ten-

such as African chicken, Portuguese sausages, green vegetable soup, king prawns, Macau sole and double doses of olive oil, on Coloane try the famous **Fernando's** ✆ (853) 328 264 at Hac Sa beach and, by the entrance to Coloane Park, **Balichao** ✆ (853) 870 098. On Taipa, **Pinocchio's** ✆ (853) 827 128.

SIGHTSEEING

Macau is so small that it's a place for walking, bicycling, or tooling comfortably around in its own form of individual tour-

nis courts, children's playground and roller skating.

Most up-market hotels have discos — the **Green Parrot** at the Hyatt is a popular place for the young and not-so-young swingers and the Presidente has nightly cabaret and dancing in the **Skylight Disco and Nightclub.** If you want a touch of the more exotic, the Lisboa features the famous **Crazy Paris Show,** a nude revue which is quite exciting if your tastes run to **Miss Green's School for Dance and Deportment for Semi-Naked Young Ladies.**

Macau is a great place for eating and drinking — Portuguese wine is still incredibly cheap — and restaurants are everywhere. For Portuguese and Macanese food

ist transport, a Mini-Moke. They rent at HK$280 to HK$320 a day (discounts at weekends), and you can book them from Hong Kong at **Macau Mokes** ✆ 2543 4190, fax: 2851 8081, or in Macau at **Rua de Malaca** ✆ (853) 378 851, fax: (853) 555 433. Or, through **Avis Rent a Car in Hong Kong** ✆ 2541 2011, fax: 2541 3254, and in Macau at the **Mandarin Oriental** ✆ (853) 336 789 ext. 3004, fax: (853) 314 112.

The sightseeing is interesting if for nothing else than the fact that you're studying another example of two alien cultures that have managed to live fairly peacefully alongside each other for centuries. You can see it in the contrast of Buddhist and Taoist temples and Roman Catholic churches, and in the accommodation that the two societies have reached on philosophy and lifestyle — the bustling grab-happy Cantonese character snoozing beneath the trees along the waterfront *praia* during the afternoon siesta. In the shopping streets of the downtown area, you're also taking a look at Hong Kong, say, 20 years ago, before it began leaping towards the twenty-first century.

There are many temples, most of them Buddhist and ornately decorated, headed by the **A-Ma Temple** at Barra Point, from which Macau derives its name, A-Ma Gau

Among the many churches, **St Paul's,** built in 1602, is the most prominent one — the remains of its towering stone façade and grand staircase on Rua de Sao Paulo is one of the most popular tourist symbols of Macau. The Cathedral on Largo de Sto. Agostinho, re-built in 1937, features magnificent stained-glass windows and is the focal point of Macau's principal religious events, especially the huge parades and masses of Easter. The **Chapel of St Francis Xavier** on the island of Coloane rates a special visit because of its baroque cream and

or Bay of A-Ma. It's dedicated to a peasant girl who miraculously survived a violent storm on her way to Guangzhou in the early sixteenth century, and subsequently re-appeared in Macau as a goddess. The monastery features several images of her, along with Buddhist and Taoist statues, and a model of an ancient war-junk.

Another fascinating temple is **Kun Iam Tong,** on the Avenida do Coronel Mesquita, dedicated to the Goddess of Mercy and featuring the deity herself costumed in embroidered silk and flanked by 18 Buddha images. There are also images of the Three Precious Buddhas in pavilions and halls placed among elaborately landscaped gardens and fountains.

white, oval-windowed architecture and its relics of the disastrous attempt to Christianize Japan — a crusade which ended with the massacre of hundreds of foreign and Japanese missionaries, priests and followers in 1597 and 1637.

For more information contact **Macau Government Tourist Office** © (853) 315 566, fax: (853) 510 104, at 9 Largo Do Senado, Macau. In Hong Kong they're located at 336 Shun Tak Centre, 200 Connaught Road © 2857 2287, or you can contact the **Macau Tourist Information Bureau** © 2540 8180 on the 37th floor of the same building.

The Macau Grand Prix OPPOSITE and ABOVE teenagers step out in Tsimshatsui East.

FROM MACAU TO CHINA

As with Hong Kong, Macau has had a special tourist allure over the past 30 years — its position right on the border with China. Now, of course, you don't go there to peek over at PLA border guards and their checkpoints, you can go across by bus on a 10-hour HK$760-a-head day tour (HK$800 at weekends) of Zhongshan in the Zhuhai Special Economic Zone, and go from there if you wish right through to Guangzhou.

and you can take your pick of one-day trips across the border into **Shenzhen Special Economic Zone,** three-day tours to **Guangzhou** and **Guilin** or the high-priced long-haul tours through the major cultural venues.

If you want to go there on your own, visas are quite easy to obtain. The fastest and cheapest way is to go to the **Visa Office, Ministry of Foreign Affairs of the People's Republic of China,** 5/F, 26 Harbour Road, Wanchai ✆ 2827 1881. Take along one photo with your passport — processing takes one working day and the fee is HK$100 for sin-

And if you want to do something completely different, you can book into China's "first golf course" and country club, the **Zhongshan Hot Spring Resort** a half an hour from the border, and bang your way around the Scottish links fair ways in between tennis, spa bathing, local sightseeing or just relaxing in the club's traditionally-landscaped water gardens. For more information, contact International Tours ✆ 2541 2011 or **CITS** in Hong Kong.

THE CHINA TRAIL

Hong Kong is still the main staging point for the once-in-a-lifetime China pilgrimage,

gle entry, HK$250 if you need it the same day. You can also go to **China International Travel Service (CITS)** ✆ 2732 5888, **China Travel Service (CTS)** ✆ 2853 3888 or any travel agent, but expect to pay a little more, who will also arrange your tour or just get you by train to Guangzhou, where you can plot and book your itinerary from there. After traveling as an "individual" on the trains through 20 cities myself, handling my own bookings as I went, I can promise you that, apart from the immense people-pressure along the routes, you can travel alone and unaided in China as well as in any other country. Trains depart for Lowu at Hong Kong's border, or direct to Guangzhou, on a regular basis from the **Kowloon-Canton**

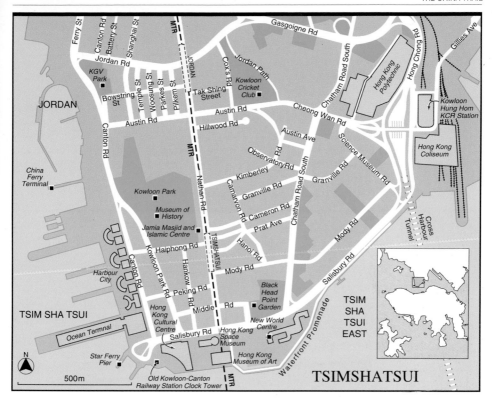

Map of Tsimshatsui showing Jordan, Tsim Sha Tsui, and Tsim Sha Tsui East. Labels include: Gasgoigne Rd, Gillies Ave, Ferry St, Canton Rd, Battery St, Shanghai St, MTR, Jordan Rd, Cox's Rd, Jordan Path, Hong Kong Chong Rd, KGV Park, Kowloon Cricket Club, Hong Kong Polytechnic, Kowloon Hung Hom KCR Station, JORDAN, Bowstring St, Temple St, Woosung St, Parkes St, Pilkem St, Tak Shing Street, Kowloon Cricket Club, Cheong Wan Rd, Chatham Road South, Austin Rd, Hillwood Rd, Austin Ave, Austin Rd, Science Museum Rd, Hong Kong Coliseum, China Ferry Terminal, Canton Rd, Observatory Rd, Kimberley, Granville Rd, Chatham Road South, Kowloon Park, Nathan Rd, Museum of History, Carnarvon Rd, Granville Rd, Cameron Rd, Prat Ave, Mody Rd, Cross Harbour Tunnel, Jamia Masjid and Islamic Centre, Haiphong Rd, TSIMSHATSUI, Hanoi Rd, Mody Rd, Salisbury Rd, TSIM SHA TSUI EAST, Harbour City, Canton Rd, Hankow Rd, Peking Rd, Black Head Point Garden, Waterfront Promenade, TSIM SHA TSUI, Kowloon Park Rd, Middle Rd, New World Centre, TSIM SHA TSUI EAST, Ocean Terminal, Hong Kong Cultural Centre, Salisbury Rd, Hong Kong Space Museum, Hong Kong Museum of Art, Star Ferry Pier, 500m, Old Kowloon-Canton Railway Station Clock Tower, MTR, N, TSIMSHATSUI

Railway's (KCR) (Hung Hom Terminus) next to the Cross Harbour Tunnel's Kowloon exit. For more information ℂ 2602 7799

Besides the train there are several other ways of traveling into China. By air, the **Chinese National airline, CNAC (CAAC)** fly directly to most cities in China and cover virtually the entire country from Guangzhou. For reservations ℂ 2861 0322 and for ticketing go to G/F Gloucester Tower, the Landmark, 17 Queen's Road Central. Dragonair flies directly to 14 destinations, such as Beijing, Guilin, Kunming, Shanghai and Xian, along with stopover packages. They're located at 9/F World-Wide House, 19 Des Voeux Road Central, or call reservations ℂ 2590 1188, ticketing ℂ 2868 6777 and for information on tours ℂ 2590 1133.

Journeys by sea can be booked through CITS, CTS, a travel agent or from the China Ferry Terminal, China Hong Kong City, 33 Canton Road, Tsimshatsui, where hovercraft and steamers leave daily for Shenzhen, Shekou, Guangzhou and many other cities in southern China. Or you can take a leisurely two-day cruise to Shanghai aboard

the cargo liners *Shanghai, Hai Xing* and *Hai Hua* which offer comfortable staterooms, cabins and berths. Amenities include lounge and disco, bar, coffee shop, swimming pool, barber and beauty salon and cinema.

Air-conditioned buses leave daily to Shenzhen from the Admiralty bus terminus in Central and from outside China Hong Kong City in Tsimshatsui. Contact **CityBus** ℂ 2604 6120.

The addresses of CITS, CTS and some major tour operators follow:
CITS (Head Office), 6/F, Tower II, South Seas Centre, 75 Mody Road, Tsimshatsui ℂ 2732 5888, fax: 2721 7154; Central branch — 1018 Swire House, **9 Connaught Road** ℂ 2810 4282, fax: 2868 1057.

CTS (Head Office), CTS House, 78-83 Connaught Road Central ℂ 2853 3888, fax: 2877 2033 or China Travel Building, 77 Queen's Road Central ℂ 2522 0450, fax: 2877 2033; Kowloon branch — 1/F Alpha House,

OPPOSITE Aerial view of Star Ferry and the Cultural Centre in Tsimshatsui.

27-33 Nathan Road, Tsimshatsui ✆ 2721 1331, fax: 2721 7757.

Hong Kong

Concorde Travel, ✆ 2526 3391, fax: 2845 0485, 7/F (China tours), 8-10 On Lan Street, Central.
Swire Travel, ✆ 2579 6688, fax: 2590 0099, 18/F Devon House, 979 King's Road, North Point.
Thomas Cook Travel Services, ✆ 2545 4399, fax: 2545 7477, 18/F Vicwood Plaza, 199 Des Voeux Road Central.

KOWLOON

TSIMSHATSUI

Kowloon and Tsimshatsui, the main tourist dormitory, shopping district and playground, have none of the dramatic beauty of Hong Kong Island but make up for it with excitement. To stand at night in the crowded Middle Road, behind the Peninsula Hotel, or Peking or Canton roads, is to be almost overwhelmed by the blaze of

Tulips Travel, ✆ 2810 1131, fax: 2810 1559, 809 Yip Fung Building, 2-18 D'Aguilar Street, Central,.
Wallem Travel, ✆ 2865 1618, fax: 2865 2652, 46/F Hopewell Centre, 183 Queen's Road East.

Kowloon

Associated Tours, ✆ 2722 1216, fax: 2369 5687811-814 Wing On Plaza, 62 Mody Road, Tsimshatsui East.
Morning Star Travel, ✆ 2736 8368, fax: 2375 5100, G/F, 5C Star House, 3 Salisbury Road, Tsimshatsui.
Silkway Travel, ✆ 2724 0888, fax: 2721 7646, 15/F Kaiseng Commercial Centre, 426 Hankow Road.

neon light, a kind of frozen fireworks display of rich colors and a kaleidoscopic clash of ornate signs.

As does Central District, Tsimshatsui starts at the Star Ferry terminal, with the added convenience of an HKTA bureau on the concourse offering advice, maps and guide booklets on all aspects of tourism in Hong Kong, along with fairly classy souvenirs.

From there, three routes lead into the heart of this people-packed high-rise funland — you can head up the escalator into the mammoth **Harbour City** complex of shops, restaurants and hotels, or you can stroll along the harbor promenade all the way to Tsimshatsui East to more hotels, shopping plazas, nightclubs and restaurants, or walk directly along Salisbury Road and pay your respects to the Grand Duchess of tourism in Hong Kong, the lady who's virtually seen it all, the **Peninsula Hotel.**

Built in 1928, the Peninsula reigned supreme as the center of high society life in Hong Kong through to the late 1970s, and even had the dubious distinction of being the headquarters of the Japanese military administration during the occupation in World War II. It's seen some of the most distinguished and most flamboyant names

day after the face-lift and immediately remarked: "You've changed the pub!" Today, the lobby has been renovated again and a 30-storey tower of luxury rooms connected to the hotel has been added.

To my mind, any outing in Tsimshatsui should start with morning coffee mid the columns, crisp linen and heavy silver tableware, soaring ceiling, potted plants and equally crisp and precise service staff of the **Peninsula Lobby.**

If you begin your walk at the seafront promenade by Star Ferry, you can study

of the twentieth century come and go, and even today it's a place where you can play "Place the Face" in its ornate and renowned Lobby, trying to recall the name of the features that just passed you by, and what they were doing when you last saw them on TV.

The Peninsula's columned architecture has survived with much dignity the latter-day explosion of steel and glass in Tsimshatsui, but only just. In the 1970s, after a proposal to tear the old dowager down was quashed, the rooms and suites were renovated and redesigned to update the establishment without harming the outside frills. But even then, one of her greatest devotees, the ill-fated Harold Holt, Prime Minister of Australia, arrived to stay one

another contrast of tradition and tearaway progress in Hong Kong, the old Kowloon-Canton Railway Station's **Clock Tower,** preserved after much public protest and beside it the **Hong Kong Cultural Centre.** Within the complex there's the world-class **Hong Kong Museum of Art** © 2734 2167, which has a superb collection of oil paintings, lithographs of old Hong Kong along with other exhibitions of Chinese fine art and historical pictures, etc. Next door the domed **Space Museum** has one of the most

OPPOSITE One of the new shopping plazas that have sprung up in Tsimshatsui East. Huge hotels like the New World ABOVE have sprung up in Tsimshatsui East, an entirely new tourist city built on reclaimed land on the Kowloon Peninsula.

advanced planetariums in the world, and features a sky theater with computerized projection which is so vivid that you actually feel as though you're journeying through outer space. There are performances in English, but only on certain days and at certain times, so it is best to check with the museum beforehand © 2734 2722.

Heading along the waterfront you can take a leisurely stroll to the end of the promenade to **Hung Hom** — the building that you'll see looking like an upturned pyramid is the **Hong Kong Coliseum.** Next to

this is the Kowloon-Canton Railway Terminus (KCR), where the suburban trains serve Kowloon and the New Territories centers up to the border with China, and the expresses go right through to Guangzhou (Canton), the jumpoff point for almost the entire China trail.

This walk is a must at night, when Hong Kong is lit up, and especially when there's a full, rising moon; and it's a dazzling, romantic sight that I never get tired of.

Alternatively, you can take the pedestrian bridge just past the **New World Centre** across Salisbury Road to the shopping and hotel district the **Regal Meridien, Holiday Inn Crowne Plaza Harbour View, Shangri-La, Nikko** and **Royal Garden** with

its scenic inside elevators — of Tsimshatsui East. Also located here is the **Hong Kong Science Museum** © 2732 3232, which has around 500 exhibits, more than half of them "hands-on," at 2 Science Museum Road. This high-tech playground is every bit as interesting as the one you may have visited in Toronto, Canada — complete with robots, a flight simulator, satellite weather shows, animated skeletons of everything from the human DNA structure to dinosaurs, virtual reality demonstrations, various scientific exhibits and, hanging above it all, Cathay Pacific's first aircraft, a DC-3 called Betsy.

From Tsimshatsui East you can head west back to Tsimshatsui via Granville Road, stopping at **Kowloon Park** on Nathan Road for a much deserved break. The park has extensive sports and recreation facilities — restaurants, an indoor heated Olympic swimming pool, games hall, playground, aviary, Chinese Garden, bird lake and other ponds and gardens. You'll also find the **Museum of History** © 2367 1124, where relics of Hong Kong are on display, and the **Jamia Masjid and Islamic Centre,** which was built in 1984 for the Muslims in Hong Kong. Guided tours can be arranged, but by appointment only. © 2724 0095 for more details.

Also, it's another ideal place to watch tai chi exercises in the morning, along with the bird-fanciers who bring their caged birds here to air them, show them off, compare them with other birds and listen to their song. Some of the finches, thrushes and more exotic lovebirds and parakeets change hands at up to HK$1,000 each, and the passion with which they're regarded by the Chinese — in Hong Kong and indeed throughout China — can be seen in the elegant wicker and bamboo cages, some of which cost HK$10,000 alone, and the delicate little ceramic water and seed pots.

If you're visiting the park on a Sunday, local amateur musicians put on a variety show, free of charge, from 2:00 to 5:00 pm.

AROUND KOWLOON

Getting There

All of these areas are easily reached by MTR. For those interested in just wandering around Yaumatei and Mongkok on foot, checkout HKTA's Yaumatei Walking Tour book.

Yaumatei

As previously mentioned, one of the most popular places to visit at night is Temple Street, not only for bargain shopping but to watch the street theater of Chinese opera, fortune tellers and street dentists. Close by, on the corner of **Nathan Road** and **Public Square Street**, but best visited during the day, you'll find **Tin Hau Temple**,

a complex of four temples originally built in the late 1870s but refurbished in 1972 after a fire destroyed the roof and rafters. Two blocks west, **Jade Market** sprawls its precious wares right across the sidewalks everyday from 10:00 am until around 3:30 pm. But as I've already advised, unless you know all about jade, that is jadeite or nephrite, be careful about buying as there are many other stones which look like jade.

Mongkok

In **Hon Lok Street,** near the Hon Lok Street MTR exit, you'll find a whole lane devoted to bird shops, and you may even witness a "bird-fight" in which two prized warblers,

put together in a cage, will try to bully each other into submission — without actually touching each other.

Shamshuipo

Further down the MTR line at **Cheung Sha Wan,** a five-minute walk from the station will take you to an area of street markets which cluster around one of Hong Kong's proudest but often neglected cultural sites, **Lei Cheng Uk** ✆ 2386 2863 on **Tonkin Street** in Lei Cheng UK resettlement estate. This museum marks the site of a Han dynasty

tomb dating from the years 206 BC to 220 AD. When the vault was discovered in 1955 some pottery and bronzeware were found inside.

Laichikok

The next stop is to two of the best tourist spots in Kowloon, offering culture with a splash of fun — **Laichikok Amusement Park** ✆ 2741 4281, featuring fairground rides

OPPOSITE The minaret of the new Kowloon Mosque in Nathan Road. Many shades and shapes of jade are displayed in the Temple Street jade market ABOVE but care is needed if true jade is the quest. ABOVE RIGHT Wan Loy Teahouse in Mongkok is a popular rendez-vous where proud bird fanciers display their warbling caged finches.

and Chinese opera performances, and the adjacent **Sung Dynasty Village** © 2741 5111, a colorful and charming little historical hamlet complete with a "river," huge traditional restaurant and hall, stores and temple. When you see it you immediately wonder how it could have been built slap-bang in the middle of soaring estates and still give the feeling of antiquity.

A lot of it has to do with the staff, who masquerade in the colorful and gaudy costumes of that time, and the shows that they present for visiting tours — a traditional

"wedding," kung-fu acrobatics, dances and a magic show. When they're not performing, they play hawkers and vendors in the shops and stalls, or fortune-tellers, joss stick makers and calligraphers. Tours are conducted four times a day, but they're pricey — about HK$ 120 a shot, including an "authentic" Song (Sung) dynasty lunch or dinner. It's worth a visit, but be prepared for little twinges of disappointment. As one tour trundles through, another is on the way, and a lot of the staff act so fed-up and bored that they'll often turn their heads away when you try to photograph them, despite the fact that they're actually there to be photographed! For those not on a tour, the village can be reached by taking the

MTR to **Mei Foo** station (two stops after Cheung Sha Wan), but as it's at least a 20-minute walk from there it's probably better to take a No 6A Kowloon Motor Bus (KMB) from Kowloon Star Ferry, which will take you directly to the park.

Wong Tai Sin

A much more satisfying place, to my mind, is the **Wong Tai Sin Temple** on **Lung Cheung Road** near the MTR station of the same name, dedicated to the deity who's become the patron saint of horserace punt-

ers. Glittering in the midst of high-rises, it was built in 1973 on the site of an original place of worship, its most treasured relic being a portrait of Wong Tai Sin brought to Hong Kong from China's southern Guangdong province 70 years ago.

What makes the temple particularly fascinating is a surrounding cluster of stalls selling joss sticks, colorful paper offerings and souvenir paper windmills — which the Chinese believe will blow away bad luck— and a nearby arcade full of soothsayers and palmists. It's here, along with the Man Mo Temple in Central District, that you can have your own fortune told in the traditional way by shaking the *chim,* a bamboo canister full of tapers, each of which has a number in Chinese on it. You shake and shake until one detaches itself, and its number is written on a scrap of paper. You take this to one of the soothsayers nearby.

You can put the powers of Wong Tai Sin to the test by shaking out two numbers, the race and the runner, and taking them along to the nearest off-course betting shop. You never know.

THE NEW TERRITORIES

SHATIN

The Wong Tai Sin Temple comes under enormous worship pressure in the autumn and winter months when the horses are running at the huge Shatin Racecourse, first major stop on the trail through the New Territories. The racetrack's size and technological grandeur have already been dealt with — see THE SPORTS TRAIL, page 184.

Shatin is also the home of the huge **New Town Plaza**, a good spot for luxury bargain shopping, featuring the Yohan department store with its vast basement food art, and indoor computer-controlled musical fountain, an outdoor amphitheater for cultural shows and orchestral concerts, a mini-golf course, children's playground and tennis courts.

An even more spectacular local facility is the **Hong Kong Sports Institute** © 2605 1212 near the racecourse, a giant Olympic-standard complex that includes a 250-meter velodrome, athletics field, "energy room "full of weightlifting equipment, a hall for table tennis and fencing, a 25-square-meter training pool, 12 squash courts, a judo hall, indoor sports hall with room for two tennis courts or eight badminton courts, a huge gymnasium, 15 outdoor tennis courts, and restaurants and snack bars. It's the pride of Hong Kong's sporting world, described by the President of the International Olympic Committee as the best he'd seen in 130 countries, and it's open everyday for visitors from 8 am to 10 pm. The trouble is, you can't use it. Most of its facilities are booked out by major multi-nationals and corporations in Hong Kong.

One place you'll have no trouble visiting and spending some time in is the remarkable **Ten Thousand Buddhas Monastery** behind the Shatin Railway Station. It takes a half an hour to get to it, climbing 431 steps, but it's worth the effort. In the main hall you'll find not 10,000 but 12,800 Buddha images lining the walls, and the human effigy of the temple's founding abbot, Yuet Kai, preserved and covered with gold leaf in a glass showcase. Along with large gilded Buddhas which preside over the main altar, there are also tall decorated images of the 18 *Lohans*, the disciples of Sakyamuni Buddha. You'll also find a fierce mounted image of Mo, or Kwan Kung, the God of War, standing guard in one of the halls, along with the God of Wisdom riding a huge blue lion and the Goddess of Mercy, Guan Yin. In **Tai Wai**, just west of Shatin, there's an interesting walled village called **Tsang Tai Uk,** which was built as a stronghold by the Tsang clan in 1859, and a few minutes walk away, **Che Kung Temple**.

Shatin is also the home of the **Chinese University**, which has a superb collection of more than a thousand Chinese paintings and calligraphy, 300 Han and pre-Han bronze seals and 400 jade flower carvings in its Art Gallery © 2609 7416.

Getting There

To reach Tsang Tai Uk, take the KCR to Tai Wai station. From there, the monastery is the next stop down the line at Shatin and the stop after that will take you to the **Shatin Racecourse** at Fo Tan.

TSUEN WAN

From Shatin, the New Territories trail leads to the **Chuk Lam Shim Yuen Monastery** at Tsuen Wan, also known as the "Bamboo Forest Monastery" because it was first established in a bamboo mat shed in 1927. Now an ornate, sprawling temple with a sweeping, curved and tiled roof, it houses three of the biggest images of Hong Kong. Another venue of interest is the **Sun Tung Uk Museum** © 2411 2001, on Kwu Uk Kane, which features relics and a re-created

OPPOSITE Visitors step back into ancient times at replica of Sung Dynasty Village in Laichikok.

traditional village of the most colorful of the Chinese clans in the New Territories, the Hakkas, who migrated into southern China from the north several centuries ago. You'll see the Hakka women all over the New Territories, distinctive for their wide-brimmed and fringed black hats, and on the construction sites in the urban areas, where they've made it a tradition to work as laborers. A short taxi ride from the MTR station will take you to **Lo Wai Village** and to the **Yuen Yuen Institute,** a temple complex dedicated to Buddhism, Taoism and Confucianism. Vegetarian food is available.

Getting There
Tsuen Wan is easily reached by MTR.

TUEN MUN

In the center of Tuen Mun's high-rise housing estates you'll reach two of the most interesting places of worship in Hong Kong, the **Ching Chung Koon Temple** at Tuen Mun and the **Miu Fat Monastery** at nearby Castle Peak. Ching Chung Koon is a purely Taoist temple, also known as the "Temple of Green Pines," and packed with garish images and altar guardians that were carved in Beijing 300 years ago. It's dedicated to Liu Tung Bun, one of the Taoist Eight Immortals, legendary beings who have been deified as superior human spirits, or fairies, and have the power to become invisible and bring the dead back to life.

Among Ching Chung Koon's other treasures are its famous bonsai collection, a series of lanterns, more than 200 years old, which once decorated the Imperial Palace in Beijing, a 1,000-year-old jade seal and a library of 3,872 books covering 4,000 years of Taoist history. The temple is also a sanctuary for old people without homes or families, who live in a building in the grounds and are supported by visitors' donations.

At Castle Peak's Miu Fat Monastery you're confronted by what could, without irreverence, be called Buddhism Inc. It's a huge, multi-storied temple, packed on most days with worshipers and visitors

OPPOSITE Sunrise over New Territories fish farms.

and virtually lined throughout with thousands of small Buddha images and niches paid for by the faithful to gain merit and to keep the establishment in the style to which it has become accustomed. And that style, judging from its latest renovations, is considerably up-market.

Miu Fat has many treasures, including beautiful gilded images of the Three Precious Buddhas on the altar in the main temple — the founding Sakyamuni Buddha flanked by the Lord of the Western Paradise, the Chinese Buddhist version of Nirvana, and the Healing Buddha. There's also a large vegetarian restaurant where the lunch menu is as good as any in Hong Kong. Going from the old to the new, the **Gold Coast Hotel** ✆ 2452 8888, 1 Castle Peak Road, Castle Peak Bay, has to be seen to believed and like everything else in Hong Kong it's big. Situated on the coast in 40.5 hectares of landscaped gardens, the HK$600 million, 18-storey, 450-room luxury resort's facilities include fine restaurants, a spa, adult and children's swimming pool, chip and putt golf and driving range, watersports, squash and tennis courts, fitness center, disco, business center and conference facilities. The hotel also has its own hoverferry service from Tsimshatsui East.

Getting There

From Hong Kong Island, take the Tuen Mun ferry from the Central Harbour Ferry Services Pier in Central; from Kowloon, the MTR to Tsuen Wan, then bus No. 66M, or bus 68X from the Jordan Road terminus. From Tuen Mun the Light Rail Transit (LRT) will take you to both destinations to reach Ching Chung Koon Temple alight at Ching Chung station and to reach Miu Fat Monastery go to Lam Tei station.

YUEN LONG

For another look at traditional Chinese life, the **Kun Ting Study Hall** and **Tang Ancestral Hall** in Ping Shan, just west of Yuen Long. The ancestral hall is one of the largest in the New Territories, with three halls and two internal courtyards, and today is still used by the Tang clan. The study hall was built around 1870 mainly for education and

ancestral worship. Nearby, you'll find the ancient, hexagonal **Tsui Shing Lau Pagoda**, first built in the fourteenth century to ward off evil spirits. Somewhat diminished in size from seven storeys to three, the pagoda used to rise up out of a rustic swathe of duck farms and rice paddies — today most of the farms have disappeared and the pagoda is now dwarfed by high-rises.

East of Yuen Long, **Kam Tin Walled Village**, or **Kat Hing Wai**, has all the character, sights and smells of Old China. Surrounded by high brick walls and a moat, it was built

in the 1600s by the Tang clan, and it was obviously fortified as protection both against the pirates who operated from Hong Kong and Kowloon and warring factions in this, a peripheral southern area which has always lain far beyond the centers of imperial authority to the north. There was also a "walled" city in urban Kowloon, near Kai Tak airport, but it was established for a far different reason. It was left exempt from the colonial lease on the New Territories to provide a safe haven, or

OPPOSITE Hong Kong imports most of its food from China but much of the fresh market vegetables seen locally is grown on New Territories plots as here. ABOVE Incense burner and Buddhist deity.

diplomatic quarters, where Chinese Government officials could reside and conduct business as ambassadors to the colony.

Until the early 90s, when it was completely demolished, it was home to more than 50,000 people.

Getting There
From Hong Kong Island, take the Tuen Mun ferry from Central Harbour Ferry Services Pier, then the LRT to Ping Shan station. From there the ancestral hall is about a 30-minute walk along Ping Ha Road so if you

ship is built on discarded oyster shells — it's been the center of the oyster farming industry in Hong Kong for many years.

Getting There
From Yuen Long, bus No. 655, or take a taxi.

THE BORDER AREAS

Further north at Santin there are more ancestral halls, **Man Lun-Fung** and **Man Shek Tong,** along with a stately traditional Chinese official's house, **Tai Fu Tai**, which has

see a taxi, grab it. If you're coming from Kowloon, it would be best to take the MTR to Tsuen Wan station then bus No. 68M to Yuen Long. You can also catch bus No. 68X from the Jordan Road terminus but the journey is quite long, taking about one and a half hours. Once in Yuen Long, take the LRT to Ping Shan station, or go by taxi. To reach the walled village, take a taxi from Yuen Long.

LAU FAU SHAN

On the edge of Deep Bay and the western border with China, **Lau Fau Shan** is an interesting little fishing settlement where you may still catch sight of a traditional sailing junk or two. You'll also find that the town-

been beautifully restored. Built in 1865 by the Man clan, the mansion is decorated with wood carvings, murals and terra-cotta figures. Just beyond San Tin you'll reach **Lok Ma Chau** lookout point, which for more than three decades was the closest most foreigners were able to get to China. Along with the Lo Wu Bridge to the east, it was the point where tour groups could mount observation towers and look across rice paddies, duck farms and the Zhenzhen River and boast later that they actually saw "Red China." Nowadays, of course, the rice paddies and the ducks are the only things worth watching — with the China door wide open to tourism, you can get a visa in 24 hours and see the real thing.

Heading east you'll arrive at **Fanling**, on the main KCR railway line, once just a farming community but now a booming town. But despite its progress, Fanling has still managed to retain some of its past which can be seen at **Luen Wo Market** a traditional rural market with stalls selling dried fish and mushrooms, 1,000-year-old eggs, herbal medicines, bean curd, gold fish and paper offerings. You'll also find the recently restored **Tang Chung Ling Ancestral Hall**, which is believed to have been constructed in 1525.

to **Sha Tau Kok** at the mouth of the bay, but again, you can just as easily get a bus or jetfoil to the Shenzhen Special Economic Zone or the train to Guangzhou and spend a couple of days in China itself instead of peeking over the back fence.

Getting There
To get to Lok Ma Chau, take a taxi from Sheung Shui KCR station. San Tin and Tai Fu Tai are also best reached by taxi from either Sheung Shui or Yuen Long. Luk Keng Bird Sanctuary isn't as difficult to get to as

In Fanling itself, you can visit the famous **Po Sang Yuen Bee Farm,** which produces the most exquisite honey and invigorating honey drinks. The farm is near the KCR station and to arrange a visit © 2669 5840.

A short taxi ride from the town center, the **Royal Hong Kong Golf Club** has three championship courses, which are open to visitors, but on weekdays only. For more details see THE SPORTS TRAIL, p184.

For naturalists, the Luk Keng bird sanctuary at Starling Inlet in the far northeast of the New Territories combines a study of egrets and herons, and their breeding season from March to September, with another vantage point for views of China. To get even closer to the border, you can carry on

you would expect — from Fanling KCR station minibus No. 56K takes you right there.

PLOVER COVE

If you're interested in engineering, the **Plover Cove Reservoir** north of Tolo Harbour is something of a marvel of water conservation. It was once part of the sea. In the early 1970s the inlet was closed off, the entire bay sealed, the seawater pumped out — and the monsoon rains did the rest. Now,

OPPOSITE and ABOVE Oyster shells festoon the waterfront and streets of Lau Fau Shan in the New Territories.

The Broad Highway

it's one of Hong Kong's main guarantees against its old summer time agony, either too much rain, with accompanying land slips and death and injury, or not enough, with accompanying strict water rationing. On your way to the reservoir suggest you call in to **Tai Mei Tuk Visitors Centre** on **Bride's Pool Road** for information on country walks and nature trails and the area's most popular attraction, **Bride's Pool Waterfalls.**

Getting There
From Tai Po KCR station bus No. 75K will

stored — one is near the Railway Museum on Fu Shin Street and the other across the river on Ting Kok Road.

At Shek Kong, west of Tai Po, you'll find **Kadoorie Experimental Farm** on the north-western slope of Hong Kong's tallest mountain, **Tai Mo Shan.** Established in 1951, it was originally set up to teach modern agricultural techniques to refugees from over the border. The farm is beautifully landscaped with steep terraces of pools, crops and trees, and the view from the top of the slope is magnificent. Livestock such as pigs

take you to Tai Mai Tuk village, which is close to the reservoir, or take a taxi.

Tai Po

From Plover Cove, the New Territories trail ends up virtually where it began, at **Tai Po**, a former pleasant market town north of Shatin and now a fast-changing New Town. For railway enthusiasts, the old Tai Po Market station has been preserved and tarted up and turned into the **Hong Kong Railway Museum** ✆ 2653 3339, featuring an exhibition gallery, old coaches and a mock-up of a modern-day electric-powered coach. It's open daily from 9 am to 4 pm. Nearby, two Tin Hau temples have also been re-

and ducks are specially reared. If you're interested in visiting, please give the farm at least two day's notice. For inquiries ✆ 2488 1317.

Sai Kung Peninsula

There's one other interesting place to visit on the "other side" and that's Hebe Haven and **Sai Kung,** where a cluster of old villages around the shallow bay are gradually being transformed into marine resorts. If you feel like taking a rest from the shopping plazas and packed streets of the urban tourist districts, or feel the need to lay back and get your feet up after your New Territories tour, you'll find relative tranquillity, wind-surfing and other water-sports, blazing sunsets, interesting fishing communities, wonderful hiking in the country parks and a pleasant place to stay — the Beach Resort © 2791 1068, Lot 1780 DD221, Tai Mong Tsui Road, Sai Kung, which has its own beach, swimming pool and recreational amenities.

Getting There
From Choi Hung MTR station in Kowloon bus No. 92 or minibus No. 1 goes to Sai Kung town via Hebe Haven.

CLEAR WATER PENINSULA

Clear Water Bay is another quite dramatic area of beaches, country parks and fishing communities, along with the **Tin Hau Temple** in **Joss House Bay.** The temple, which has been restored a number of times, is thought to have been built in the thirteenth century, toward the end of the Song (Sung) dynasty. If you happen to be in Hong Kong for the Tin Hau Festival, held each year to celebrate the birthday of Tin Hau (Goddess of the Sea), on the 23rd day of the third lunar month that is, April or May — then head for Joss House Bay where you'll see thousands of fisherfolk in festively decorated boats paying their respects to the goddess.

Getting There
From Choi Hung MTR station take bus No. 91 to the entrance of the Clearwater Bay Golf Club. From there follow the signposts to the temple.

THE TOUR TRAIL

For those who don't want the hassle of public transport, HKTA offers a number of New Territories tours to most of the sights already mentioned. Their Land Between Tour, for example, takes in such attractions as the near Tsuen Wan, Bamboo Forest Monastery near Tai Mo Shan mountain, the fish and duck farms of Shek Kong, the golf club at Fanling, Luen Wo market, the bird sanctuary at Luk Keng, Plover Cove Reservoir, a fishing village in Tolo Harbour, Tai Po, the Chinese University and Shatin.

It's an interesting tour and quite reasonably priced at HK$295 for adults and HK$245 for children, considering the distance it covers. But it's also becoming increasingly difficult to promote and sustain as rural adventure with the amount of new development that's going on throughout the area. In many places, especially around the gigantic New Towns, the old rustic paddy life is scarred by major construction, new roads and drainage systems, and some of the traditional tranquillity can only be glimpsed through convoys of huge dump-trucks and their clouds of exhaust. But then, development is as much a matter of pride in

Hong Kong as the lingering tradition and antiquity.

You can also try their Heritage Tours, which cover temples, museums and ancestral halls.

THE OUTLYING ISLANDS

For some reason, Lantau, Lamma and Cheung Chau are called the Outlying Islands. But they're not as outlying as the name suggests they can be clearly seen from

OPPOSITE Surrounding "moat" of village near China border. ABOVE Campers at the Sai Kung Peninsula.

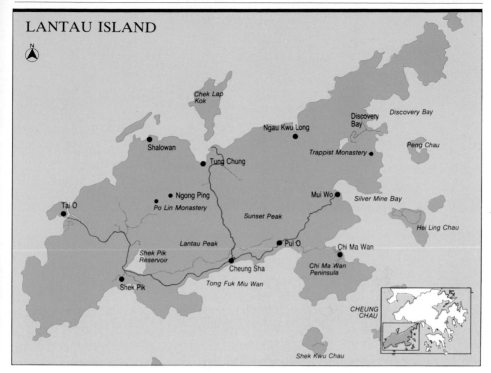

LANTAU ISLAND

N

Chek Lap Kok

Shalowan

Tung Chung

Ngau Kwu Long

Discovery Bay

Discovery Bay

Peng Chau

Trappist Monastery

Tai O

Ngong Ping
Po Lin Monastery

Mui Wo

Silver Mine Bay

Sunset Peak

Hei Ling Chau

Lantau Peak

Shek Pik Reservoir

Pul O

Chi Ma Wan

Shek Pik

Cheung Sha

Chi Ma Wan Peninsula

Tong Fuk Miu Wan

CHEUNG CHAU

Shek Kwu Chau

Hong Kong and Kowloon and are not more than one-hour away by ferry. Lantau and Lamma, in particular, offer beautiful countryside for walking and hiking, as well as old temples and interesting fishing villages. In fact the Hong Kong Tourist Association is encouraging visitors to "Stay an extra day" to explore the other side of Hong Kong that most tourists don't even know exists.

Ferries and hoverferries to Lantau, Peng Chau and Cheung Chau leave from the Outlying District Services Pier and the Government Pier, and to Lamma from the Central Harbour Services Pier on Connaught Road Central, west of Star Ferry.

LANTAU

Lantau is, in fact, a whole new Hong Kong. It's nearly twice the size of Hong Kong Island, and for the time being until the Chek Lap Kok International Airport is completed — quite undeveloped, offers magnificent hiking, camping, fishing and other recreational pursuits, features a colossal Buddha statue, monasteries, temples, a fort and even has a small tea plantation. The island broods just beyond the urban jungle of

Hong Kong — dark and silent and huge and almost mysterious at night, a rustic green rolling switchback of hills in the day's sun.

The ferries from Central take you to **Silvermine Bay,** also known by its Chinese name, Mui Wo, or "Five Petal," the island's major township. It's named after a silver mine which once operated north of the town. The town has a small beach resort, the **Silvermine Beach Hotel** ℂ 2984 8295 with water sports and other recreational amenities.

But the prime reason for visiting Lantau is to climb to the beautiful **Po Lin ("Precious Lotus") Buddhist Monastery,** which lies on the high Ngong Ping Plateau close to Lantau Peak. To get there you take a bus from Silvermine Bay, passing the **Shek Pik Reservoir** and Hong Kong's one and only tea plantation along the way.

Po Lin was first established in 1905 by a group of reclusive Buddhist monks, and the present temple complex dates back to 1927. It's the most important Buddhist center in

OPPOSITE Fish traps abound the foreshores of Po Toi O Bay in the New Territories.

Hong Kong, and once every three years it attracts hundreds of novice monks from all over Asia for special study and prayer. The main temple features three magnificent bronze Buddha images — Sakyamuni, the Healing Buddha and the Lord of the Western Paradise; and an even more spectacular one — the "world's largest" outdoor bronze Buddha statue (34 meters high and weighing 250 tonnes) which, on a clear day, can be see from as far away as Macau — stands by the monastery. Vegetarian food is available.

Down below at the **Tea Gardens** ✆ 2985 5161 — Hong Kong's only commercial tea plantation — you can stop off for a cup of Chinese tea, or even stay overnight in one of their (very basic) bungalows if you wish and spend the next day watching the picking and processing of several varieties of tea, climb to the monastery and, if you have the time and energy, enjoy horse riding and roller-skating as well.

From Silvermine Bay you can also go by bus to the northwestern shoreline of the island, to **Tai O,** a small fishing and market town which for more than a century was the center of the salt-panning industry in Hong Kong. Now, it's more famous for its seafood restaurants, which cluster along the waterfront, its rope-drawn sampan ride across the creek and its eighteenth century **Kwan Tai Temple**, dedicated to the God of War and Righteousness, a deified general who lived in the Three Kingdoms Period (220– 265) and is remembered for his crusades against injustice and corruption. Two other temples have recently been renovated, **Han Wong**, overlooking the bay, and **Kwan Yum** just outside the village. There's also a direct ferry service to Tai O from Central District during the weekends and on Public Holidays only which calls in at several small coastal villages along the way.

Another route from Silvermine Bay takes you to the foot of **Sunset Peak,** a 869 m (2,851 ft) mountain which offers blissful solitude and rest for those who find the clamor of Hong Kong too much to take. It's an arduous three-hour climb to the peak, up a winding path that leads through woodlands and misty meadows, but once there you stand close to clouds, enjoying cool breezes and panoramic views of Lantau

Island and a great deal of the rest of the territory. You can camp up there, and awake in the mornings to the clang of cow-bells among a herd of dairy cattle that feed on the lush hilltop grasses. You'll also find a series of old stone huts that various companies and community groups rent for employees and members who need a break from it all.

Down below, in the village of **Pui O**, you can round off your Sunset Peak expedition with a meal and bottle of wine in one of Hong Kong's most unusual and most popular "outlying" restaurants. If you alight from

the bus near the Pui O village school and walk up the hill that rises from the right hand side of the road you'll find **Charlie's,** which offers quite a remarkable menu that ranges from Cantonese food to fish and chips, to curries and even to lemon pancakes, with an outstanding wine list that also includes champagne, port and liqueurs.

Another hoverferry and high-speed ferry service goes from Star Ferry in Central District to the **Discovery Bay** residential resort on the northeastern coastline of

Two faces of Lantau Island — twice the size of Hong Kong Island and only marginally settled and developed. So far it has remained one of the territory's main areas of open-air recreation.

Lantau. It's a new executive-class dormitory of high-rise blocks and two- and three-storey beachfront condominiums with a sweeping man-made beach where you can rent a wind-surfer or sailing dinghy for the day or just sit and broil in the sun. It also has 27-hole top-class golf course and for more details see THE SPORTS TRAIL, p184.

Behind Discovery a path leads up and over the steep mountainsides to another of Lantau's main cultural attractions, the **Trappist Monastery of our Lady of Liesse.** Built in 1956 by Cistercian monks, the mon-

LAMMA ISLAND

Lamma Island is the closest of Hong Kong's other islands, and again it's largely undeveloped — except for the Hong Kong Electric Power Station on the northwest waterfront — and still nods sleepily in a rustic atmosphere of small villages and fishing havens. The ferries go to two destinations, Yung Shue Wan, or "Banyan Tree Bay" in the north near the power plant, and **Sok Kwu Wan** which lies in the island's narrow central spine.

astery supports itself through a dairy farm at Yuen Long which provides fresh milk to some of Hong Kong's major hotels. It welcomes visitors, and offers cheap accommodation at about HK$120 a day — for inquiries © 2987 6292. And it offers peace, too — there are signs at the entrance which appeal for "No Radios" and "Silence." Another way to reach the monastery is to go to Peng Chau island on the Silvermine Bay ferry (but make sure it's the one going via Peng Chau) from Central, and then crossing by small motorized boat, or kaido, to the hillside on which the monastery stands. If you have time in Peng Chau, take a wander — the island has a 200-year-old Tin Hau Temple and shops selling hand-painted porcelain.

Lamma features several good beaches, many countryside walks, including a strenuous climb up its main peak, Mount Stenhouse, interesting village life and two Tin Hau temples, one in each major town. But it's famous above all for its seafood restaurants which virtually line the waterfront in both Yung Shue Wan and Sok Kwu Wan. Those in Sok Kwu Wan are probably the most popular because the environment is more pleasant — a bay filled with fish-traps rather than the distant stacks of the power station. At weekends, tourists and local residents flock there to pack the covered alfresco eating places, feasting off deep-fried spiced crab, prawns, mussels, oysters and prawns.

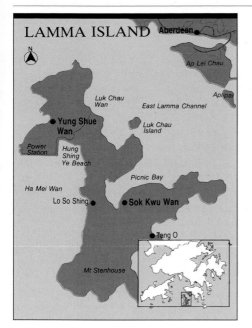

CHEUNG CHAU

There's another crowded and popular huddle of seafood restaurants on the main waterfront, or Praya, of Cheung Chau, a strangely shaped island which lies close to Lantau. There's also a huge fishing and trading fleet, including many junks, that sits off the promenade, along with the last of the great traditional boat-building yards of Hong Kong, where fishing junks, elegant teak and yakal pleasure junks and the new fishing trawlers are constructed in a confusion of crowded slipways, Tin Hau temples and others dedicated to a number of popular deities.

Cheung Chau was once a thriving port, watering place and market town for junks plying the South China Coast to and from Macau, and had a busy, well-developed society long before Hong Kong itself was settled. Much of that society remains — clans and trade guilds still dominate the island's industrious but carefully paced fishing and business life. For some years the island has been a place of retreat for foreign writers, photographers and other "media types" anxious for a more relaxed lifestyle than that of the urbanized main island and Kowloon.

But all that peace and quiet pace explodes each April or early May during the week-long Bun Festival, held to appease the spirits of victims of a plague which swept Cheung Chau in the later 1880s. As huge towers loaded with buns loom over the island's most famous cultural monument, the Pak Tai Temple to the north of the Praya, parades, dragon and lion dances and processions clash, bang and howl along the waterfront day after day, highlighted by children in ornate traditional costumes supported by children harnessed on tall poles so that they seem to be floating over the melee. An altar near the Pak Tai Temple bears giant papier-mâché effigies of the God of the Earth, God of the Mountains and the black-faced Lord of the Ghosts. Throughout the festival, no meat is eaten on the island, so the restaurant fare is strictly vegetarian.

At other times, Cheung Chau is a place for strolling, especially through the market stalls and narrow streets of the waterfront area, where you'll find small factories and workshops engaged in traditional arts and

OPPOSITE For centuries boat-building has been one of the traditional occupations of the villagers of the outlying islands.

crafts. Its main temples are quite dramatic — the **Pak Tai Temple,** built in 1783, features images of its supreme deity, the Spirit of the North, also known as the Supreme Emperor of the Dark Heaven and Protector of all Seafarers, along with the attendant gods Thousand Mile Eye and Favorable Wind Ear.

A sampan ride from the Praya to Sai Wan will take you to a **Tin Hau Temple** and the **Cave of Cheung Po Tsai,** a notorious pirate who once menaced the seas from Cheung Chau. Inland from the Praya there's another small temple, the **Kwan Kung Pavilion,** dedicated to the martial god, Mo, of the Man Mo Temple on Hong Kong Island. The Kwun Yum Temple, to the east of the pavilion, commemorates Guan Yin, the Goddess of Mercy, and the Kwai Yuen Monastery is another interesting place of worship to the south.

Cheung Chau, one of the main "Outlying Islands" referred to in the Central District ferry pier of that name. The air-conditioned ferry takes 50 minutes.

Off the
Beaten
Track

THE SPORTS TRAIL

Although Hong Kong has a variety of sports to offer, many of the facilities available to the public are in heavy demand; and as a result you may have to join the queue or book your time several days or more in advance. So if don't have the time to wait around but are desperate for a game of golf, tennis, badminton, squash, table tennis or just a swim and a Finnish sauna, HKTA offers a **Sports and Recreation Tour** at the exclusive Clearwater Bay Golf and Country Club on the Clear Water Bay Peninsula. But, depending on what sport you choose, it can be expensive and on top of HKTA's tour fee of about US$48 for air-conditioned coach, guide, lunch and admission fee to the club, if you want to play golf, for example, you'll have to pay an extra US$192 for green fee, golf club and cart charges. But for a game of tennis, badminton or squash the cost is reasonable — about US$12 per hour.

BEACHES AND SWIMMING

Hong Kong has many charming beaches, but these days many of them are quite dangerously polluted and during the summer months the easiest-to-reach ones are packed with people. On Hong Kong Island they're all located on the south side, with **Repulse Bay** the largest and most popular, followed by **Deep Water Bay, Chung Hom Kok, Stanley Main Beach** and, at the southeastern extremity of the island, **Shek-O** and **Big Wave Bay**. You can also try **Lantau, Cheung Chau** and **Lamma** islands. The best beaches, though, are in the New Territories around Sai Kung and Clear Water Bay peninsulas — but to reach the most secluded and least polluted you'll have to walk an hour or so through the country parks, which may mean climbing over a mountain or two.

For more details, the Hong Kong Government publication *Gazetted Beaches in Hong Kong* lists more than 30 beaches which have lifeguards and changing facilities; and for a check on the quality of the water, look on the beach notice board, or ask HKTA ✆ 2801 7177 before you go.

The most centrally located indoor and outdoor swimming pools are, on Hong Kong Island, **Victoria Park Swimming Pool** ✆ 2570 4682 in Causeway Bay; **Morrison Hill Swimming Pool** ✆ 2575 3028 in Wanchai; and the **Pao Yue Kong Swimming Pool** ✆ 2553 3617 in Aberdeen. In Kowloon, **Lai Chi Kok Park Swimming Pool** ✆ 2745 5234; and the **Kowloon Indoor Games Hall and Swimming Pool** ✆ 2724 4522 in Kowloon Park.

BOATING AND SAILING

If you belong to a sailing club, the chances are you'll be able to join a crew in Hong Kong, as the **Royal Hong Kong Yacht Club (RHKYC)** has reciprocal arrangements

With a number of larger overseas clubs. For more information call © 2832 2817 or write to the RHKYC, Kellet Island, Hong Kong.

Pleasure junks can be chartered but they're not cheap — the charge, whether it's for a full day or a minimum of two and a half hours, is approximately US$580. You can try Duk Ling © 2851 9601, or contact HKTA for other charterers.

COUNTRY WALKS AND HIKES

Walking and hiking are favorite pastimes in Hong Kong and Hong Kong is surprisingly well endowed with trails — almost 640 km (400 miles) in its 21 large, protected Country Parks, rural, recreational lungs which cover more than 40 percent of the terri-

tory's land area. The longest of these, the **MacLehose Trail** is a three-day trek weaving in and around the mountain spine that surrounds the Kowloon peninsula. There is also a **Hong Kong Trail** and **Lantau Trail.** Details of walks and treks can be obtained from the HKTA or the Government Publications Centre next to the General Post Office in Connaught Place, Hong Kong.

GOLF

Although golf clubs in Hong Kong are private, visitors are welcome to play — except on weekends and public holidays.

ABOVE Outlying Islands ferry glides through lighters and fishing trawlers off central "bottleneck" of Cheung Chau Island.

The most popular venue is the three-course layout of the **Royal Hong Kong Golf Club (RHKGC)** ✆ 2670 1211 at Fanling in the New Territories. The green fees for 18 holes cost HK$1,200, but are subject to change, and it's best to book in advance. RHKGC also has a nine-hole course at **Deep Water Bay** ✆ 2812 7070 on Hong Kong Island. There's another course (27 holes) high above the Discovery Bay residential development on Lantau Island. Ferries run frequently from Star Ferry in Central, and there's a bus to take you up to the course. To

lar routes are in Victoria Park, at the **Happy Valley Racetrack** and, best of all, along the scenic **Bowen Road** path in the Mid-Levels, which runs for several kilometers above Wanchai and around into **Happy Valley** to the roundabout at Stubbs and Tai Hang roads. The Hash House Harriers sally forth on a hue and cry each week and are remarkable, aside from their stamina, for the considerable amounts of liquid replenishment that they take after each run.

Amateurs runners are also welcome to take part in Hong Kong's two annual mara-

check in advance call the **Discovery Bag Golf Club** direct on ✆ 2987 7271.

ICE SKATING

Two venues you can try are the **Whampoa Super Ice** ✆ 2774 4899 in Hung Hom, Kowloon, and, on the island, **Cityplaza Ice Palace** ✆ 2885 4697 at Taikoo Shing.

JOGGING

Despite the heat and the urban crush, Hong Kong has a large army of joggers and a number of good jogging routes. A spectacular city route is along the waterfront promenade in Tsimshatsui. On the island, popu-

thons, the **Coast of China Marathon** on the first Sunday of March, and the **International Marathon** in January. For details about the China Marathon, write to **Athletics Promotions Ltd,** G/F 16 Wood Road, Wanchai, Hong Kong or ✆ 2573 5292; and for the International Marathon, call the **Hong Kong Amateur Athletics Association** ✆ 2574 6845.

MARTIAL ARTS

If you're interested in Martial Arts, the **Hong Kong Chinese Martial Arts Association** ✆ 2394 4803 will do their best to arrange a time for demonstrations of kung fu, tai chi chuan (Chinese shadow boxing), Thai boxing and others.

RACQUET SPORTS

Tennis, squash and badminton are very popular in Hong Kong, and trying to find an available court may not be easy. Your best bet for squash is the **Hong Kong Squash Centre** © 2521 5072, located at the entrance to Hong Kong Park, opposite the Peak Tram, at 23 Cotton Tree Drive in Central, but you can also try **Queen Elizabeth Stadium** © 2591 1346 in Wanchai and, in Kowloon, **Kowloon Tsai Park** © 2336 7878

and **Lai Chi Kok Indoor Games Sports Hall** © 2745 2796. For tennis, on the island, Victoria Park © 2570 6186 in Causeway Bay and the **Tennis Centre** © 2574 9122 at Wongneichong Gap Road; in Kowloon, **King's Park** © 2385 8985. For badminton, **Queen Elizabeth Stadium**.

SOFTBALL

If you're an American and you pine for a touch of hometown sport and bonhomie, there's a sponsored softball league that plays amid the tenements and neon through the winter months. If you're interested, contact the **Softball Association** © 2711 1167, Tin Kwong Road, Homantin, Kowloon.

WATER-SKIING AND WINDSURFING

For water-skiing contact the **Deep Water Bay Speedboat Company** © 2812 0391.

Windsurfing can be arranged by hire at a number of beaches, particularly on Cheung Chau island at the **Cheung Chau Windsurfing Centre** © 2981 8316, and at **Kent Windsurfing Centre** © 2813 0596 or **Windsurfing Promotions Centre** © 2813 2372 in Stanley. **The Windsurfing Association of Hong Kong** © 2866 3232 conducts

regattas and competitions in the balmy "dry" months of November and December each year.

For other activities such as diving, cycling, fishing, football, roller skating, tenpin bowling and lawn bowls, check out HKTA's *The Official Hong Kong Guide*, which has a detailed sports section plus other tourist information.

OPPOSITE Urban clamor and skyline of Hong Kong is contrasted by the tranquillity of some of the best beaches in Southeast Asia. ABOVE Two faces of Hong Kong's sports — snooker hall draws young hustlers, and greens of Hong Kong Golf Club at Fanling attract more sedate hopefuls.

Travelers' Tips

VISAS

Hong Kong is a British colony, and so all British subjects are given a six-month stay with no visa. Commonwealth citizens are given three months with no visa. Americans, along with the citizens of some 25 other Western nations, are allowed one-month visa-free permits. All visitors must have a valid passport, and must fill out a landing card, either on the plane to Hong Kong or on arrival there, to be presented

60 milliliters of perfume and 250 milliliters of toilet water.

HEALTH

Unless you've been in an infected area in the previous 14 days you won't need a cholera certificate, or any other vaccination stamp. Hong Kong itself has very high health and hygiene standards — you can safely drink the water — but the high summer temperatures and humidity can cause

at the immigration counter.All residents of Hong Kong are required to carry an identity card and visitors are advised to also carry some identification with a photo at all times.

skin and fungal problems, called "Hong Kong Foot," if you stay for any length of time. On a short visit, with your tolerance for tropical germs quite low, it's advisable to stay away from cooked food stalls.

CUSTOMS

Hong Kong is a free port, but that doesn't mean you can bring in anything you like. The usual strict restrictions on firearms, dangerous items, drugs and what have you apply here as elsewhere, and as far as duty-free goods are concerned you can carry in a one-liter bottle of alcohol, 200 cigarettes (or 50 cigars or 250 gm of tobacco),

COMMUNICATIONS

Hong Kong has a very efficient telephone system, and local calls are free if they're made from a private phone. Some hotels charge for local calls, however, and there are also public phones that cost HK$1 a call. Most hotels have International Direct Dialing (IDD). Cardphones for IDD are located at some 500 sites and operate on stored-value phonecards available at most Telecom CSL shops, Hong Kong Telecom Service Centres and HKTA and other public locations in three denominations: HK$50, HK$100 and HK$250. There are also Creditcardphones and Coinphones for IDD calls. For more details call International Customer Services on 103.

TRANSPORTATION

AIRPORT BUS SERVICE

For airport arrivals, three air-conditioned Airbus coach services feed travelers cheaply to Tsimshatsui, Causeway Bay and Central District, calling at most major hotels along the way. The A1 service does a shuttle service around Tsimshatsui for a flat fare of HK$9; A2 (HK$14) covers Central District, terminating at the Victoria Hotel and the Macau Ferry Terminal; A3 (HK$14) serves Causeway Bay and Wanchai; and A5 (HK$14) Taikoo Shing. The service operates at 15- to 20-minute intervals from 7:00 am till midnight.

TRAINS

MTR (Underground)

The Mass Transit Railway (MTR) operates three lines: one on Hong Kong Island, between Sheung Wan in Western District and Chai-wan in the east, which passes through Central District, Wanchai, Causeway Bay, North Point, Quarry Bay, Taikoo Shing and Shau-kei-wan. The second line shoots across the harbor to Tsimshatsui, though Yau-ma-tei, Mongkok, Shamshuipo and Lai-chi-kok to as far as Tsuen Wan in western Kowloon. The third line connects eastern Hong Kong with eastern Kowloon, and from Quarry Bay crosses the harbor to Lam Tin, continuing northwest through Kwun Tong, Choi Hung, Wong Tai Sin and Kowloon Tong and then south to Mongkok and Yaumatei. Trains run from 6:00 am to 1:00 pm, every two minutes during rush hour. For more information ✆ 2750 0170 or you can collect an MTR handbook, free of charge, from any MTR ticket office.

KCR (Overground)

From Hung Hom, the Kowloon-Canton Railway (KCR) runs through Kowloon and the New Territories, with access to such places as Mongkok, Shatin, Taipo, Fanling and Sheung Shui, to Lowu at the Chinese border. But unless you have a China visa, Sheung Shui is the last stop as Lowu is a restricted area. MTR tickets can be used on the KCR, which connects with the MTR at Kowloon Tong. Trains run from 5:35 am to 12:25 am about every six minutes. For enquiries ✆ 2602 7799.

LRT (Overground)

The Light Rail Transit (LRT) operates in the western New Territories between Tuen Mun ferry pier and Yuen Long. The LRT has a number of lines, which can be a bit confusing, so be sure to study the route map before getting on any train. For information ✆ 2468 7788.

TAXIS

Taxis are plentiful, and reasonably cheap, on both sides of the harbor, operating on a HK$6.50 flagfall for the first two kilometers and HK$1.00 for each 200 metres thereafter. There are a growing number of orderly taxi ranks in Central, Tsimshatsui and other major centers, but otherwise it's everyone for himself at the kerbsides — and I've yet to meet any visiting Westerner who can outsmart a Cantonese when it comes to hailing and grabbing one. The worst times to try to get a cab are around 4 pm each day, when the fleets change drivers, and on race days. If you cross the harbor you often pay an extra HK$20 for the Cross Harbour Tunnel fee — it's actually $10 each way, the driver gets to keep the extra HK$10 for his return toll. Aside from the occasional young hot-rodder, the drivers are quite expert and most speak a little English. If you're not happy with their service there's a police hotline that you can call — ✆ 2527 7177.

OPPOSITE The Bank of China building dominates the skyline above the Star Ferry's Central terminus.

BUSES

Public buses are also plentiful, both on the island and in Kowloon, and the HKTA provides timetables and information on routes. The main bus terminals are just west of Exchange Square on the island and the Star Ferry in Tsimshatsui. Fares are cheap, but you must have the exact fare. There are also mini-buses that dart in and out of the mainstream transport, picking passengers up wherever they're hailed, rather like taxis,

Tsimshatsui for HK$1.50 first class from 6:30 am to 11:30 pm. In addition, there is also a service between Central District and Hung Hom via Whampoa Garden and another between Central District and Wanchai. If you want to reach the outlying islands and Tuen Mun in the New Territories, the Hong Kong Ferry Company © 2542 3081 operates from three piers — Government, Outlying Districts and Central Harbour Ferry Services — west of Star Ferry on the island harborfront, along with a hoverferry service between Central and

and feeding awkward or distant destinations. Maxi-cabs, a green and yellow version of these "service" vehicles, provide direct access to distinct points — the Star Ferry terminal in Central to the Mid-Levels, Aberdeen and Ocean Park, for example.

For more information on routes, fares and other enquiries, call Kowloon Motor Bus Company (KMB) © 2745 4466, and for Hong Kong Island, China Motor Bus Company (CMB) © 2565 8556 and Citybus © 2736 3888.

FERRIES

The Star Ferry © 2366 2576 shuttles back and forth between Central District and

Tsimshatsui East, departing from Queen's Pier, in front of City Hall.

TRAMS

For the cheapest scenic land transport, there is little to beat the 90-year-old tram service that runs from Kennedy Town in Western District right through the heart of Central, Wanchai and Causeway Bay and then heads east into the re-developing centers of North Point, Quarry Bay and Shaukeiwan. The fare is cheap and all it costs is HK$1.20. But don't use them if you're trying to get somewhere in a hurry — they're slow. Trams run down from 6:00 am to midnight.

PEAK TRAM

On Hong Kong Island the Peak Tram runs from 7:00 am to midnight, every 10 minutes, from its lower terminus on Garden Road in Central, taking about eight minutes to reach the Peak Terminus 397 meters up Victoria Peak. Each way the fare for adults is HK$10, but if you buy a return ticket HK$16. Children pay HK$4 each (HK$6 return). From Star Ferry a free, open-air double-decker shuttle-bus service runs to the lower terminus every 20 minutes from 9:00 am to 7:00 pm.

RICKSHAW

What was once the cheapest form of travel in Hong Kong, the rickshaw, is now one of the most expensive. Now all but phased out, they're there mainly for tourist snapshots, and for a short run around the block. Negotiate first — if you're lucky, you just might be able to get a photo for HK$50 and a ride for HK$100. But be warned: these drivers are aggressive and greedy.

HELICOPTER

Helicopters can be chartered for sightseeing and for more details and prices contact Heliservices © 2802 0200, Fenwick Street Pier Heliport, Central. For flights to Macau, East Asia Helicopters © 2859 3359.

CAR RENTAL

Chauffeur-driven cars are widely used in Hong Kong. Most major hotels have limousines available for guests, or you can call Avis Rent-a-Car © 2890 6988. For those thinking of self-driving, I suggest you forget it — street parking spaces are few and far between, and car parks are nearly always full.

MEDIA

NEWSPAPERS

Six English-language dailies are printed here — the *South China Morning Post*, *Hongkong Standard*, *Eastern Express* (which commenced publishing in February 1994), *USA Today International*, the *Asian Wall Street Journal* and the *International Herald Tribune*. For weekly regional news, *Asiaweek* and the *Far Eastern Economic Review*.

TELEVISION

Satellite television seems to expand by the day and for the moment the choices are Star TV's Star Plus, MTV, Prime Sports and the BBC; ESPN1 (an American sports network),

CNN1 and Australian Television's ATV1. Some hotels feature HKTA's Explore Hong Kong and The Hongkong Channel's video guides.

RADIO

The main English-language radio stations are the Radio Television Hong Kong's (RTHK) British-style Radio 3 AM/FM, Radio 4 AM/FM (classical music) and Radio 6 AM (BBC World Service Relay);

OPPOSITE Hong Kong's lifestyle is fast-paced, whether it's public transport or ABOVE the remarkably vast range of printed media that hits the news stands each day.

Commercial Radio's Quote AM, which sounds like a British Station trying to go West Coast; BFBS FM (the British Forces Broadcasting Service); and Metro Plus AM and FM Select.

LANGUAGE

The language of 98 percent of the Hong Kong population is, of course, Chinese, and the dialect is Cantonese. It's completely different in tone and vocabulary to the national tongue of China itself, Mandarin. But before you begin rushing for English-Chinese phrase books and dictionaries, rest assured that most Chinese who you'll come into direct contact with as a tourist in Hong Kong will speak reasonable or fluent English. In the streets there are special English-speaking Chinese police officers, identified by a red flash under the numbers on their shoulders.

ELECTRICITY

All electrical appliances in Hong Kong work on 200/220 volts, 50 cycles, and American appliances and plugs need transformers and adapters. Most hotels provide shaver adapters.

CURRENCY

The Hong Kong dollar is linked to the American dollar and its banknotes come in denominations of $1,000, 500, 100, 50, 20 and 10. Don't be confused by the different designs — they are issued by both the major banks, the Hongkong and Shanghai Bank and the Standard Chartered. There are also silver coins in $5, $2 and $1 denominations, and bronze coins for 50¢, 20¢ and 10¢. Most banks are open Monday to Friday from around 9:00 am to 4:30 pm, and on Saturdays till 12:30 pm.

If you want to change your currency, generally speaking, the banks give the best exchange rates. You'll find that the hotel desks and the shop-front money-changers charge a commission.

TIPPING

Most major restaurants include a 10 percent service charge in the check— and expect to keep some of the change. Elsewhere, my advice is to tip everyone from bellboys to toilet attendants if they offer a genuine service, but not more than HK$5. Also, add a dollar to the meter fare to keep the taxi drivers happy.

DEPARTURE

At Kai Tak Airport, remember to have enough money left to pay the airport tax of HK$50 for adults and children 12 years and above (free for those younger than 12 years) when you check in to leave.

ACCOMMODATION

Hong Kong's hotels are among the best and most luxurious in the world, and their rates are among the highest, too. However, there is a fairly varied choice of accommodation and prices ranging from five-star right down to hostel class, catering both for the "discerning" and budget traveler.

EXPENSIVE (ABOVE US$200)

HONG KONG
Conrad, ✆ 2521 3838, fax: 2521 3888, Pacific Place, 88 Queensway, Central.
Furama Kempinski, ✆ 2525 5111, fax: 2845 9339, 1 Connaught Road Central.
Grand Hyatt, ✆ 2588 1234, fax: 2802 0677, 1 Harbour Road, Wanchai.
Hongkong Hilton, ✆ 2523 3111, fax: 2845 2590, 2 Queen's Road Central.
Island Shangri-La, ✆ 2877 3838, fax: 2521 8742, Pacific Place, 88 Queensway, Central.
J.W. Marriott, ✆ 2810 8366, fax: 2845 0737, Pacific Place, 88 Queensway, Central.
Mandarin Oriental, ✆ 2522 0111, fax: 2810 6190, 5 Connaught Road Central.

OPPOSITE Traditional fan dancer in demurely attractive pose.

Ritz Carlton, ✆ 2877 6666, fax: 2877 6778, 3 Connaught Road, Central.

KOWLOON
Hong Kong Renaissance, ✆ 2375 1133, fax: 2375 6611, 8 Peking Road, Tsimshatsui.
Hotel Nikko, ✆ 2739 1111, fax: 2311 3122, 72 Mody Road, Tsimshatsui East.
Kowloon Shangri-La, ✆ 2721 2111, fax: 2723 8686, 64 Mody Road, Tsimshatsui East.
New World, ✆ 2369 4111, fax: 2369 9387, New World Centre, 22 Salisbury Road, Tsimshatsui.
Peninsula, ✆ 2366 6251, fax: 2722 4170, Salisbury Road, Tsimshatsui.
Regent, ✆ 2721 1211, fax: 2739 4546, 18 Salisbury Road, Tsimshatsui,.
Royal Garden, ✆ 2721 5215, fax: 2369 9976, 69 Mody Road, Tsimshatsui East.
Sheraton Hong Kong Hotel & Towers, ✆ 2369 1111, fax: 2739 8707, 20 Nathan Road, Tsimshatsui.

MODERATE (US$150 TO $200)

HONG KONG
Century Hong Kong, ✆ 2598 8888, fax: 2598 8866, 238 Jaffe Road, Wanchai.
Charterhouse, ✆ 2833 5566, fax: 2833 5888, 209-219 Wanchai Road, Wanchai.
Excelsior, ✆ 2894 8888, fax: 2895 6459, 281 Gloucester Road, Causeway Bay.
Luk Kwok, ✆ 2866 2166, fax: 2866 262, 272 Gloucester Road, Wanchai.
Park Lane, ✆ 2890 3355, fax: 2576 7853, 310 Gloucester Road, Causeway Bay.
Victoria Hotel, ✆ 2540 7228, fax: 8258 3398, Shun Tak Centre, 200 Connaught Road Central.

KOWLOON
Holiday Inn, Crowne Plaza Harbour View, ✆ 2721 5161, fax: 2369 5672, 70 Mody Road, Tsimshatsui East.
Holiday Inn Golden Mile, ✆ 2369 3111, fax: 2369 8016, 46-52 Nathan Road, Tsimshatsui.
Omni The Hongkong, ✆ 2736 0088, fax: 2736 0011, Harbour City, 3 Canton Road, Tsimshatsui.
Omni Marco Polo, ✆ 2736 0888, fax: 2736 0022, Harbour City, Canton Road.
Omni Prince, ✆ 2736 1888, fax: 2736 0066, Harbour City, Canton Road, Tsimshatsui.
Ramada, ✆ 2311 1100, fax: 2311 6000, 73-75 Chatham Road South, Tsimshatsui.
Regal Airport, ✆ 2718 0333, fax: 2718 4111, Sa Pa Road, Kowloon City.
Regal Kowloon, ✆ 2722 1818, 2369 6950, 71 Mody Road, Tsimshatsui East.

NEW TERRITORIES
Gold Coast Hotel, ✆ 2452 8888, fax: 2440 7783, 1 Castle Peak Road, Castle Peak Bay, Tuen Mun.
Regal Riverside, ✆ 2649 7878, fax: 2637 4748, Tai Chung Kiu Road, Shatin.

AVERAGE (US$80 TO $149)

HONG KONG
Evergreen Plaza, ✆ 2866 9111, fax: 2861 3121, 33 Hennessy Road, Wanchai.
Grand Plaza, ✆ 2886 0011, fax: 2886 1738, 2 Kornhill Road, Quarry Bay.
Newton Hotel, ✆ 2807 2333, fax: 2807 1221, 218 Electric Road, North Point.
Wesley, ✆ 2866 6688, fax: 2866 6633, 22 Hennessy Road, Wanchai.

KOWLOON
Eaton, ✆ 2782 1818, fax: 2782 5563, 380 Nathan Road, Yaumatei.
Grand Tower, ✆ 2789 0011, fax: 2789 0945, 627-641 Nathan Road, Mongkok.
Guangdong, ✆ 2739 3311, fax: 2721 1137, 18 Prat Avenue, Tsimshatsui.
Imperial, ✆ 2366 2201, fax: 2311 2360, 30-34 Nathan Road, Tsimshatsui.
Kimberley, ✆ 2723 3888, fax: 2723 1318, 28 Kimberley Road, Tsimshatsui.
Kowloon, ✆ 2369 8698, fax: 2739 9811, 19-21 Nathan Road, Tsimshatsui.
Metropole, ✆ 2761 1711, fax: 2761 0769, 75 Waterloo Road, Yaumatei.
The Salisbury YMCA, ✆ 2369 2211, fax: 2739 9315, 41 Salisbury Road, Tsimshatsui.

INEXPENSIVE (US$60 TO $79)

HONG KONG
Garden View International YWCA, ✆ 2877 3737, fax: 2845 62631, Macdonnell Road, Central.

KOWLOON
Caritas Bianchi Lodge, ✆ 2388 1111, fax: 2770 666, 94 Cliff Road, Yaumatei.
Caritas Lodge, 134 Boundary Street, ✆ 2339 3777, fax: 2338 2864.
Hong Kong YWCA Anne Black Guest House, ✆ 2713 9211, fax: 2761 1269, 5 Man Fuk Road, Waterloo Hill Road, Mongkok.
YMCA International House, ✆ 2771 9111, fax: 2388 5926, 23 Waterloo Road, Yaumatei.

CHEAP (BELOW US$60)

KOWLOON
Booth Lodge (The Salvation Army), ✆ 2771 9266, fax: 2385 1140, 11 Wing Sing Lane, Yaumatei.
Chungking House, ✆ 2366 5352, fax: 2721 3570, Blk A, 4/F, Chung King Mansions, 40 Nathan Road, Tsimshatsui.
Holy Carpenter Guest House, ✆ 2362 0301, fax: 2362 2193, 1 Dyer Avenue, Hung Hom.
STB Hostel, ✆ 2710 9199, fax: 2385 0153, 2/F Great Eastern Mansion, 255-261 Reclamation Street, Mongkok.

TOURS AND TOURIST INFORMATION

The **Hong Kong Tourist Association (HKTA)** will provide advice, and books, on shopping, sightseeing, culture, dining and entertainment. They also advise visitors to shop and eat only in places that display their sign — all HKTA members are required to give value for money, an accurate representation of products sold and a reliable and polite service. HKTA also publish loads of other books and brochures, some in different languages, such as maps, *Hong Kong This Week, The Official Hong Kong Guide*, guides on public transport, walking tours, hotels, consumer electronics and jewelry.

HKTA offer many interesting tours (or will put you directly in touch the tour company) — Sunset and Dinner Cruises, Cocktail Cruises, a Family Insight Tour, Hong Kong City Tour with Lunch, Aberdeen Sampan Tour, Aberdeen and Islands Lunch Cruise, Kowloon and the New Territories Tour, to name but a few, along with their Sports and Recreation Tour, Heritage and Land Between Tours and a Come Horseracing Tour.

The trams and Star ferries are also available for tours or private charter. Harbor journeys range from a Noon Day Gun Cruise and Afternoon Chinese Tea Cruise to a Sundown Cocktail Cruise and a Harbour Lights Dinner Cruise. Tram Tours, from daytime to dinner excursions, are on a special open-top antique tram. All tours include drinks on board, a souvenir, lucky draw and entertainment. For private hire, the tram takes in three routes starting from the depot in Western: Causeway Bay-Happy Valley and back (two hours); North Point and back (two hours); and North Point-Happy Valley (three hours). For more details — MP Tours ✆ 2366 7024, or call into their Star Ferry booking counters, at Star Ferry on both sides of the harbor. You can also contact HKTA.

You'll find HKTA's Tourist Information Office and Gift Centres at the following locations:

Kowloon
Star Ferry Concourse, Tsimshatsui.
Hong Kong International Airport (on arrival only).

Hong Kong
Shop 8, Basement, Jardine House, 1 Connaught Place, Central, Hong Kong. Head Office: 35/F Jardine House, 1 Connaught Place, Central, Hong Kong.

For any information ✆ 2801 7177 (multilingual).
For tours ✆ 2877 2599.
INFOFAX (facsimile information service — English only): 2177 1128.
For general shopping advice and inquiries about HKTA members ✆ 2801 7278.
HKTA has sixteen offices worldwide and a selection of addresses follow:

Australia ✆ (02) 521 3167, Level 5, 55 Harrington Street, The Rocks, Sydney, NSW 2000.
Canada ✆ (416) 366 2389, Suite 909, 347 Bay Street, Toronto, Ontario M5H 2R7.
France ✆ (01) 4720 3964, 38 Avenue George

V, (entree 53 rue Francois ler 7 etage), 75008, Paris.

Germany ✆ (069) 722 841, Wiesenau 1, 6000 Frankfurt/Main 1.

Singapore ✆ (65) 532 3668, 13-08 Ocean Building, 10 Collyer Quay 0104.

United Kingdom ✆ (071) 930 4775, 4-5/F, 125 Pall Mall, London.

United States of America ✆ (212) 869 5008/9, 5/F, 590 Fifth Avenue, New York, NY; ✆ (310) 208 4582, Suite 1220, 10940 Wilshire Boulevard, Los Angeles, CA 90024-3915.

CONSULATES & COMMISSIONS

There are at least 89 Consulates and Commissions in Hong Kong and contact numbers for some of the major ones follow:
Australia ✆ 827 881, fax: 827 6583

Belgium ✆ 524 3111, fax: 868 5997
Canada ✆ 810 4321, fax: 810 6736
Denmark ✆ 827 8101, fax: 827 4555
Finland ✆ 525 5385, fax: 810 1232
France ✆ 529 4351, fax: 866 9693
Germany ✆ 529 8855, fax: 865 2033
Greece ✆ 774 1682, fax: 334 2738
Italy ✆ 522 0033, fax: 845 9678
Luxembourg ✆ 877 1018, fax: 869 6623
Netherlands ✆ 522 5127, fax: 868 5388
New Zealand ✆ 525 5044, fax: 845 2915
Portugal ✆ 523 1338, fax: 845 7944
Singapore ✆ 527 2212, fax: 861 3595
Spain ✆ 525 3041, fax: 877 2407
Sweden ✆ 521 1212, fax: 596 0308
Switzerland ✆ 522 7147, fax: 845 2619
United Kingdom ✆ 523 0176, fax: 845 2870
United States of America ✆ 523 9011, fax: 845 1598

Selected Reading List

JOAN REID AHRENI/RUTH LOR MALLOY, *Hong Kong Gems and Jewelry*, Hong Kong, Delta Dragon Publications, 1986.

FRENA BLOOMFIELD, *The Occult World of Hong Kong*, Hong Kong, Hong Kong Publishing Company, 1980.

TIM CAREW, *The Fall of Hong Kong*, London, Pan Books, 1976.

PETER CHANCELLOR, *Shades of Hong Kong*, London, International Fine Arts Publications, 1983.

T. K. GHOSE, *The Banking System of Hong Kong*, Singapore, Butterworth, 1987.

DANA GOETZ, *Hong Kong Factory Bargains*, Hong Kong, Delta Dragon Publications, 1987.

Hong Kong Guidemaps, Hong Kong, Universal Publications Ltd, 1987.

Hong Kong Streets & Places, Vol 2, Hong Kong, Hong Kong Government Printer, 1983.

RICHARD HUGHES, *Borrowed Place, Borrowed Time*, London, André Deutsch, 1976.

SUSAN JEFFREY, *Drummond's Hong Kong Guide to Art & Antique Dealers*, Hong Kong, Drummond's, 1986.

DEREK KEMP, *Twelve Hong Kong Walks*, Hong Kong, Oxford University Press, 1985.

T. C. LAI, *Chinese Painting – Its Mystic Essence*, Hong Kong, Swindon Book Company, 1974.

LYN PAN, *The New Chinese Revolution*, London, Hamish Hamilton, 1987.

SUSAN THOMAS SCHNEIDER, *Born to Shop – Hong Kong*, New York, Bantam Books, 1986.

JOHN WARNER, *Fragrant Harbour*, Hong Kong, John Warner Publications, 1986.

PETER WESLEY-SMITH, *Unequal Treaty – 1898-1997*, Hong Kong, Oxford University Press, 1984.

Photo Credits

All photos by **Nik Wheeler** except those below:

Alain Evrard: 8, 14, 24, 29, 37, 39, 52, 55, 61, 62-3, 64, 67, 68, 70-71, 97, 99, 101, 105, 108, 109, 111, 151, 152, 153, 155, 156, 164 *left*, 168, 170, 171, 177, 185, back cover *top left* and *bottom right*.

Adina Tovy: 11 *right*, 13, 43, 93, 150 *right*.

John Kwong: 35.

Hong Kong Museum of History, Urban Council: 10

The Public Records Office of Hong Kong: 11 *left*, 40.

The Stock House: Robin Moyer, 51; Paul Von Stroheim, 117

Profile Photo Library: Neil Farrin, 18, 158; Rex A. Butcher, 28, 142-143; Philip Young, 30-31; Airphoto International Ltd, 72-73, 141, 146; Alain Evrard, 124; A. M. MacKillop, 126-127, 144, 190; Paul Thomson, 132-133; Hans Linburg, 142; Kenny Ip, 26.

Quick Reference A-Z Guide
to Places and Topics of Interest with Listed Accommodation, Restaurants and Useful Telephone Numbers

Central District –
  Al's Diner (American)
    © 2869 1869   96
  Ashoka (Indian) © 2524 9623   94
  The Benkay (Japanese)
    © 2521 3344   94
  Beirut (Lebanese) © 2804 6611   96
  Bentley's Seafood Restaurant and
    Oyster Bar © 2868 0881   96
  Blue Heaven (Cantonese)
    © 2524 3608   92
  La Bodega (Spanish)
    © 2877 3101   96
  Brown's (Western) © 2523 7003   95
  Bull & Bear (Western)
    © 2525 7436   95, 96
  La Cafe (American) © 2526 6863   96
  Cafe Afrikan (African)
    © 2868 9299   96
  Cafe de Paris (French)
    © 2524 7521   96
  California (Western)
    © 2521 1345   95
  Chiu Chow Garden
    (Chui Chow) © 2525 8246   94
  City Hall Restaurant (Cantonese)
    © 2521 1303   92
  Club 1997 © 2810 9333   95
  Club Sri Lanka (Sri Lankan)
    © 2526 6554   94
  DeliFrance (Western)   95
  Eagle's Nest (Cantonese)
    © 2523 3111   93
  Fountainside Restaurant (Western)
    © 2526 4018   95
  Genji (Japanese) © 2523 3111   94
  Golden Leaf (Cantonese)
    © 2521 3838   93
  Graffiti (Western) © 2521 2202   95
  Grappa's Ristorante (Italian)
    © 2521 4028   96
  Hanagushi (Japanese)
    © 2521 0868   94
  Hunan Garden (Hunan)
    © 2868 2880   93
  Indochine (Vietnamese)
    © 2869 7399   96
  Jade Garden (Cantonese)
    © 2524 5098   92
  Jim's Eurodiner (Western)
    © 2868 6886   95
  Jimmy's Kitchen (mixed)
    © 2526 5293   96

  Koh-I-Noor (Indian)
    © 2877 9706   94
  Luk Yu Tea-House (Cantonese)
    © 2523 2973   92
  Mad Dogs in the Basement
    (English) © 2810 9333   96
  Mandarin Grill (Western)
    © 2522 0111   96
  Man Ho (Cantonese)
    © 2810 8366   93
  Man Wah (Cantonese)
    © 2522 0111   93
  Mecca 97 (Middle Eastern)   95
  Michelle's at The Fringe
    (Mediterranean) © 2877 4000   96
  Mozart Stub'n (German)
    © 2522 1763   96
  Nadaman (Japanese)
    © 2820 8570   94
  Noble House (Peking)
    © 2877 3993   94
  Papillon (French) © 2526 5965   96
  Peking Garden Restaurant (Peking)
    © 2526 6456   94
  Phukets Seafood Grill (Thailand)
    © 2868 9672   94
  The Pierrot (French)
    © 2522 0111   96
  Pomeroy's Wine Bar and
    Restaurant © 2810 1162   96
  Prince's Tavern (Creole and Cajun)
    © 2523 9352   96
  Ristorante Il Mercato (Italian)
    © 2868 3068   96
  La Ronda © 2525 5111   97
  Schnurrbart (German)
    © 2537 1677   96
  Shalimar (Indian) © 2522 8489   94
  Shanghai Garden (Shanghai)
    © 2524 8181   94
  Sichuan Garden (Sichuan)
    © 2521 4433   93
  Summer Palace (Cantonese)
    © 2820 8520   93
  Supatra's Thai Gourmet (Thailand)
    © 2522 5073   94
  Tai Woo Seafood Restaurant
    (Cantonese) © 2524 5618   92
  Tandoor (Indian) © 2521 8363   94
  La Taverna (Italian) © 2522 8904   96
  La Terrazza (Western)
    © 2526 4200   94
  Trios (American) © 2877 9773   96

Tsui Hang Village Restaurant (Cantonese) ✆ 2524 2012   92

Va Bene "stile veneziano" ✆ 2845 5577   96

Victoria Hotel (mixed) ✆ 2540 7228   97

Yat Chau Health Restaurant (Cantonese) ✆ 2545 8688   92-3

Yorohachi (Japanese) ✆ 2524 1251   94

Yung Kee Restaurant (Cantonese) ✆ 2522 1624   92

Causeway Bay –

Ah Yee Leng Tong ✆ 2573 0402   99

Baan Thai (Thai) ✆ 2831 9155   100

Banana Leaf (Indo-Malaysian) ✆ 2573 8187   100

Cammino (Italian) ✆ 2837 6780   102

Carriana (Chui Chow) ✆ 2511 1282   99

Casa Mexicana (Mexican) ✆ 2566 5560   102

Chui Chow Garden Restaurant ✆ 2577 3391   99

Cleveland Szechuan Restaurant ✆ 2576 3876   99

Excelsior Hotel Coffee Shop (Western) ✆ 2894 8888   102

Hong Kong Chung Chuk Lau (Mongolian) ✆ 2577 4914   99

Ichiban (Japanese) ✆ 2890 7580   100

Kanetanaka (Japanese) ✆ 2833 6018   100

Koreana (Korean) ✆ 2577 5145   100

Kung Tak Lam (Shanghai) ✆ 2890 3127   100

Maharaja I (Indian) ✆ 2574 9838   100

New American Restaurant (Peking) ✆ 2575 0458   99

Paterson Vietnamese Restaurant ✆ 2890 6146   100

Rangoon (Burmese) ✆ 2892 1182   100

Red Pepper (Sichuan) ✆ 2577 6346   99

Revolving 66 (Western) ✆ 2862 6166   102

Shanghai Grand Restaurant (Chiu Chow)   99

Sunning Unicorn (Cantonese) ✆ 2577 6620   98

Sui Sha Ya (Japanese) ✆ 2838 1808   100

Sze Chuan Lau (Sichuan) ✆ 2891 9027   99

Texas Rib House (Western) ✆ 2566 5560   102

Tin Tin Hot Pot (Cantonese) ✆ 2895 3883/2890 9966   98

Tomokazu (Japanese) ✆ 2891 2898/2833 6339   100

The Shinta (Indonesian) ✆ 2527 8780   100

Vegi Food Kitchen (Vegetarian) ✆ 2890 6660   100

Wishful Cottage (Vegetarian) ✆ 2573 5645   100

Happy Valley –

Amigo Restaurant (French) ✆ 2577 2202   102

Arirang (Korean) ✆ 2572 3027   100

Pep 'N Chilli (Sichuan) ✆ 2573 8251   99

other areas on Hong Kong Island

Beaches (Western) ✆ 2813 7313   108

Cafe Deco Bar & Grill (Asian/Western) ✆ 2849 5111   108, 145

Hei Fung Terrace Chinese Restaurant (Cantonese) ✆ 2812 2622   108

Peak Cafe (Asian/American) ✆ 2849 7868   108, 145

Peak 100 (Mediterranean) ✆ 2849 7788   108

Seaview (Cantonese) ✆ 2812 2803   108

Spices (Asian) ✆ 2812 2711   108

Stanley's (French) ✆ 2812 8873   108

Stanley's Oriental (Asian/Western) ✆ 2813 9988   109

Tai Pak (Cantonese) ✆ 2552 5953   108

Verandah (Continental) ✆ 2812 2722   108

Wanchai –

La Bella Donna (Italian) ✆ 2802 9972   102

Brett's Seafood Restaurant (Western) ✆ 2866 6608   102

Canton Room (Cantonese) ✆ 2866 2166   98

Chilli Club (Thai) ✆ 2527 2872   100

Chrysanthemum Chinese Restaurant (Cantonese) ✆ 2838 2222   98

Cinta (Indonesian) ✆ 2527 1199   100

East Ocean Seafood Restaurant (Cantonese) ✆ 2827 8887   98

Illustrated Blueprints to Travel Enjoyment

INSIDER'S GUIDES

The Guides That Lead